The Beast
of Revelation

Other Books by Dr. Kenneth L. Gentry

God Gave Wine

"Reformed Theology and Six Day Creation"
    in *Creation According to the Scriptures*

Perilous Times: A Study in Eschatological Evil

The Great Tribulation: Past or Future? (with Thomas D. Ice)

"The Postmillennial View,"
    in *Three Views on the Millennium and Beyond*

"The Case for Preterism," in *Always Reforming*

"A Preterist View of Revelation"
    in *Four Views on the Book of Revelation*

Before Jerusalem Fell: Dating the Book of Revelation

He Shall Have Dominion: A Postmillennial Eschatology

*The Greatness of the Great Commission: The Christian Enterprise
    in a Fallen World*

*God's Law in the Modern World: The Continuing Relevance
    of Old Testament Law*

Lord of the Saved: Getting to the Heart of the Lordship Debate

"Civil Sanctions in the New Testament"
    in *Theonomy: An Informed Response*

The Christian Case Against Abortion

The Charismatic Gift of Prophecy: A Reformed Analysis

House Divided: The Break-Up of Dispensational Theology
    (with Greg L. Bahnsen)

"Problems with Public Welfare" in *The Welfare State*

The Beast of Revelation

Kenneth L. Gentry, Jr., Th.D.

AMERICAN VISION
Powder Springs, Georgia

Unless otherwise noted, Scripture quotations are taken from the *New American
Standard Bible®,* © Copyright The Lockman Foundation 1960, 1962, 1963,
1968, 1971, 1972, 1973, 1975, 1977, 1995, Used by permission.
www.Lockman.org.

ISBN: 0-915815-41-9
Printed in the United States of America

02 03 04 05 06   5 4 3 2 1

For current information about all releases from American Vision, visit our websites:
www.americanvision.org and www.prophecybooks.com
Or write: American Vision
            Box 220
            Powder Springs, GA 30127

Telephone: 1-800-628-9460
email: avpress@mindspring.com

Dedicated to John Franek
A strong witness for Christ
A great encouragement to me

TABLE OF CONTENTS

Preface to Second Edition

I am most grateful for the reception *The Beast of Revelation* has received within the Christian community for the past decade. As I stated in the first edition, in some ways this book is a condensation of my much larger, more detailed, exhaustively footnoted doctoral dissertation, which was released as *Before Jerusalem Fell*.[1] Nevertheless, though *The Beast* served as something of a basic summary of *Before Jerusalem Fell* for those who wanted a more introductory presentation, it was not simply an abstract of that book. In fact, two distinctives of *The Beast of Revelation* set it apart from *Before Jerusalem Fell*.

First, the material was ordered differently, focusing on the question of the identity and role of the Beast particularly, whereas *Before Jerusalem Fell* was more wide ranging in its concerns. Second, some material appears in *The Beast of Revelation* that did not make it into the larger work. Consequently, the interested student of Scripture will benefit from reading both volumes.

The first edition of *The Beast of Revelation* went out of print in 1998. I am thankful for Gary DeMar and American Vision for their interest in re-releasing it. And with Gary's encouragement, I have made numerous changes in this presentation making it truly a *new* edition. The 1994 re-print was offered as a "second printing with corrections," removing only minor typographical errors but leaving the text virtually intact. But this American Vision re-release makes many easily noticeable and very important emendations. Consequently, the nature of the changes should easily justify the re-purchase of this title by any who are interested in the continuing debate.

I must also thank my good friend Blake Davis. Blake gave much of his time to reading through the second printing of *The Beast*. He caught numerous typographical errors and made several valuable suggestions for strengthening the argument. In addition, I want to thank Arnold Jagt for his quick and gracious recovery of the published text. Over the years the compuer files of the chapters had been lost. Arnold graciously devoted his time and expertise to scanning the book then converting it to text that could be edited. Without his able assistance this new edition would have been a much more difficult and time consuming task to complete.

Interest in Revelation

A new edition of the present work seems most opportune in that Revelation study among evangelicals appears to be undergoing a resurgence. This revival of interest is evident to me from several lines of evidence:

First, *negatively* the enormous success of the *Left Behind* series demonstrates a wide-spread (though wrong-headed) evangelical interest in the prophecies of Revelation. This series of novels (the ideal genre for the whole theological system from which it springs) sold more than forty million copies between 1996 and 2001.[2] Such a publishing event clearly highlights the tragic, naive, and embarrassing confusion reigning among evangelicals over the majestic Revelation of Jesus Christ. One would think that enthusiasm would have dissipated after numerous date-setting failures from this school of thought. The list is legion: Hal Lindsey's *1980s: Countdown to Armageddon* and *Planet Earth— 2000: Will Mankind Survive?*; Lester Sumrall, *I Predict 2000*; Steve Terrell's *The 90's: Decade of the Apocalypse*; Ed Dobson, *The End: Why Jesus Could Return by A.D. 2000*; and other such titles by self-proclaimed "prophecy experts." In the original story Chicken Little eventually lost her credibility.

Second, positively though, a growing number of works has begun impacting the evangelical community and chipping away at dispensationalism's stony resistance. Books such as my *The Beast of Revelation* and *Before Jerusalem Fell*; DeMar's *Last Days Madness* and his detailed response to *Left Behind, End Times Fiction*; Gregg's *Revelation: Four Views: A Parallel Commentary*; Pate's *Doomsday Delusions* and *Four Views on the Book of Revelation*; Sproul's *The Last Days According to Jesus*; Mathison's *Postmillennialism*;[3] and other preterist or preterist-sympathetic studies underscore a renewed desire not only to reflect more seriously upon Revelation but to consider more carefully the preterist approach.

Third, not only is there a growing body of preterist materials (which is cause for hope), but several *major* Christian publishers have witnessed the growing enthusiasm for evangelical preterism (which is cause for confidence). Gregg's *Revelation: Four Views* is published by one of the leading Christian publishers, Thomas Nelson—as is DeMar's *End Times Fiction*. Gregg's commentary (which appreciatively cites my *Beast*) continues to enjoy a large distribution. R. C. Sproul's *The Last Days According to Jesus* (which interacts with my writings) is published by Baker Book House and has gone through numerous printings. Contributors to Pate's *Four Views on the Book of Revelation* (which includes my section on the preterist approach) were recently sent a certificate of appreciation for entering its fifth printing from Zondervan, perhaps the largest circulation Christian publisher. The yeoman work of smaller presses such as American Vision, Institute for Christian Economics, and Covenant Media Foundation is paying off.

Fourth, I am receiving more invitations to speak on Revelation and eschatology in conferences and seminars than I can accept. Radio interviews are also multiplying, and often have to be turned down due to time pressures. My debate book with Thomas Ice, *The Great Tribulation: Past or Future?*

(which touches upon Revelation) was even published by a notable dispensational publisher, Kregel.[4] I have received almost 100 responses from readers, and only one of them expressed sympathy with Ice's argument; many of them confessed to abandoning the dispensational view.

Changes in the New Edition

But now, what changes have been made in *The Beast of Revelation* to justify purchasing this new edition? I will list a few of the more noticeable changes, with brief explanatory comments. Rest assured that *every* chapter has been edited, and almost every *paragraph*—with Chapters 1–3 and 5–8 undergoing the most substantial expansion and change. Note that some chapter titles have changed (Chapters 8, and 13–15).

First, the original edition of *The Beast of Revelation* was released in 1989. This new edition has updated all of the bibliographical references where necessary. For instance, the more recent editions of Revelation commentaries have been employed (e.g., those by Mounce and Morris); the newer edition of certain reference works have been consulted (e.g., Guthrie's latest *New Testament Introduction*); and so forth. Thus, the bibliography and footnotes are updated for easier consultation.

Second, in addition, I have interacted with altogether new resources (e.g., the important multi-volume *Compendium of Contemporary Biblical Scholarship* published by InterVarsity Press, 1993–2000; the latest editions of scholarly biblical and theological dictionaries). I interact with several new sources that directly respond to my earlier works (e.g., Thomas's two-volume, *Revelation: An Exegetical Commentary* [1992, 1995]; Beale's massive *The Book of Revelation: New International Greek Testament Commentary* [1999]; Kistemaker's important *Journal of the Evangelical Theological Society* article [September 2000]). In several places, I incorporate quotations from newer resources while dropping out those from older ones, bringing those arguments into the contemporary debate. I have also expanded the list of scholars promoting an early-date (e.g., noting Ellis's important *The Making of the New Testament Documents* [1999], as well as works by Rowland, Wilson, and others).

Third, I have dropped mistaken observations and have modified deficient arguments. For instance, in Chapter 2 I stumbled exegetically at Revelation 1:19, which reads: "Write therefore the things which you have seen, and the things which are, and the things which shall take place after these things." I previously argued that the Greek verb *mello* should be translated "about to," thus rendering the phrase "and the things *about to* take place after these things." Although *mello* can speak of temporal nearness in some texts, it does not do so here (as I note at the proper place below).

I also originally argued in Chapter 5 that the reference to "the tribulation" in Revelation 1:9 referred to the "great tribulation" of Matthew 24 and Revelation 7. But that could not be, for John was *already* in this "tribulation" while he was writing (which trial fell upon Christians beginning in A.D. 64), whereas he was prophesying the still *future* "great tribulation" (which judgment was to be upon the Jews beginning in A.D. 67). Unfortunately, I argued that the definite article "the" modified only "tribulation" (seemingly making it refer to *the* tribulation, i.e., the "great tribulation"). Syntactically though, the Granville Sharp rule of the article in Greek has it governing all three of the nouns (tribulation, kingdom, perseverance), thereby not highlighting *the* tribulation.

Furthermore, some of my statements may have been overstated. For instance, in Chapter 5 I argued dogmatically that the Neronic persecution lasted forty-two months, as a relentless, actively-engaged pogrom against Christianity. Though some historians argue such, I now allow that Nero's persecution, once begun, may have been intermittent until his death, existing as more of a *state of siege*, even if not a relentless hunting down of Christians. In addition, some readers understood me to imply in Chapter 10 that Julius Caesar was actually an emperor. In the present work I make clear that Julius was *not* formally an emperor, though he virtually functioned as one.

Fourth, I have added much new material along the way. As I continue to research Revelation studies, first-century history, apocalyptic literature, Jewish-Christian relations and the like, I am frequently uncovering additional and exciting information. The new material helps flesh out the argument, giving it more weight. In a variety of contexts I have multiplied Scripture references for additional biblical support.

Fifth, I have labored to polish my writing style over the past decade. Consequently, the presentation within is a little zestier and less cumbersome than the original. Previously my focus was so much on the formal argument that stylistic matters were not as much of a concern for me. With further study in the art of writing as a form of communication and persuasion, I have learned the value of a freer writing style.[5] Also in some places I have added new headings or reformulated clunky older headings to allow the reader to visualize the structure of my presentation more easily.

So once again I present to the Christian community a challenge to the dispensational hegemony respecting Revelation. "Come, let us reason together!"

Kenneth L. Gentry, Jr., Th.D.
Westminster Classical College
Elkton, Maryland
Pearl Harbor Day, December 7, 2001

Notes

[1] Kenneth L. Gentry, Jr., *Before Jerusalem Fell: Dating the Book of Revelation*, 3rd ed. (Atlanta: American Vision, 1998).

[2] Corrie Cutrer, "Left Behind Series Puts Tyndale Ahead," *Christianity Today* 44:13 (November 13, 2000), 26–27. For an analysis of the *Left Behind* series, see Gary DeMar, *End Times Fiction: A Biblical Consideration of the Left Behind Theology* (Nashville: Thomas Nelson, 2001).

[3] Gary DeMar, *Last Days Madness: Obsession of the Modern Church*, 4th ed. (Powder Springs, Ga.: American Vision, 1999); DeMar, *End Times Fiction* (Nashville: Thomas Nelson, 2001); Steve Gregg, *Revelation: Four Views: A Parallel Commentary* (Nashville: Thomas Nelson, 1996); C. Marvin Pate and Calvin B. Haines, Jr., *Doomsday Delusions: What's Wrong with Predictions About the End of the World* (Downer's Grove, Ill.: InterVarsity, 1995); C. Marvin Pate, ed., *Four Views on the Book of Revelation* (Grand Rapids: Zondervan, 1998); R. C. Sproul, *The Last Days According to Jesus: When Did Jesus Say He Would Return?* (Grand Rapids: Baker, 1998); Keith A. Mathison, *Postmillennialism: An Eschatology of Hope* (Phillipsburg, N.J.: Presbyterian and Reformed, 1999).

[4] Thomas Ice and Kenneth L. Gentry, Jr., *The Great Tribulation: Past or Future?* (Grand Rapids: Kregel, 1999).

[5] In fact, I have established a writing ministry with a correspondence course: *Righteous Writing*. For more information, see my website: www.kennethgentry.com or write me at P. O. Box 832, Elkton, MD 21921.

Part One
Who is the Beast?

Introduction

Blessed is he who reads and those who hear the words of the
prophecy, and heed the things which are written in it. Rev. 1:3a

---

Revelation is one of the most fascinating and intriguing books in the
Bible. Evidently this has always been the case, for it was one of the most
widely circulated of New Testament books in the early centuries of
Christianity.[1] Following upon this early interest, the Middle Ages
and the Reformation era experienced an explosion of commentaries
on Revelation.[2]

Nor does interest in Revelation show any sign of slackening today.
In fact, in the 1990s many Christians viewed the year 2000 with ex-
cited prophetic anticipation, generating a reinvigorated interest in John's
magnificent prophecy.[3] Check any Christian bookstore and you will
discover a vast selection of books on eschatology in general and Revelation in particular. And—despite the continuing dismal failures of popular
prophecy writers who interpret the Bible through the pages of today's
newspapers—millions of evangelicals live with the deep expectation
that we are living on the very brink of Revelation's events. Scholarly
investigation regarding apocalyptic literature also demonstrates the keen
interest in Revelation and other prophecy studies. Aune's massive bibliography presents fifteen full pages of scholarly bibliography on Revelation studies—and Beale's surpasses him with eleven additional pages.[4]

One of the most intriguing questions debated in Revelation regards the identity of the Beast of Revelation (Chapters 13 and 17).

Michaels is surely correct: "No other figure in the book of Revelation has captured readers' imaginations quite like the beast of chapter 13."[5] This terrifying enemy of God and his Church has fascinated both the Christian and non-Christian mind down through the ages.

Who is this nefarious personage?
What is his role in biblical eschatology?
Does his foreboding visage haunt our future?

These questions are frequently asked by contemporary Christians. And the biblical answer must arise from the one book in Holy Scripture where this evil figure looms large: Revelation. In the Book of Revelation we find God-inspired information regarding the Beast, and the essential definitive data to guide us in our unmasking of his identity. Unfortunately, there is a great deal of misinformation floating around.

Confusion Regarding Revelation

Revelation has been not only one of the most widely circulated, but certainly the most vigorously debated and variously understood of New Testament books. Revelation has proved to be as perplexing as it has been popular. Lamentably, the vast majority of the prophetic literature, media presentations, films, conferences, seminars, and so forth from our era is ill-conceived. Most of it stands as a source of positive embarrassment to the apologetic integrity of the Scriptures, and the intellectual credibility of the Christian witness.

Three of the most penetrating exposes of the false expectations generated by the modern prophecy movement are Dwight Wilson's 1977 classic, *Armageddon Now!*, Paul Boyer's important *When Time Shall Be No More*, and Francis Gumerlock's recent *The Day and the Hour*.[6] They profusely document a multitude of failed predictions based on careless interpretations of Scripture by well-meaning, Bible-believing Christians both in our own century (Wilson and Boyer) and throughout church history (Gumerlock). Most of these failures have been related either directly or indirectly to a radical misunderstanding of the Book of Revelation.

Much of this problem is traceable to a frustrating tendency which David Chilton laments: "Many rush from their first profession of faith to the last book in the Bible . . . finding, ultimately, only a reflection of their own prejudices."[7] The dangers of such a "rush" are magnified due to the great difficulty in interpreting Revelation (see next section below). Thus, there is a ripe market for tantalizing and dramatic expositions of Revelation. Scripture has a name for this syndrome: "itching ears" (2 Tim. 4:3). The modern evangelical bookmarket also has an apt description of such works: "best seller."

Reasons for Revelation's Difficulty

Undoubtedly, a major reason for Revelation's interpretive difficulty is due to its literary form. It is not simple historical narrative or didactic instruction. Rather, it contains fearsome visions and strange symbols, employing imagery drawn from Old Testament prophecy and ancient Near Eastern culture. Its literary style (apocalyptic) understandably renders Revelation a difficult work, particularly for modern, Western Christians.[8]

Much of the data concerning the Beast perplexes us because of the symbolic *style* John employs. The terrifying visual appearance of the Beast in Revelation 13:1–2 is obviously symbolic, as even dispensationalists agree.[9] But why does John employ such imagery? The death and resurrection of the Beast in Revelation 13:3 indicate something quite dramatic. But what? The rendering of the Beast's name in numerals in Revelation 13:18 is a unique feature in Scripture. But how are we to decipher it? The Great Harlot in Revelation 17:1–6 is quite mysterious, and is somehow related to the Beast. But who is she and what is their relationship?

Beyond the widely recognized difficulty of style, an equally serious matter confronts the would-be interpreter: the date of the writing of Revelation. Basically two possibilities regarding the *date* of Revelation's composition are open to evangelical Christians: John may have written Revelation prior to the destruction of the Temple in A.D. 70. Or possibly he composed it a generation later, around A.D. 95–96, in the last days of the emperor Domitian. The second view is the majority opinion among contemporary commentators. The first view is the conviction of the present writer and a growing minority of biblical scholars, including such noted names as John A. T. Robinson and E. Earle Ellis (see Chapter 8 below). In fact, the late-date is not as secure a conclusion among scholars as many assume. Indeed, one of the pre-eminent Revelation commentators admits that "the early date could be right, but the cumulative weight of evidence points to the late date."[10]

Few Christians-in-the-pew realize the importance of this matter for the interpretation of Revelation. This is partially due to most of the popular literature on Revelation either ignoring the issue of dating altogether or too lightly glossing over it.[11] Even some of the more technical modern commentaries on Revelation appeal to a majority opinion or parrot the insufficient evidence for the popular, but erroneous date of Revelation.[12] Yet determining Revelation's date of composition is absolutely crucial to the correct understanding of the book.

Despite the majority opinion, I will make two bold claims regarding Revelation's date. First, misapprehending its date can effectively turn Revelation on its head. Whereas the problem of Apocalyptic style renders the exposition of its *details* difficult, adopting a wrong date renders its *specific* meaning impossible. If Revelation prophesies events related to the destruction of the Temple in Jerusalem in A.D. 70, then holding a date of composition *after* that event would miss John's whole point.

Second, Revelation provides more concrete internal information pointing to its date than does any other New Testament book. As I will show, a major reason for dating the book more than a quarter of a century too late is not due to internal indications within Revelation itself, but to church tradition. Unfortunately, the self-witness of Revelation oftentimes does not receive the attention it should, while an inconsistent tradition arising more than a century after its writing predominates the discussion. This is tantamount to "neglecting the word of God" and holding "to the tradition of men" (to paraphrase Mark 7:8).

My Purpose

My main purpose herein is to ascertain the identity of the Beast of Revelation.[13] I believe that the evidence clearly identifies the very name and historical circumstances of the Beast. I also believe that as the reader carefully considers the material I present, he will find the identification not only persuasive, but surprisingly easy and quite startling. Due to the enormous interest in Revelation among evangelicals, though, this will be difficult to accomplish because "none of us reads [Revelation] fresh in the Garden of Eden. We receive it in a tradition of readers who connect us to the text—often through complicated, unrecognized links—and who shape what we see."[14]

An auxiliary purpose is to provide the reader with a synopsis of several of the arguments for the proper dating of Revelation. As will become evident, the matter of dating is all-important to the identity of the Beast. The concerned student should consult the more extensive and technical research provided in my doctoral dissertation, *The Date of Revelation: An Exegetical and Historical Argument for a Pre-A.D. 70 Composition.* That dissertation, submitted to Whitefield Theological Seminary in Lakeland, Florida, in March, 1988, is now available in its third edition from American Vision, and is titled *Before Jerusalem Fell: Dating the Book of Revelation.*

Notes

[1] Robert Mounce, *The Book of Revelation*, 2nd ed. (Grand Rapids: Eerdmans, 1998), 21; Walter F. Adeney, *New Testament*, vol. 2 of *A Biblical Introduction* (London: Methuen, 1911), 461.

[2] Henry B. Swete, *Commentary on Revelation* (Grand Rapids: Kregel, [1911] 1977), cxcvii.

[3] Hal Lindsey, *Planet Earth—2000: Will Mankind Survive?* (Palos Verdes, Calif.: Western Front, 1994). Lester Sumrall, *I Predict 2000* (South Bend: LeSea, 1987). David Allen Lewis, *Prophecy 2000: Rushing to Armageddon* (Green Forest, Ark.: Green Leaf, 1990). Ed Dobson, *The End: Why Jesus Could Return by A.D. 2000* (Grand Rapids: Zondervan, 1997). Peter and Paul LaLonde, *2000 A.D.: Are You Ready?* (Nashville: Thomas Nelson, 1997). Jack Van Impe, *2001: On the Edge of Eternity* (Nashville: Word, 1996).

[4] David E. Aune, *Revelation 1–5* (Dallas: Word, 1997), xxx-xlv. Greg K. Beale, *The Book of Revelation* (NIGTC) (Grand Rapids: Eerdmans, 1999).

[5] J. Ramsey Michaels, *Revelation* (Downers Grove, Ill.: InterVarsity Press, 1997), 156.

[6] Dwight Wilson, *Armageddon Now: The Premillenarian Response to Russia and Israel Since 1917* (Grand Rapids: Baker, 1977). Paul Boyer, *When Time Shall Be No More: Prophecy Belief in Modern American Culture* (Cambridge, Mass.: Belknap, 1992). Francis X. Gumerlock, *The Day and the Hour: Christianity's Perennial Fascination with Predicting the End of the World* (Atlanta: American Vision, 2000).

[7] David Chilton, *Paradise Restored* (Fort Worth, Tex.: Dominion Press, 1985), 153.

[8] See the wealth of scholarly literature on the challenge of apocalyptic. Consult Bible encyclopedias and dictionaries, and especially introductions to technical Revelation commentaries, for a sampling. See particularly, G. K. Beale, *The Use of Daniel in Jewish Apocalyptic Literature and in the Revelation of St. John* (Lanham, Mary.: University Press of America, 1984); David E. Aune, *Prophecy in Early Christianity and the Ancient Mediterranean World* (Grand Rapids: Eerdmans, 1983); James H. Charlesworth, *Old Testament Pseudepigrapha*, 2. vols. (Garden City, N.Y.: Doubleday, 1983).

[9] "The symbolic connotation of *therion* [beast] is in question." (Robert L. Thomas, *Revelation 8–22: An Exegetical Commentary* (Chicago: Moody, 1995), 152.

[10] Beale, *The Book of Revelation*, 4.

[11] See Charles Caldwell Ryrie, *Revelation* (Chicago: Moody Press, 1968), 7–8; William Hendriksen, *More Than Conquerors* (Grand Rapids: Baker: 1967), 19–20; John F. Walvoord, *The Revelation of Jesus Christ* (Chicago: Moody Press, 1966), 13–14; Herman Hoeksema, *Behold, He Cometh!* (Grand Rapids: Kregel, 1969), 33.

[12] See George Eldon Ladd, *A Commentary on the Revelation of John* (Grand Rapids: Eerdmans, 1972), 8; G. R. Beasley-Murray, *The Book of Revelation* (Grand Rapids: Eerdmans, 1978), 17–38; Alan F. Johnson, *Revelation* (Grand Rapids: Zondervan, l983), 12.

[13] Also see my *Perilous Times: A Study in Eschatological Evil* (Texarkana, Ark.: Covenant Media Press, 1999), ch. 5, as well as my soon-to-be released commentary *The Tale of Two Cities*

[14] Leonard L. Thompson, *The Book of Revelation: Apocalypse and Empire* (New York: Oxford, 1990), 3

The Identity of the Beast

Who is like the Beast, and who is able to wage war with him?
If anyone has an ear, let him hear
Rev. 13:4b, 9

Those readers who like to read the last pages of a book to discover the conclusion to the story will be disappointed in my approach. In this opening chapter I will identify the Beast. I do this so that you might have his identity in mind as you consider the evidence while it is being presented. For those who expect the Beast to appear on the scene of history at any moment, another surprise awaits. The material in Revelation is quite clear: The Beast has already intruded upon the scene of history in our distant past.

All Revelation students are familiar with the "number of the Beast" (Rev. 13:18a), which is "the number of his name" (Rev. 13:17b). That dreaded number is "666," six hundred and sixty-six. This number contains the specific identity of the Beast, an identity confirmed by various additional lines of evidence within Revelation itself.

Interpretive Principles

Although I will deal specifically with the number of the Beast in Chapter 3, we must keep in mind several interpretive principles regarding that number. As is evident from the history of the interpretation of 666, we certainly need *something* to confine our thinking to the realm of the reasonable. Those necessary, textually derived limiting principles are:

1. *The Beast's number is that of a man.* According to John, the name-number 666 must be "that of a *man*" (Rev. 13:18b).[1] Beckwith argues, not only grammatically but logically, that the number must be that of "a man" in that any other denotation "would not aid the solution of the problem, for the Beast's name could be anything, the sum of whose letters amounts to 666, however unlike names known to men. . . . It means then the number denoting a man."[2] Below I will also note that in antiquity the names of men are frequently reduced to numbers. This human designation excludes any interpretation involving demonic beings, philosophical ideas, political movements, or anything other than an individual human person. In fact, the Beast eventually is cast into hell (Rev. 19:20), denoting his personal existence (though this evidence does not exclude his being a supernatural demon).

2. *The Beast is an evil man of debased character.* Indeed, he must be someone of an evil, idolatrous, and blasphemous nature. His character traits and evil activities outlined in Revelation 13 (particularly verses 4–7) clearly portray him thus. He not only appears under the grotesque imagery of a compound of three wild carnivores (Rev. 13:2) and wages war against the saints (13:7), but demands worship for himself (13:8, 12, 15) while arrogantly blaspheming God (13:5–6). Furthermore, he somehow carries about with him a despicable harlot (17:3–4) drunk on the blood of the saints (17:6; 18:24).

3. *The Beast possesses "great authority"* (Rev. 13:2, 7). This certainly demands that he be a political figure, particularly in that upon his heads

are "ten diadems" (13:1b) and he possesses a "throne" (13:2b). Indeed, his great authority is "over every tribe and people and tongue and nation" (13:7).

These first three principles are fairly widely held among evangelical Revelation commentators. The two remaining ones are largely overlooked, which almost certainly causes a radical misidentification of the Beast and his mission. These will be simply listed and stated at this juncture; later chapters will establish their veracity.

4. *The Beast is one of John's contemporaries.* John's temporal expectation clearly requires his contemporary presence. The events of Revelation must occur "shortly" (Rev. 1:1; 22:6); John insists that "the time is at hand" (1:3; 22:10). Numerous other temporal indicators appear within (see Ch. 2 below) and fit perfectly with John's first century imagery. This principle alone will eliminate 99.9% of the suggestions by both prophecy populists and even competent commentators. (Unfortunately, it also eliminates the same percentage of market-share for evangelical publications defending the proper view.)

5. *The Beast is relevant to the first century Christians.* John writes to Christians in seven historical churches (Rev. 1:4, 11). He expects them to heed what he writes (1:3) and to calculate the Beast's number (13:18). They are under serious trials (1:9; 2:3, 9–10, 13; 3:10; 6:10–11; 14:13) and would surely be unconcerned with events thousands of years in the future. How could they give heed to John and calculate the identity of the Beast if it were some shadowy figure far removed from their own situation? Sadly, most "interpreters have been concerned to show that the beast has finally arisen in their own day."[3] We should, however, be "suspicious of interpretations that are blatantly narcissistic; this way of understanding the book maintains that the entire course of human history has now culminated in us!"[4] Revelation is not, as Thompson warns, "a floating specter"[5]; rather we must understand him as a figure securely rooted in the first century.

The early establishment of Principles 4 and 5 is essential to the correct understanding of the identity of the Beast. Consequently, I will deal with them at length in Chapter 2.

The Importance of the Limiting Principles

One illustration of the hopeless results caused by ignoring this set of limiting principles is found in a dispensational work of the 1970s. In this work we read a vain attempt to explain the number 666: "At all times Satan has had to have one or more Antichrist candidates waiting in the wings, lest the Rapture come suddenly and find him unprepared. That is why so many malevolent world leaders have had names whose letters added up to 666 when combined in certain ways. (Depending on which 666 formula is used, at any given moment there, are several hundred thousand men in the world whose names add up to 666. It is from this large pool of candidates that Satan has traditionally chosen his 'man of the moment'.)"[6]

Contrary to as competent a scholar as Leon Morris, we doubt that "the possibilities are almost endless."[7] And despite the fact that "the list of conjectures concerning the meaning of the number . . . is almost as long as the list of commentators on the book,"[8] the limiting factors derived from Revelation's text greatly restrict the realm of possibility.

Dual Imagery

Before I actually point to the person that John's number indicates, I must note a widely recognized problem regarding the Beast imagery. Most commentators agree that the Beast in Revelation shifts between the generic and the specific. That is, sometimes the Beast pictures a kingdom, sometimes a particular, individual leader of that kingdom. Nevertheless, we should understand that the number 666 is itself applied to a particular individual king in that kingdom (Rev. 13:18).

At some places the Beast has seven heads, which are seven kings collectively considered. In Revelation 13:1 John states that he "saw a beast coming up out of the sea, having ten horns and seven heads." Revelation 17:10 specifically declares that the seven heads represent "seven kings." These seven kings arise in chronological succession; some have already died, one is now reigning, one is yet to come (17:10–11). Thus, the *Beast* is generically portrayed as a *kingdom*.

So we see the Beast represented as the generic kingdom in some places. But in the very same contexts John speaks of it as an individual. John urges his readers to "calculate the number of the beast, for the number is that of *a man*" (Rev. 13:18). In Revelation 17:11 the interpretive angel informs John and his readers "the beast which was and is not, is himself also an eighth, and *is one of the seven*." This feature, as frustrating as it may be, is recognized by many commentators of various schools of interpretation.[9] Interestingly, of the emperor Augustus, the Roman poet Ovid (43 B.C.–A.D. 18) writes: "the state is Caesar."[10] In fact, this compound idea of generic/specific is not unprecedented in Scripture. For instance, "man" is generic, whereas "Adam" is the specific representative of man. The "body of Christ" often refers to the Church corporate, whereas it also refers to the corporeal individual himself.

Introducing the Beast

With these introductory considerations before us I will now state what I believe the Beast to be, in regard to both his generic and his specific identity. I will establish the generic identity in a little more detail at this juncture. Then after only briefly identifying his specific identity, I will develop the proofs of that specific, individual identity in the following chapters.

His Generic Identity

The generic identity of the Beast is the ancient Roman Empire of the first century. This is the political entity under which Christ was crucified and Christianity was born, and during which John wrote and his audience received his Revelation. According to Revelation 17:9, the seven heads of the Beast represent "seven mountains." The seven heads, then, seem clearly to specify a prominent geographical feature associated with the generic kingdom. Perhaps no point is more obvious in Revelation than this one: *Imperial Rome is here symbolized by the seven mountains.* After all, *Rome* (the capital of the Empire) is the one city in history distinguished by and recognized for its seven mountains. The famous seven hills of Rome are the Palatine, Aventine, Caelian, Esquiine, Viminal, Quirinal, and Capitoline hills.

The Roman writers Suetonius and Plutarch refer to the first century festival in Rome called *Septimontium, i.e.* the feast of "the seven hilled city."[11] Archaeologists have discovered the Coin of Vespasian (emperor A.D. 69–79) picturing the goddess *Roma* as a woman seated on seven hills.[12] The famed seven hills of Rome are mentioned time and again by ancient pagan writers such as Ovid, Claudian, Statius, Pliny, Virgil, Horace, Propertius, Martial, and Cicero.[13] The seven hills are mentioned by such Christian writers as Tertullian and Jerome, as well as in several of the Sibylline Oracles.[14]

This fact—that Rome was universally recognized as the city on seven hills—is widely recognized by both critical and conservative commentators as exercising a bearing upon our passage. The referent is virtually beyond doubt: This vision of the seven-headed Beast portrays Rome, the capital of the Empire. By everyone's dating Revelation was written *sometime* during the period of the Roman Empire.

Furthermore, both secular and ecclesiastical history record that the first imperial persecution of Christianity began in this seven-hilled city under the emperor Nero Caesar in A.D. 64.[15] John himself informs us that he is writing Revelation to seven historical churches in Asia Minor (Rev. 1:4, 11) that exist in an age of great trouble (1:9; 2:10; 3:10). As Ramsey and Hemer demonstrate, the letters to the seven churches betray intimate details of the first century setting of those Christians.[16] Moreover, John exhorts these churches to read, hear, and heed the book (1:3; 2:7; 2:11, 17, 29; 3:6, 13, 22; 22:7). The subject matter of Revelation was urgent for and relevant to those churches, for John writes forcefully of the imminent approach of Revelation's catastrophes (1:1, 3; 3:10; 22:6ff.).[17]

The matter of audience relevance in Revelation 17 should be a paramount concern for the serious interpreter. In light of the circumstances outlined above, is it at all likely that when John mentioned "the seven mountains" he was not speaking of the Roman Empire? Put yourself in first century sandals: Would you think John might be speaking of events occurring untold centuries after the collapse of the Empire which was presently persecuting you? Would you surmise that he was not really relating a message about Imperial Rome? Impossible! Again: John exhorted the people to read, hear, and heed the book (Rev. 1:3). He surely was speaking of the first century Roman Empire, headquartered in the seven-hilled city of Rome. The Empire possessed such "great authority" that it fielded "one of the greatest and most formidable armies that has ever existed,"[18] an army of which "their opponents cannot match these qualities" and to which "victory is the invariable and certain consequence."[19]

His Specific Identity

But now we must ask: Who is the Beast *individually* considered? The Beast of Revelation in his personal incarnation is none other than the infamous Lucius Domitius Ahenobarbus. Though you probably do not know him by his birth name, you certainly will recognize his adoptive name: Nero Claudius Caesar. He and he alone fits the bill as the specific or personal manifestation of the Beast. This vile character fulfills all the requirements of the principles derived from the very text of Revelation. The Roman philosopher and political counselor of Nero,

Seneca (4 B.C.–A.D. 65) wrote in the first person of Nero's great power: "I have been given the power of life and death over all the nations. To determine the condition and to control the destinies of every race and of every individual is my absolute prerogative."[20]

Excluding Julius Caesar, probably no other Roman emperor's name is as well known to the average Christian today as Nero's. Yet his large role *in Revelation* is virtually unknown among contemporary evangelicals. Perhaps a brief history of Nero's tumultuous life would serve well in preparing you for the proofs of my identification, which will be presented in Chapters 2–7.

Nero's Birth and Early Life

The father of Nero[21] was one Enaeus Domitius Ahenobarbus, a vicious man from a noted, but cruel Roman family. The entire family was "notorious for instability, treachery and licentiousness."[22] Nero's father is spoken of as "hateful in every walk of life."[23] Nero's famous, conniving, and ill-fated mother was Agrippina, the sister of the emperor Gaius (also known as "Caligula") and niece (and wife!) of the emperor Claudius.

Nero was born in Antium on December 15, A.D. 37, just nine months after the death of Emperor Tiberius, under whom Christ was crucified. He was born with bright red hair, as was common to his lineage (the name "Ahenobarbus" meant "red-beard").[24] Nero came into the world feet first; among a superstitious and pagan people this was an evil omen. This omen did not go unnoticed by Roman historians of the day.[25] Many astrologers "at once made many direful predictions from his horoscope."[26] On the day of his birth even Nero's father predicted that this offspring could only be abominable and disastrous for the public.[27]

Nero's cruel character evidenced itself quite early. On February 25, A.D. 50, at twelve years of age Nero was adopted by the emperor Claudius Caesar. Soon thereafter he began accusing his brother

Britannicus of being a "changeling," in order to bring him into disfavor before the emperor. At the same time he even served as a public witness in a trial against his aunt Lepida, in order to ruin her.[28] The next year, on March 5 Nero was officially declared an adult.

Agrippina, his mother, plotted and schemed to secure Nero a high position in imperial Rome. Upon the death of the wife of the emperor Claudius she began to make her moves.[29] She arranged Nero's marriage to the daughter of Claudius, labored to get the Roman law changed to allow her to marry Claudius (her uncle), prompted the adoption of Nero by the emperor (A.D. 49), maneuvered to get Nero certain high titles to secure his succession to the emperorship, and caused the exile and death of any supporters of Nero's brother, Britannicus. When it became evident that Claudius did not like leaving Britannicus out of his will, as was urged by Agrippina, she poisoned Claudius.[30]

Nero's Adult Years

On the death of Emperor Claudius, the seventeen year old Nero had his entry to the Palace to assume the emperorship carefully planned for a specific time. This timing was due to certain bad omens throughout the day.[31] He began to reign on October 13, AD. 54.

The first five years of Nero's reign were characterized by remarkably good government and prudence. This was due not to his own wisdom or character, but his being guided by the wise tutors Seneca and Burrus.[32] This era, known as the *quinquennium Neronis,* probably helps us understand Paul's very favorable attitude to the government of the day in Romans 13:1.[33] These tutors attempted to cut off the evil influence of Nero's mother over him. She then began trying to maneuver his brother Britannicus into position as the rightful heir to Claudius. Nero responded by poisoning Britannicus.

Seneca and Burrus recognized the evil bent in Nero's nature and attempted to let it have expression through private base pleasures, hoping to keep him from causing public harm. Suetonius notes that: "Although at first his acts of wantonness, lust, extravagance, avarice and cruelty were gradual and secret. Yet even then their nature was such that no one doubted that they were defects of his character and not due to his time of life."[34] But Nero descended more deeply into degrading conduct: "He castrated the boy Sporus and actually tried to make a woman of him; and he married him with all the usual ceremonies . . . and treated him as his wife."[35] Suetonius continues: "He even devised a kind of game, in which, covered with the skin of some wild animal, he was let loose from a cage and attacked the private parts of men and women, who were bound to stakes."[36]

Nero even plotted and secured his own mother's murder, despite the fact she was responsible for bringing him to power.[37] Not long after that Burrus died. Later, Nero ordered Seneca to commit suicide, which he did.

Nero divorced his first wife Octavia to marry his mistress, Poppaea. Octavia was banished to an island upon Poppaea's orders and was soon beheaded (A.D. 62). Three years later Poppaea, while pregnant and ill, was kicked to death by Nero.[38]

By enormous, self-glorifying building projects and profligate living, Nero exhausted the imperial treasures inherited from the frugal Claudius. Thereupon he began to accuse Roman nobles falsely of various crimes in order to confiscate their estates.[39] Tacitus records that "Nero having butchered so many illustrious men, at last desired to exterminate virtue itself by the death of Thrasea Paetus and Barea Soranus."[40] Suetonius writes that "he showed neither discrimination nor moderation in putting to death whomsoever he pleased on any pretext whatever."[41]

On July 19, A.D. 64, the great Roman fire broke out, destroying most of Rome.[42] Although he was out of Rome at the time, suspicion was cast upon Nero for causing the fire. Many were convinced that since he deplored the ugliness of Rome he intended to destroy it to make room for more of his own building projects.[43] In order to turn attention away from himself, he falsely accused Christians of starting the fire[44] and punished them for being "given to a new and mischievous superstition."[45]

Nero was a lover of music, theater, and the circus, vainly fancying himself to be one of the world's greatest musicians, actors, and charioteers.[46] Suetonius records that "while he was singing no one was allowed to leave the theatre even for the most urgent reasons. And so it is said that some women gave birth to children there, while many who were worn out with listening and applauding . . . feigned death and were carried out as if for burial."[47] The great general and future emperor, Vespasian, "narrowly escaped trouble by falling asleep while the emperor was singing."[48] Nero even virtually abandoned direct rule of Rome for a two year visit to Greece (A.D. 67–68) in order to appear in their music festivals.

Nero's Death

Disgusted with his absence from Rome, his excesses in life, and enormous political abuses, a series of revolts against Nero arose in A.D. 68. Tacitus records one army officer's lament to Nero: "I began detesting you when you murdered your mother and wife and became a charioteer, actor, and incendiary."[49] Julius Vindex in Gaul revolted first; this was followed quickly with military uprisings by Servius Galba in Spain and Cladius Macer in Africa. Vindex's revolt was quickly put down, but Galba's presented a more serious and ultimately destructive threat to Nero.[50] Torn with indecision as to what to do in such pressing circumstances, Nero hesitated in acting against Galba. When the revolt had gathered too much strength he talked of suicide, but was too cowardly and again hesitated.[51]

As he desperately reflected upon his dire circumstances and the ever quickening approach of certain death, he lamented: "What an art-ist the world is losing!"[52] Finally, upon learning that the Senate had voted to put him to death by cruel and shameful means, he secured the assistance of his secretary Epaphroditus to run a sword through his throat.[53] His suicide occurred at the age of 31 on June 9, A.D. 68. Suetonius records that "in the widespread general rejoicing, citizens ran through the streets wearing caps of liberty."[54] Tacitus comments that "the death of Nero had been welcomed initially by a surge of relief."[55]

But with his death the line of Julius Caesar was cut off. And for the first time an emperor of Rome was appointed from outside Rome—an ominous and potentially destabilizing reality.[56]

Conclusion

In this work I will show that the emperor Nero Caesar is the Beast of Revelation specifically considered and that the imperial Roman government is the Beast generically considered. As our quick survey of his life demonstrates, Nero was a horrible character even by Rome's sordid standards. Church historian Philip Schaff speaks of him as "a demon in human shape."[57] As will be shown in the pages to follow, he was the very one whom John had in mind when he wrote of the Beast.

The view I present and defend below is contrary to what the vast majority of Christians believe today. Almost certainly you have been taught a radically different view at some point in your Christian journey. You may even be tempted to scoff at its very suggestion at this point. Nevertheless, I challenge you to bear with me as we wade through the evidence on this matter in Revelation. I am convinced that you will find the flood of evidence becoming a "river that no man can cross."

As we begin our interpretive journey through this issue, may we bear in mind the exhortation of Paul who wrote: "Let God be found true, though every man be found a liar" (Rom. 3:4). May we with the faithful Bereans of old "examine the Scriptures daily, to see whether these things be so" (Acts 17:11).

Notes

1. NRSV, NKJV, NASB. See arguments in: Isbon T. Beckwith, *The Apocalypse of John: Studies in Introduction with a Critical and Exegetical Commentary* (Grand Rapids: Baker, [1919] 1979), 642-43. R. H. Charles, *A Critical and Exegetical Commentary on The Revelation of St. John* (Edinburgh: T & T Clark, 1920), 1:364–65. David E. Aune, *Revelation 6–16* (Nashville: Thomas Nelson, 1998), 769–70. Robert H. Mounce, *The Book of Revelation*, 2nd ed. (Grand Rapids: Eerdmans, 1998), 261. A. T. Robertson, *Word Pictures in the New Testament* (Nashville: Broadman, 1930), 6:406.

2. Beckwith, *Apocalypse of John*, 642.

3. Bart D. Ehrman, *The New Testament: A Historical Introduction to the Early Christian Writings* (New York: Oxford, 2000), 436

4. Ehrman, *New Testament*, 434.

5. Leonard L. Thompson, *The Book of Revelation: Apocalypse and Empire* (New York: Oxford, 1990), 11.

6. Raymond Schafer, *After the Rapture* (Santa Ana, Calif.: Vision House, 1977), 55.

7. Leon Morris, *The Revelation of St. John*, 2nd ed. (Grand Rapids: Eerdmans, 1987), 169.

8. Alan F. Johnson, "Revelation," *The Expositor's Bible Commentary*, ed. Frank E. Gaebelein (Grand Rapids: Zondervan/Regency, 1981), 12:533.

9. For example: John F. Walvoord, *The Revelation of Jesus Christ* (Chicago: Moody Press, 1966), 200; Charles, *Revelation*, 1:349; Philip Mauro, *Things Which Soon Must Come to Pass*, rev. ed. (Swengel, Penn.: Reiner Publications, n.d.), 402; Charles Caldwell Ryrie, *Revelation* (Chicago: Moody, 1968), 82; G. R. Beasley-Murray, *The Book of Revelation* (Grand Rapids: Eerdmans, 1974), 206; J. Ramsey Michaels, *Revelation* (Downers Grove, Ill.: InterVarsity Press, 1997), 157.

10. Cited in Michael Grant, *The Twelve Caesars* (New York: Barnes and Noble, [1975] rep. 1996), 95.

11. See for example: Suetonius, *Domitian* 4.

12. Ehrman, *The New Testament*, 437; Fig. 28.4

13. Ovid, *De Trislia* 1:5:69 and *Elegies* 4; Claudian, *In Praise of Stilicon* 3:135; Statius, *Silvae* 1; 2:191; Pliny, *Natural History* 3:5, 9; Virgil, *Aeneid* 6:782 and *Georgics* 2:535; Horace, *Carmen Secularae* 7; Propertius 3:10, 57; Martial 4:64; Cicero, *Ad Atticum* 6:5.

14. Tertullian, *Apology* 35; Jerome, *Letter to Marcella;* and *Sibylline Oracles* 2:18; 11:114; 13:45; 14:108.

15. See Chapter 5.

16. W. M. Ramsey, *The Letters to the Seven Churches*, ed. by Mark W. Wilson (Peabody, Mass.: Hendrikson, [1904] 1994) and Colin J. Hemer, *A Study of the Letters to the Seven Churches of Asia with Special Reference to Their Local Background* (Unpublished dissertation: University of Manchester, 1969).

17. See Chapter 2.

18. Michael Grant, *The Army of the Caesars* (New York: Charles Scribner's, 1974), xv.

19. Josephus, *Wars* 3:5:7.

20. Seneca, *On Clemency* 1:2.

21. I will call Nero by his familiar adoptive name, although it was not granted him until he was twelve years old.

22. Arthur Weigall, *Nero: Emperor of Rome* (London: Thornton Butterworth, 1933), 24.

23. Suetonius, *Nero* 5.

24. Weigall, *Nero*, 25.

25. Suetonius, *Gaius* 24.

26. Suetonius, *Gaius* 24.

27. Suetonius, *Nero* 6.

28. Suetonius, *Nero* 7.

29. For more information on the behind-the-scenes machinations of Agrippina and their relevance to Paul's "man of lawlessness," see my *Perilous Times: A Study in Eschatological Evil* (Texarkana, Ark.: Covenant Media Press, 1999), 106–107.

30. S. Angus, "Nero" in James Orr, ed., *The International Standard Bible Encyclopedia* (Grand Rapids: Eerdmans, [1929] 1956), 3:2134.

31. Suetonius, *Nero* 3; Tacitus, *Annals* 12:68.

32. E. M. Blailock, "Nero," in Merrill C. Tenney and Steven Barabas eds., *The Zondervan Pictorial Encyclopedia of the Bible* (Grand Rapids: Zondervan, 1976), 4:411.

33. See Donald B. Guthrie, *New Testament Introduction*, 3rd ed. (Downers Grove, Ill.: Inter-Varsity Press, 1970), 397; and Greg L. Bahnsen, *Theonomy in Christian Ethics* (Nutley, N. J.: Craig Press, 1977), 366–373.

34. Suetonius, *Nero* 26. Michael Grant, *Nero* (New York: Dorset, 1970), 47–53.

35. Suetonius, *Nero* 28. An amusing comment is recorded by Suetonius in light of this particularly atrocious activity of Nero: "And the witty jest that someone made is still current, that it would have been well for the world if Nero's father Domitius had had that kind of wife."

36. Suetonius, *Nero* 29.

37. Suetonius, *Nero* 34.

38. Suetonius, *Nero* 35.

39. Suetonius, *Nero* 30-32.

40. Tacitus, *Annals* 16:21ff.

41. Suetonius, *Nero* 37.

42. Philip Schaff, *History of the Christian Church*, 7 vols., 3rd ed. (Grand Rapids: Eerdmans, 1910), 1:379; B. W. Henderson, *The Life and Principate of Nero* (London: Methuen, 1903), 237.

43. Suetonius, *Nero*, 18; Tacitus, *Annals* 15:38ff. Many historians accept the reliability of the story of Nero returning to Rome during the fire and playing the lyre and singing while the city burned. Grant, *Nero*, 126–27.

44. Tacitus, *Annals* 15:44.

45. Suetonius, *Nero* 16.

46. Suetonius, *Nero* 23–25. See Miriam T. Griffin, *Nero: The End of a Dynasty* (New Haven: Yale University Press, 1984), ch. 9. Grant, *Nero*, ch. 5.

47. Suetonius, *Nero* 23.

48. Grant, *The Twelve Caesars*, 211.

49. Tacitus, *Annals* 15:67.

50. Suetonius, *Nero* 10ff.

51. Apollinius states that Nero was "cowardly and supine." Philostratus, *Life of Apollinius*, 5:33.

52. Suetonius, *Nero* 49.

53. Suetonius, *Nero* 49.

54. Suetoniius, *Nero* 57.

55. Tacitus, *Histories* 1:4.

56. See: Suetonius, *Galba* and Tacitus, *Histories* 1.

57. Schaff, *History* 1:379

2

The Relevance of the Beast

The Revelation of Jesus Christ, which God gave Him to show to His
bond-servants, the things which must shortly take place; and He
sent and communicated it by His angel to His bond-servant John
Rev. 1:1

One of the most important clues for the proper understanding of
Revelation is simultaneously one of the most overlooked and neglected.
This clue is also a significant key for opening up the identity of the
Beast. I am speaking of the stated *expectation* of John regarding the time
of the fulfillment of the prophecies.

The truth is: John specifically states that the prophecies of Revelation (a number of which involve the Beast) would begin transpiring
within *a very short period of time.* He clearly declares that the events of
Revelation were "shortly to take place" and that "the time is near." And
as if to insure that we not miss the point—which many commentators
have—he emphasizes this truth in a variety of ways. Read the following
passages with an openness to the text itself and see if you agree.

Emphasis on the Expectation

First, John emphasizes the nearness of his prophecy by *strategic placement* of the time references: He places his boldest time statements in both the introduction and conclusion to Revelation. Remarkably, many recent commentators have missed it literally coming and going.

The statement of expectancy is found two times in the first three verses: Revelation 1:1, 3. The same idea is found four times in his concluding remarks: Revelation 22:6, 7, 12, 20. John seems carefully to bracket his entire work to avoid any confusion. Significantly, these statements occur in the more historical and didactic sections of Revelation, before and after the major dramatic-symbolic visions. You should take time to just quickly read these verses in order to sense John's expectancy. We will look carefully at these below.

Second, his temporal expectation receives *frequent repetition.* His anticipation appears six times in the opening and closing sections of Revelation, at least three times in the letters to the seven churches (Rev. 2:16; 3:10, 11), and at least twice more as significant notices in the body of Revelation (6:17; 10:6b). According to the unambiguous statement of the text, the events were "at hand." John was telling the seven historical churches (1:4, 11; 2:1, 8, 12, 18; 3:1, 7, 14; 22:16) in his era to expect the events of his prophecy at any moment. He continually repeats the point for emphasis.

Third, he carefully *varies his manner of expression,* as if to avoid any potential confusion regarding his meaning. A brief survey of the two main terms he employs will be helpful in ascertaining his meaning.

John's Varied Expressions of Anticipation

1. "Shortly." The first of the terms we come upon in Revelation is the Greek word *tachos,* translated "shortly." John explains the purpose of his writing in Revelation 1:1: "The Revelation of Jesus Christ, which God gave Him to show to His bond-servant, the things which must *shortly* [*tachos*] take place; and He sent and communicated it by His angel to His bond-servant John." The standard Greek lexicon of our era lists the following meanings under the *tachos* entry for Revelation 1:1 and 22:6: "soon, in a short time."[1] Balz and Schneider's *Exegetical Dictionary of the New Testament* list the following translations: "In the NT only in the combination *en tachei, immediately, without delay* . . . ; *soon.*" Then they specifically mention Revelation 1:1 and 22:6, translating thus: "what must *soon/in a short time* take place."[2]

If you look up Revelation 1:1 in *any* modern translation you will find temporal proximity clearly exhibited. This term also occurs in Revelation 2:16; 3:11; and 22:6, 7, 12, 20. Even a cursory reading of these verses unavoidably leads to the conclusion that John expected these things to happen "shortly" or "soon."

2. *"Near."* Another term John uses is *eggus* (pronounced *engus)*, which means "near" (Rev. 1:3; 22:10). In Revelation 1:3 we read: "Blessed is he who reads and those who hear the words of the prophecy, and heeds the things which are written in it; for the time is *near* [*eggus*]." When used of spatial relationships it signifies geographical proximity: "near," "close to," "close by." When used of temporal relationships it means: "near," "soon."[3] This term literally means "at hand."[4] Therefore, its import in our context is clearly that of temporal nearness. The events bracketed by these statements were expected, by the holy apostle John, to begin taking place at any moment.[5]

John's Parallel with New Testament Eschatology

The temporal expectation in Revelation parallels New Testament teaching elsewhere. For instance, Robert Thomas parallels Revelation 6 with Matthew 24: "Jesus in His discourse was clearly anticipating what he was to show John in much greater detail." Pate concurs.[6] I agree. Interestingly, in Matthew 24:34 Jesus holds the same expectancy as John: "Assuredly, I say to you, this generation will by no means pass away till all these things take place" (cp. Matt. 23:36). He urges his hearers, as John does his readers, to expect these judgments in their own lifetimes.

In Mark 9:1 Jesus promises that some of his hearers would not "taste of death" before witnessing the "coming of the kingdom with power." This almost certainly refers to the destruction of the temple at the behest of Christ (rather than to the transfiguration which is only six days away). Similar notes of the temporal proximity of divinely-governed crises abound in the New Testament: Matthew 26:64; Acts 2:16–20, 40; Romans 13:11,12; 16:20; 1 Corinthians 7:26, 29-31; Colossians 3:6; 1 Thessalonians 2:16; Hebrews 10:25, 37; James 5:8, 9; and 1 Peter 4:5, 7. How else could the New Testament express nearness more clearly? As these verses so evidently show, dramatic divine judgments are: "soon," "near," "at hand," "at the door," "present"; because "the hour has come"; "the time is short"; "the wrath of God is coming"; "the day is approaching" in "just a little while." These judgments are to occur in "this generation," before "some of you standing here taste of death."

Liberal exegetes easily recognize John meant "near." But they write it off as error. Of Revelation's expectation Boring comments: "Does this mean he was wrong? Yes. Christians who reverence the Bible as Scripture, the vehicle of God's word, ought not to hesitate to acknowledge that its authors made errors. . . . The error should not continue."[7] Shreckenberg and Schubert imagine a shift in the Church's historical consciousness in this regard: "Only after the expectation of the imminent Parousia and the concomitant telescoping of time had subsided by the second century at the latest, was there room for a thorough-going historical and church-historical interest. Coming to terms with the world for a longer period than at first supposed, perhaps even permanently, seemed unavoidable."[8]

The remarkable nature of our preterist assertion regarding the events of Revelation is met with bewilderment by most evangelicals today. Yet the evidence is there for all to see.

John's Expectation and Our Theological Predispositions

Unfortunately, right in the very first verse of Revelation certain commentators begin straining to reinterpret the obvious. Commentators employ various desperate maneuvers to get around the clear meaning of these two terms:

Some, such as Walvoord and Ice, understand these words as indicating that whenever the events do start coming to pass, they will occur with great speed, following one upon the other with great *rapidity*.[9] Others, such as Mounce and Johnson, view them as teaching that the events are always *imminent*.[10] That is, they are always ready to occur, though they may not actually transpire until thousands of years later. Still others, such as Swete and Morris, see John's references as a measure of *God's time*, not man's.[11] That is, John is informing us that these events will come to pass "shortly" *from God's perspective*, but we must remember that "a day with the Lord is as a thousand years" (2 Pet. 3:8).

Each of these approaches is destroyed by the very fact that John repeats and varies his terms as if to dispel any confusion. Think of it: If these words in these verses do not indicate that John expected the events to occur soon, *what words could John have used to express such?* How could he have stated it more plainly? John even distinguishes his experience from Daniel's on the basis of their differing temporal outlooks— Daniel "seals" his work because of the great distance in time; John does *not* seal his work because of the nearness of the time (Dan. 12:4; Rev. 22:6).

Another detriment to the strained interpretations listed above is that John is writing to historical churches existing in his own day (Rev. 1:4, 11; 2–3). He and they are presently suffering "tribulation" (1:9a). John's message (ultimately from Christ, 1:1; 2:1; 22:16) calls upon each to give careful, spiritual attention to his words (2:7, 11, 17, 29; 3:6, 13, 22). John is deeply concerned with the expectant cry of the martyrs and the divine promise of their soon vindication (6:10; cp. 5:3–5). He would be cruelly mocking their circumstances (while committing a "verbal scam," according to Mounce[12]) were he telling them that when help comes it will come with swiftness—even though it may not come until two or three thousand years later. Or that the events are always imminent—though the readers and their great, great grandchildren may never experience them. Or that God will send help soon—according to the way the Eternal God measures time.

We must never forget that Revelation was written *to and for* first-century Christians. Proper hermeneutics recognizes the significance of an ancient work's original audience: "The identities of a book's author and his first audience are important considerations for an interpreter."[13] Indeed, Revelation functions as an "occasional epistle,"[14] that is, as a letter dealing with real-life, historical occasions in the lives of the original recipients: it was

> a letter to Christians [John] knew and for whom he felt a pastoral responsibility. . . . Just as we will certainly misunderstand Paul if we ignore the particularities of the situation in first-century Corinth, so we will misunderstand Revelation if we read it as though it were written directly to us. . . . As a letter, Revelation is not a collection of "ideas" or "general principles" but a particular message to a particular situation.[15]

The Revelation and the Coming of Christ

Perhaps one of the contextual matters that causes the most confusion is that several of the passages before us refer to Christ's "coming" (Rev. 2:16; 3:11; 22:7, 12, 20). "Behold, I am coming quickly" resounds in these verses. Surely we do not believe the Second Advent came in the first century, do we? No orthodox Christian holds such a position.[16]

Unfortunately, a good deal of unnecessary confusion arises at this juncture. Actually Christ "comes" in a number of ways. In fact, as

Morris notes of the beloved Apostle: "John uses the idea of 'coming' in more ways than one."[17] Certainly the Lord will come at the end of history, bringing about the resurrection and the judgment (e.g., Acts 1:11; 1 Thess. 4: 13–17; 1 Cor. 15:20–26).

But Scripture also teaches that Christ comes to his people in other ways.[18] He comes to individuals personally in the Holy Spirit (John 14:18, 23),[19] in fellowship or discipline by his presence in the Church (Matt. 18:20: Rev. 3:20), to believers at death (John 14:l–3),[20] to God the Father in heaven to receive his kingdom (Dan. 7:13), and in judicial judgment upon men in history (Matt. 21:40, 41; Rev. 2:5).[21]

But which "coming" does John have in mind here in Revelation?

The references in Revelation speak of his coming in judgment— *particularly upon Israel* (cf. Ch. 9 below for more detail). This is evident in the theme verse of Revelation: "Behold, He is coming with the clouds, and every eye will see Him, even those who pierced Him; and all the tribes of the earth will mourn over Him. Even so. Amen" (Rev. 1:7). This cloud-coming of Christ in judgment reminds us of Old Testament cloud-comings of God in judgment upon ancient historical people and nations (Pss. 18:7–15; 104:3; Isa. 19:l; Joel 2:1, 2; Hab. 1:2ff.; Zeph. 1:14, 15). For example, Isaiah 19:1 speaks of an historical, Old Testament judgment upon Egypt: "The oracle concerning Egypt. Behold, the Lord is riding on a swift cloud, and is about to come to Egypt; the idols of Egypt will tremble at His presence, and the heart of the Egyptians will melt within them."

Furthermore, this coming focuses upon first century Israel. Revelation 1:7 says he is coming upon "those who pierced Him." John even adds that as a consequence all "the tribes of the earth [or Land]" will mourn. The New Testament emphatically points to first century Israel as responsible for crucifying Christ (John 19:6, 15; Acts 2:22–23, 36; 3:13–15; 5:30; 7:52; 1 Thess. 2:14–15).[22]

Jesus even warns the Jewish leaders that they would personally witness this judgment-coming (Matt. 26:64).[23] This coming (Matt.

24:30)[24] would occur in his generation (Matt. 24:34; cp. Matt. 23:31–36). It was to be witnessed by men who stood and listened to Jesus and was to be the kingdom's coming with power (*en dunami*, Mark 9:1).[25]

The Jewish War with Rome (formally engaged by imperial decree from A.D. 67 to 70) brought about the deaths of tens of thousands of the Jews in Judea (those who "pierced Christ," Rev. 1:7), and the enslavement of thousands upon thousands more. The Jewish historian Flavius Josephus, who was an eyewitness, records that 1,100,000 Jews perished in the siege of Jerusalem, though this figure is disputed. J. L von Mosheim, the great ecclesiastical historian, wrote that "throughout the whole history of the human race, we meet with but few, if any, instances of slaughter and devastation at all to be compared with this."[26] In the very opening words of *Wars of the Jews*, Josephus laments: "Whereas the war which the Jews made with the Romans hath been the greatest of all those, not only that have been in our times, but, in a manner, of those that ever were heard of."[27] In fact, Mendels observes that "the Great War against Rome was unique in the ancient Near East in terms of its scale."[28] Grant estimates that it was "one of the most terrible wars of repression that the world has ever seen."[29] Chrysostom (A.D. 347–407) comments of the Jewish War: That "those horrible events were worse than any tragedy, and that never has a war of such severity afflicted the people."[30]

But as awful as the Jewish loss of life was, the utter devastation of Jerusalem, the final destruction of the temple, and the conclusive cessation of the sacrificial system were lamented even more. According to Jewish scholar Doron Mendels, the temple was "a unifying national symbol, with its priesthood becoming more than ever the national symbol of native leadership."[31] He notes that the "literature of the time"—especially the Jewish works 4 Ezra and 2 Baruch—"show the traumatic experience of the loss of Jerusalem and the Temple." Indeed, "the most shocking and traumatic event was the destruction of Jerusalem and the

Temple."[32]   Surely "the rasing of the Temple horrified diaspora Jews as much as their Judaean compatriots. Jews outside Palestine seem to have presumed the central importance of the Temple in Jewish worship despite the physical obstacles to their frequent attendance at the cult."[33]

The covenantal significance of the temple's demise stands as the most dramatic outcome of the War. The Mishnah underscores the significance of the temple in Jewish estimation: "By three things is the world sustained: by the Law, by the [Temple-] service, and by deeds of loving-kindness."[34] With the destruction of the temple the first two elements of the world's sustaining are removed. "With the destruction of the Jewish cult the keeping of the Torah in all its details became impossible."[35] The loss of the temple was an unrepeatable loss, for it has never been rebuilt. The cessation of the Daily Sacrifice "was mourned year after year as a major calamity," and "the Jewish fast-day of 9th Ab laments the catastrophe"[36] In fact, the Western Wall of the temple remains to this day and is known as the "wall of wailing," where Jews still lament their sorrow. Hence, any Jewish calamity after A.D. 70 would pale in comparison to the redemptive-historical significance of the loss of the temple.

So then, the expectation of a judgment-coming of Christ in the first century is easily explained in terms of the biblical and historical record. Thus, the point remains: John clearly expected the events of Revelation would occur soon, within his own lifetime. Obviously, then, the Beast of Revelation must be a contemporary figure relevant to the first century audience. Certainly, Nero was a contemporary political authority who was terrifyingly relevant to John's readers.

Conclusion

In light of the clear and emphatic textual evidence, the honest interpreter of Revelation should recognize that John expected his prophecies to begin taking place very soon after he wrote. To overlook the clear, repeated, well-placed statements in Revelation in this regard is to interpret Revelation in defiance of the facts.[37]

This evidence removes all possibility of identifying the Beast with any figure beyond the first century. To assert that the Beast is any contemporary figure existing in our own time (or in our future) absolutely misses John's entire point. Of course, this evidence alone does not demand Nero Caesar as the identity of the Beast. But it does set the stage for his appearance, which will be demonstrated on other grounds.

Notes

1. F. Wilbur Gingrich and Frederick W. Danker, eds., *A Greek-English Lexicon of the New Testament and Other Early Christian Literature*, 2nd ed. (Chicago: University of Chicago Press, 1979), 807.

2. Horst Balz and Gerhard Schneider, eds., *Exegetical Dictionary of the New Testament* (Grand Rapids: Eerdmans, 1990), 3:338.

3. Gingrich and Danker, *Lexicon*, 214. Balz and Schneider, *Exegetical Dictionary*, 3:371.

4. The word is derived from the compounding of *en* (in, at) and *guion* (limb, hand). See Joseph H. Thayer, *A Greek-English Lexicon of ths New Testament*, 2nd ed. (New York: American, 1889), 164.

5. Another term that *sometimes* signifies temporal nearness is *mello*, "about to." Though this term is not conclusive, a few versions translate Revelation 3:10b in a manner suggesting imminence. For instance, the New American Standard Bible translates *mello* as "about to": "I also will keep you from the hour of testing, that hour which is *about to* come upon the whole world." The fluid nature of this term, however, makes it difficult to discern whether it signifies temporal proximity or simple futurity. I previously urged Revelation 1:19 (containing *mello*) as evidence of the nearness of Revelation's judgments (see *Before Jerusalem Fell*, 141–42). But the fact that *no* standard English translation so renders the verse along with my further lexical research have led me to drop this evidentiary datum as inconclusive. For instance, Radl notes that *mello* has four basic meanings: (1) "about to"; (2) "used periphrastically for the simple fut[ure]"; (3) "intended action"; and (4) "the necessity of an event" (Radl in Bahl and Schneider, *Exegetical Dictionary*, 2:404). Gingrich and Danker note that "w[ith] the aor[ist] inf[initive] . . . *a. be on the point of, be about to.... b. be destined, inevitable.*" They even cite Rev. 1:19 under the entry: "denoting an action that necessarily follows a divine decree *destined, must, will certainly...*" (*Lexicon*, 500–01).

6. Robert L. Thomas, *Revelation 1–7: An Exegetical Commentary* (Chicago: Moody Press, 1992), 53–54. C. Marvin Pate and Calvin B. Haines, Jr., *Doomsday Delusions: What's Wrong with Predictions About the End of the World* (Downers Grove, Ill.: InterVarsity, 1995), 44–45.

7. M. Eugene Boring, *Revelation: Interpretation: A Bible Commentary for Teaching and Preaching* (Louisville: John Knox, 1989), 73.

8. Heinz Schreckenberg and Kurt Schubert, *Jewish Historiography and Iconography in Early and Medieval Christianity* (Minneapolis: Fortress, 1992), 13. See R. C. Sproul's response to such liberal tendencies, while he himself defends the preterist view: Sproul, *The Last Days According to Jesus: When Did Jesus Say He Would Return?* (Grand Rapids: Baker, 1998).

9. John F. Walvoord, *The Revelation of Jesus Christ* (Chicago: Moody, 1966), 35. Thomas Ice in Thomas Ice and Kenneth L. Gentry, Jr., *The Great Tribulation: Past or Future?* (Grand Rapids: Kregel, 1999), 108–12. See my rebuttal to Ice in our debate book, pages 182–86.

10. Robert H. Mounce, *The Book of Revelation*, 2nd ed. (Grand Rapids: Eerdmans, 1998), 41; Alan F. Johnson in Frank E. Gaebelein, ed. *The Expositor's Bible Commentary* (Grand Rapids: Zondervan, 1990), 12:416.

11. Henry Barclay Swete, *Commentary on Revelation* (Grand Rapids: Kregel, [1906] 1977), 2. Leon Morris, *The Revelation of St. John* (Grand Rapids: Eerdmans, 1969), 45.

12. Mounce, *Revelation*, 41.

13. R. W. Wall, "James, Letter of," in Ralph P. Martin and Peter H. Davids, eds., *Dictionary of the Later New Testament & Its Developments* (Downers Grove, Ill.: InterVarsity Press, 1997), 545.

14. For a helpful discussion of the "occasional" nature of New Testament writings, see: George W. Knight, "The Scriptures were Written for Our Instruction," *Journal of the Evangelical Theological Society* 39:1 (March, 1996); 3–14.

15. Boring, *Revelation*, 5, 7.

16. A view currently gaining a cult-like popularity teaches that the total complex of end-time events transpired in the first-century: the Second Advent, the resurrection, the "rapture" of the saints, and the great judgment. This view is not supported by any creed or any council of the Church in history. A "Foreword" to a book by John Noe from this movement inadvertently highlights the (all too typical) problem: "John is not a professional theologian. He has had no formal seminary training, but that may be an advantage." Then again, lacking training in biblical languages, exegetical principles, and formal theology may not be helpful at all. The origins of this modern movement arise out of and are fueled by many either presently or previously within the Church of Christ sect (e.g., Max King, Tim King, and Ed Stevens). Some "hyper-preterists" have even become Unitarians (see Edward E. Stevens, "Wanda Shirk & PIE," *Kingdom Counsel* [April 1994–Sept. 1996]: 3–17). Others have begun to apply the biblical references to hell to the events of A.D. 70, thereby denying the doctrine of eternal punishment (see Samuel G. Dawson, *Jesus' Teaching on Hell: A Place or an Event?* [Puyallup, Wash.: Gospel Themes, 1997]). The theological foundations of the movement appear to be continually mutating, which is expected when the position has no creedal moorings and is adrift on the sea of untrained theologians. For helpful rebuttals see Kenneth L. Gentry, Jr., *He Shall Have Dominion: A Postmillennial Eschatology*, 2nd ed. (Tyler, Tex.: Institute for Christian Economics, 1997), App. C: "A Brief Theological Critique of Hyper-Preterism"; Jonathan Seraiah, *The End of All Things: A Defense of the Future* (Moscow, Ida.: Canon, 1999); R. C. Sproul, ". . . in Like Manner," *Tabletalk* 24:12 (December 2000), 4–7; Vern Crisler, "The Eschatological *A Priori* of the New Testament: A Critique of Hyper-Preterism," *Journal of Christian Reconstruction* 15 (Winter, 1998), 225–56. Keith A. Mathison, *Postmillennialism: An Eschatology of Hope* (Phillipsburg, N.J.: Presbyterian and Reformed, 1999), App. C.

17. Leon Morris, *The Gospel According to John* (NICNT) (Grand Rapids: Eerdmans, 1971), 639-40.

18. For an excellent discussion of this, see Roderick Campbell, *Israel and the New Covenant* (Tyler, Tex.: Geneva Ministries, [1954] 1983), ch. 8.

19. It should be noted that the Greek word occurring in John 14:18 is *erchomai*, which means "come." It is also the word found in Matt. 24:30; Rev. 1:7; 2:5, 16; 3:11; 16:15; 22:7, 12, 17, 20.

20. Here again the Greek word used is *erchomai*. Surely Christ has not left his disciples outside of Heaven since the first century! Note that: (1) John's context in Chapter 14 also mentions his *spiritual* coming (vv. 17, 25, 26). (2) Later revelation shows deceased believers with the Lord (Luke 23:42–43; Acts 7:59; 2 Cor. 5:8; Phil. 1:23; 1 Thess. 4:14). For helpful comments on this verse, see: A. T. Robertson, *Words Pictures in the New Testament* (Nashville: Broadman, 1930), 5:249. R. H. Lightfoot, *St. John's Gospel: A Commentary* (Oxford: Oxford University Press, 1956), 275–76. Marcus Dods, "The Gospel of St. John," in W. Robertson Nicoll and A. B. Bruce, eds., *Expositor's Greek Testament* (Grand Rapids: Eerdmans, rep. 1980), 1:822.

21. In Matthew 21:40 the Greek word is the aorist tense form of the Greek verb *erchomai.*

22. Early post-apostolic Christianity continued this theme of pointing to the Jews as the ones who pierced him. See Ignatius (A.D. 50–115), *Magnesians* 11 and *Trallians* 11. Justin Martyr (A.D. 100–165), *First Apology* ch. 35, ch. 38, and *Dialogue with Trypho* 72. More detailed information on Revelation 1:7 may be found in Chapter 9. Some liberal scholars turn the New Testament evidence in this direction into evidence of anti-Semitism. See especially Dan Cohn-Sherbok, *The Crucified Jew: Twenty Centuries of Anti-Semitism* (Grand Rapids: Eerdmans, 1992) and John Dominic Crossan, *Who Killed Jesus? Exposing the Roots of Anti-Semitism in the Gospel Story* (San Francisco: HarperSanFrancisco, 1995). Some evangelicals even mistakenly fear anti-Semitism in theologies that recognize this condemnation of the Jews in the New Testament, e.g., Hal Lindsey, *The Road to Holocaust* (New York: Bantam, 1989).

23. Jesus says they will see it "from now on" (*ap arti*). That is, "in the miracles recurring at the time of his death they shall begin to see, in his resurrection likewise, and thus onward in every manifestation of power, including especially the destruction of Jerusalem and of the Jewish nation. But *opsesthe* does not refer to physical or spiritual seeing but to experimental perception." R. C. H. Lenski, *The Interpretation of St. Matthew's Gospel* (Peabody, Mass.: Hendrickson, rep. 1943), 1065.

24. The Daniel 7:13 context—upon which Matt. 24:30 and 26:64 are based—refers to the Ascension of Christ to take up his kingly rule. The dramatic, historical judgment-experience or witness to the fact of his having ascended is the destruction of the Temple, which event is in view in these and related passages.

25. The account of Josephus on *holosis* well documents the horror of Jerusalem's fiery judgment. *Wars* 4–7.

26. John Laurence von Mosheim, *Historical Commentaries on the State of Christianity* (New York: Converse, 1854) 1:125.

27. Josephus, *Wars*, Preface 1. See identical sentiments at Preface 4 and at *Wars* 5:10:5.

28. Doron Mendels, *The Rise and Fall of Jewish Nationalism: Jewish and Christian Ethnicity in Ancient Palestine* (Grand Rapids: Eerdmans, 1992), 356.

29. Michael Grant, *The Ancient Historians* (New York: Charles Scribner's, 1970), 260.

30. Cited in Schreckenberg and Schubert, *Jewish Historiography and Iconography*, 75.

31. Mendels, *Rise and Fall*, 113.

32. Mendels, *Rise and Fall*, 371.

33. Martin Goodman, "Diaspora Reactions to the Destruction of the Temple," in James D. G. Dunn, ed., *Jews and Christians: The Parting of the Ways A.D. 70 to 135* (Grand Rapids: Eerdmans, 1992), 27.

34. Aboth 1:2.

35. Crispin H. T. Fletcher-Louis, "The Destruction of the Temple & the Relativization of the Old Covenant: Mark 13:31 & Matthew 5:18," in Kent E. Brower and Mark W. Elliott, eds., *Eschatology in Bible & Theology: Evangelical Essays at the Dawn of a New Millennium* (Downers Grove, Ill.: InterVarsity Press, 1997), 163.

36. Michael Grant, *The Jews in the Roman World* (New York: Barnes & Noble, 1973), 201. See the Mishnah at *Taanith* 4:6

37. For helpful commentaries on Revelation from this perspective, see the following: Kenneth L. Gentry, Jr., "The Preterist View," in C. Marvin Pate, ed., *Four Views on the Book of Revelation* (Grand Rapids: Zondervan, 1998), ch. 1. David Chilton, *The Days of Vengeance: An Exposition of the Book of Revelation* (Fort Worth: Dominion, 1987). Milton S. Terry, *Biblical Apocalyptics: A Study of the Most Notable Revelations of God and of Christ* (Grand Rapids: Zondervan, 1988 [1898]), ch. 19. Also see Steve Gregg, *Revelation: Four Views: A Parallel Commentary* (Nashville: Thomas Nelson, 1996).

3

The Number of the Beast

*Here is wisdom. Let him who has understanding calculate the
number of the beast, for the number is that of a man; and his
number is six hundred and sixty-six*
Rev. 13:18

ollowing upon a proper understanding of the necessity for a Beast
relevant to first century Christians, I come now to material which very
particularly points to Nero Caesar. This piece of evidence is drawn from
what is probably one of the best known features of Revelation.[1] I speak,
of course, of the number 666, which is recorded in Revelation 13:18
quoted above. Who among us has not feared $6.66 coming up on his
cash register receipt? Or worse yet, 666 appearing in his Social Security
number! Jack Van Impe certainly was alarmed when someone sent him
a picture of an Israeli tour bus license plate with 666 on it. This led him
to sound the alarm in an article titled: "Messiah 1975? The Tribulation
1976?"[2] Underneath the photo of the license plate appeared the following statement: "This Jerusalem tour bus bears awesome testimony to
Revelation 13 in the first digits of its license plates."

Nevertheless, and despite the annual alarm calls regarding the Beast, "the passage is important, and its misuses by calendarizers and religious hobbyists who regard the number 666 as something of a religious cross-word puzzle should not deter more serious interpreters from seeking its authentic meaning."[3] But how is this number helpful to our inquiry? Let us begin with some historical background.

The Function of Ancient Alphabets

The usefulness of this number derives from alphabets serving dual purposes. Letters functioned, of course, as phonetic symbols for building words in written communication. As such, they served just as our modern alphabet does. But in ancient times letters also served as numerals, in that the Arabic numbering system was a later development of history. Roman numerals are perhaps the most familiar example of this. In Roman numerals the letter "I" possesses the numerical value of 1; "V" is 5; "X" is 10; "C" is 100; and so forth. In the Greek and Hebrew the values of letters followed the order of the alphabet.[4] The first nine letters represented the values of 1–9; the next nine letters were used for tens (10, 20, 30, etc.); the remaining letters represented values of hundreds (100, 200, 300, etc.).[5]

Due to this ancient double function of alphabets, riddles employing numbers which concealed name's were common. This phenomenon is called a "cryptogram" by modern scholars. Among the Greeks it was called *isopsephia* ("numerical equality"); among the Jews it was called *gimatriya* ("mathematical").[6] Any given name could be reduced to its numerical equivalent by adding up the mathematical value of all of the letters of the name.

Archaeologists have discovered many illustrations of cryptograms as graffiti on ancient city walls that have been excavated. One example has been found in the excavations at Pompeii. There the Greek inscription reads: *"philo es arithmos φμε"* ("I love her whose number is 545").

TABLE OF ALPHABETIC NOTATION OF NUMERALS

	Hebrew	Greek
1	א	α
2	ב	β
3	ג	γ
4	ד	δ
5	ה	ε
6	ו	ϛ
7	ז	ζ
8	ח	η
9	ט	θ
10	י	ι
20	כ	κ
30	ל	λ
40	מ	μ
50	נ	ν
60	ס	ξ
70	ע	ο
80	פ	π
90	צ	ϙ
100	ק	ρ
200	ר	σ
300	ש	τ
400	ת	υ
500	ת ק	φ
600		χ
700		ψ
800		ω

Source: Geoffrey W. Bromiley, ed., The International Standard Bible Encyclopedia, 2nd ed. (Grand Rapids: Eerdmans, 1982), 3:556.

Zahn notes of this example that "The name of the lover is concealed; the beloved will know it when she recognises her name in the sum of the numerical value of the 3 letters *phi mu epsilon,* i.e., 545 (*ph* = 500 + *m* = 40 + *e* = 5). But the passing stranger does not know in the very least who the beloved is, nor does the 19th century investigator know which of the many Greek feminine names she bore."[7]

In the midst of his Latin history, Suetonius records a sample of a Greek lampoon circulated after the burning of Rome in A.D. 64: "*Neopsephon Neron idian metera apektiree.*" The translation of this lampoon is: "A calculation new. Nero his mother slew."[8] J. C. Rolfe notes in the *Loeb Classical Library* edition of Suetonius's works that "the numerical value of the Greek letters in Nero's name (1005) is the same as that of the rest of the sentence; hence we have an equation, Nero = the slayer of his own mother."[9] Interestingly then, anti-Nero cryptograms were already circulating when John wrote Revelation.

That Jewish Rabbis of old used *gimatriya* is also evident, as consulting the Babylonian Talmud and other ancient Rabbinic writings shows.[10] In addition, Christian writings often employed gematric riddles. The ancient Christian *Sibylline Oracles* has Jesus' name as equivalent to "888"[11] and makes use of number values to indicate initials of various Roman emperors, including Nero.[12]

Consequently, when John gave a numerical value as a partial concealment of the name of the Beast (Rev. 13:18), he was engaging in a common practice in his day—not our own. If we could decipher the name hidden in the number, we could point out the identity of the Beast.

As we seek to learn the identity of 666, we must recall the several principles of interpretation which I listed in Chapter 1: (1) The name-number 666 must be "that of a *man*" (Rev. 13: 18b). (2) The name must be that of someone of an evil and blasphemous nature. (3) He must also be a political figure possessing great authority (13:2, 7). (4) The name must be one of John's *contemporaries*. (5) The name must be that of someone *relevant* to the first-century Christians to whom John wrote. Ehrman aptly laments: "Most [Revelation interpreters] have been concerned to show that the beast has finally arisen in their own day. Rarely are the interpretations put forth as conjectures, of course, but almost always with the confidence of those who have the inside scoop."[13]

Much debate revolves around my first principle, which is that the number must be that of *a* man. Some scholars interpret the phrase "number of a man" as indicating merely that the number involved is a *human* number, not a supernatural one.[14] But nothing in the context suggests such. What would be John's point? Why would John tell his readers (whom he had exhorted to read and understand, Rev. 1:3) that he was going to give an intelligible, human number, as opposed to an unintelligible, supernatural one? "Surely 'the number of the beast', which is stated to be 'the number of a man', shows that behind the beast and the number there is concealed a human figure known to the hearers and readers of the text of that time. This excludes all attempts to decode the number which do not related to a human figure."[15]

Others approach the number as purely symbolic of "failure upon failure upon failure"[16] or "a persistent falling short"[17] in that this brief series of sixes falls short of the number seven, which speaks of completion or qualitative perfection.[18] In response I would note that the more natural interpretation of the phrase is "the number of *a* man." Furthermore, the number actually is "six hundred, sixty and six," not "six and six and six." Six hundred and sixty-six does not fall short of seven—it exceeds it ninety-five fold!

Identifying 666

Based on what we know of Nero's character and actions, he fits easily within the parameters of the textually derived principles stated earlier. I will show that, as a matter of fact, Nero *is* revealed in this identifying number. Two lines of evidence converge on Nero, compelling my choice of him as the candidate.

Nero's Number

Of course, the necessary condition for any candidate is that his name fit the cryptogrammatic value. If any given name does not contain the value of 666 then that name must necessarily be excluded from consideration.

Interestingly, several scholars of the nineteenth century—Fritzsche, Holtzmann, Benary, Hitzig and Reuss—each stumbled independently upon the name Nero Caesar almost simultaneously.[19] We have seen that the *Greek* spelling of Nero's name has the value 1005. A *Hebrew* spelling of his name was *Nrwn Qsr* (pronounced: Neron Kaiser). Archaeological finds have documented that a first century Hebrew spelling of Nero's name provides us with precisely the value of 666.[20] Jastrow's lexicon of the Talmud contains this very spelling.[21] The numerical valuation is as follows:

נ = 50   ר =200   ו =6   נ =50   ק =100   ס =60   ר =200

which gives:

נְרוֹן קְסַר = 666

A great number of biblical scholars recognize this name as "the most likely solution" to the problem.[22] Is it not remarkable that this most relevant emperor has a name that fits precisely the required sum? Is this sheer historical accident?

The Textual Variant 616

If you consult a Bible with marginal references you may notice something quite remarkable about Revelation 13:18. Your reference may say something to the effect: "Some manuscripts read 616." Interestingly, the number 666 in some ancient biblical manuscripts is actually changed to 616. But why? Was it changed accidentally, or on purpose?

The difference surely is no accident of sight made by an early copyist. The numbers 666 and 616 are not even similar in appearance in the original Greek—whether spelled out in words or written out as numerals. The letters representing the values for 60 and for 10 (which would make the difference between the two readings) are quite different in appearance. The letter used in the Textus Receptus as the value for 60 is ξ the letter for the value 10 is ι. If these values were originally spelled out in words as in the standard critical texts,[23] even less similarity would exist. The value for 60 would be indicated thus: *hexakonta* (ἑχαxοντα); that for 10 would read: *deka* (δεxα). There is no way a copyist could confuse the two. As many textual scholars agree, it must be intentional.[24]

But *why* does this variant appear in the textual tradition? Although we cannot be absolutely certain, a strong and most reasonable conjecture arises: As shown above, John, a Jew, used a Hebrew (or Aramaic) spelling of Nero's name in order to arrive at the figure 666. But when Revelation began circulating among those less acquainted with Hebrew, a well-meaning copyist who knew the meaning of 666 might have intended to make its deciphering easier by altering it to 616. It surely is no mere coincidence that 616 is the numerical value of "Nero Caesar," when spelled in Hebrew by transliterating it from its more common Latin spelling.

This conjecture satisfactorily explains the rationale for the divergence: so that the non-Hebrew might more readily discern the identity of the Beast. Even late-date advocate Donald Guthrie, who rejects the Nero theory, grants that this variant gives the designation Nero "a distinct advantage."[25] As renowned Greek scholar Bruce Metzger says: "Perhaps the change was intentional, seeing that the Greek form Neron Caesar written in Hebrew characters (*nrwn qsr*) is equivalent to 666, whereas the Latin form Nero Caesar (*nrw qsr*) is equivalent to 616."[26] Such a possibility offers a remarkable confirmation of the designation of Nero. As you continue reading through the chapters to follow, note how well Nero fits all the requirements of the case.

Objections to Nero

Of course, this view, though widely spread, is not accepted by all scholars. Certain problems confront the Nero designation. I will mention the two major ones.

The Silence of Early Church Fathers

Frequently, we hear that the earliest treatment of the cryptogram in Revelation 13:18 does not mention Nero as a likely candidate.[27] The reference to which I refer is *Against Heresies* by Irenaeus, Bishop of Lyons (*ca.* A.D. 180). Not only does Irenaeus not mention Nero, but he discusses several other possibilities: *Euthanos, Laetinos,* and *Teitan.*[28] If Nero was the actual meaning of the riddle, why did not Irenaeus know this, since he wrote about the matter only 100 years later? Why do no other church fathers suggest it?

This certainly is a reasonable objection to the theory.[29] In fact, it is *the* strongest argument against it. In the final analysis, however, it cannot overthrow the positive evidence for the Nero interpretation, for two reasons.

First, this argument is really a two-edged sword. The very fact that Irenaeus, writing just 100 years after Revelation, cannot be sure of the proper designation demonstrates that the true interpretation, whatever it was, had very quickly been lost. If this is true of Irenaeus in A.D. 180, it is certainly true of the later fathers.

Second, had Irenaeus offered with conviction and assurance a specific alternative, the case against the Nero theory would have been more seriously challenged. Interestingly, Irenaeus suggests the hopelessness of determining the proper understanding: "It is therefore more certain, and less hazardous, to await the fulfillment of the prophecy, than to be making surmises, and casting about for any names that may present themselves, inasmuch as many names can be found possessing the number mentioned; and the same question will, after all, remain unsolved."[30]

Irenaeus admits his own ignorance on the matter. How can that prove the Nero theory wrong? None of the later church fathers does more than guess at the solution. This proves nothing more than that the interpretation was lost early in the history of exegesis. Surely John intended *some* identification!

Thomas advances the standard argument by transforming it into *positive* evidence that the Beast "must have lain (and still lies) in the future."[31] In response, though, I would urge the following: (1) The argument is a non sequitur. It simply does not follow that because someone living 100 years later did not understand a writing, therefore the original audience did not. Nor that the prophecy must be in *our* future some 2000 years later. Thomas' response would carry some weight if we had such writings expressing confusion from within John's own day (not a century later). After all, John did intend for his original audience to understand it (1:3; 13:18). (2) This is really an argument from silence. And by their nature such *ex silencio* arguments are notoriously slippery. (3) Thomas's argument rides roughshod over the temporal delimiters John very dogmatically establishes (1:1, 3; 22:6, 10) and suppresses original audience relevance.

The Problem of the Hebrew Spelling

Some have argued that since John writes to Gentile churches in Asia Minor, the mechanical maneuver necessary to derive the name from its Hebrew spelling would be too difficult.[32] Though reasonable at first glance, this objection also fails to undermine the Nero theory.

First, although John wrote in Greek and to Gentiles, scholars have long recognized Revelation as the most "Jewish" book in the New Testament, surpassing both Matthew and Hebrews.[33] For instance, in his commentary R. H. Charles includes a major section entitled "A Short Grammar of the Apocalypse." Section 10 of this "Grammar" is entitled "The Hebraic Style of the Apocalypse."[34] There Charles well notes of

John's unusual syntax: "The reason clearly is that, *while he writes in Greek, he thinks in Hebrew.*"[35] Aune agrees.[36] As J. P. M. Sweet puts it: "The probability is that the writer, thinking in Hebrew or Aramaic, consciously or unconsciously carried over Semitic idioms into his Greek, and that his 'howlers' are deliberate attempts to reproduce the grammar of classical Hebrew at certain points."[37] Some scholars have even suggested John originally wrote it in Aramaic, a cognate language to Hebrew.[38] In other words, Gentiles readers are *always* confronted with such difficulties in Revelation.

Second, in fact other Hebraicized names appear in Revelation. For instance, the words "Abaddon" (Rev. 9:11) and "Armageddon" (16:16) are Hebrew words which are given Greek equivalents. The Hebrew word "Satan" is used by John, but is interpreted into Greek as "the devil" (12:9). Other Hebrew words appear, as well: "Amen" is said to mean "truthfully" (3:14). The Hebrew "hallelujah" is not even translated into a Greek equivalent (19:1, 3, 4, 6). Surely John's adopting a Hebraic spelling for the basis of the cryptogram would not be wholly out of character, then.

Third, Asia Minor was heavily populated by Jews. As a matter of fact, "by the time of Christ, Jews were widely dispersed throughout the cities and countryside of the Empire and beyond. . . . The regions of Mesopotamia, Syria, Asia Minor and Egypt each had more than 1 million Jewish residents. . . . There was a substantial Jewish population in virtually every town of any decent size in the Mediterranean region."[39] Indeed, "nearly one out of ten inhabitants of the Roman Empire (with a population of between six to eight million) was Jewish."[40] Grant adds that "in the eastern provinces [such as Asia Minor, KLG], the percentage was perhaps as high as twenty."[41] John's audience almost undoubtedly was composed of at least a significant minority of Jews.

And why should John not use an Hebraic riddle? Was not John himself a Jew? Was not he, the writer of Revelation, sent "to the circumcised" (Gal. 2:9)? Despite the brevity of each of the Seven Letters, in them are prominent allusions to Jewish situations (Rev. 2:9, 14; 3:9). In the book itself are very definite allusions to Jewish matters, such as the twelve tribes of Israel (chs. 7 and 14).

Conclusion

Nero Caesar looms large in the Revelational drama. As all roads lead to Rome, so do they all terminate at Nero Caesar's Golden House. The factors pointing to Nero in Revelation are numerous and varied. I have shown that his name perfectly fits the certain reading of the text in Revelation 13:18, which is 666. His name even fits the corrupted reading, 616. In later chapters I will provide additional evidences supporting the interpretation of 666 as "Nero Caesar."

Only with great difficulty may we discount the many ways in which Nero fits the expectations of Revelation. *He is the only first-century historical figure that can possibly fulfill all of the requirements.* Contrary to some commentators who fear that the key to Revelation's "666" is lost, I suggest that the key is actually in the keyhole, the last place to look.

Notes

1. Mounce introduces his discussion of Revelation 13:18 thus: "No verse in Revelation has received more attention than this one with its cryptic reference to the number of the beast." Robert Mounce, *The Book of Revelation,* 2nd ed. (Grand Rapids: Eerdmans, 1998), 261.

2. Jack Van Impe, "Messiah 1975? The Tribulation 1976?" in *The Jack Van Impe Crusade Newsletter,* 4:11 (April 1975), 2.

3. M. Eugene Boring, *Revelation: Interpretation: A Bible Commentary for Teaching and Preaching* (Louisville: John Knox, 1989), 161.

4. For Greek, see W. G. Rutherford, *The First Greek Grammar* (London: Macmillan, 1935), 143ff. For Hebrew, see E. Kautzsch, ed., A. E. Cowley, trans., *Gesenius' Hebrew Grammar,* 28th ed. (Oxford: Clarendon Press, 1946), 30.

5. For readily available evidence of these values in Hebrew and Greek, the reader may consult the appropriate letters at their entries in Francis Brown, S. R. Driver, and Charles A. Briggs, eds., *A Hebrew and English Lexicon of the Old Testament* (Oxford: Clarendon Press, 1972) and G. Abbott-Smith, *A Manual Greek Lexicon of the New Testament* (Edinburgh: T. & T. Clark, 1950). See also: "Number" in J. D. Douglas and F. F. Bruce, *New Bible Dictionary* (Downers' Grove, Ill.: InterVarsity Press, 1982), 841–43.

6. See Alfred Edersheim, *Sketches of Jewish Social Life* (Grand Rapids: Eerdmans, [1876] 1972), 289–290. "Gematria," in Jacob Neusner, ed., *Dictionary of Judaism in the Biblical Period* (Peabody, Mass.: Hendrickson, 1996). Examples of Hebrew cryptograms can be found in the ancient Jewish Talmud at *Sanhedrin* 22a, *Yoma* 20a, and *Nair* 5a.

7. Cited in Oskar Rühle, *"Arithmeo"* in Gerhard Kittel, ed., *Theological Dictionary of the New Testament,* trans. Geoffrey W Bromiley, vol. 1 (Grand Rapids: Eerdmans, 1964), 462.

8. Suetonius, *Nero* 39.

9. Suetonius, *Lives of the Twelve Caesars,* vol. 2, trans. J. C. Rolfe, ed. E. H. Warmington, *Loeb Classical Library* (Cambridge: Harvard, 1913), 158.

10. See *Yoma* 20a, *Nazir* 5a, *Sanhedrin* 22:9 and *Ukin* 12. See F. W. Farrar, *The Early Days of Christianity* (New York: Cassell, 1884), 471.

11. *Sibyllie Oracles* 1:327–329.

12. *Sibylline Oracles* 5:1–50.

13. Bart D. Ehrman, *The New Testament: A Historical Introduction to the Early Christian Writings* (New York: Oxford, 2000), 436.

14. See discussion in R. H. Charles, *A Critical and Exegetical Commentary on the Revelation of St. John,* 2 vols. (Edinburgh: T. & T. Clark, 1920) 1:364–365; and Mounce, *Revelation,* 264.

15. E. D. Schmitz, "Number," in Colin Brown, ed., *New International Dictionary of New Testament Theology* (Grand Rapids: Zondervan, 1986), 2:684.

16. William Hendriksen, *More Than Conquerors* (Grand Rapids: Baker, [1939] 1967), 182. Boring, *Revelation,* 163.

17. Leon Morris, *The Revelation of St. John,* 2nd ed. (Grand Rapids: Eerdmans, 1987), 169.

18. Henry B. Swete, *Commentary on Revelation* (Grand Rapids: Kregel, [1911] 1977), cxxxvi-cxxvii.

19. See Charles, *Revelation* 1:367 and Farrar, *Early Days,* 471, n. 4.

20. D. R. Hillers, "Revelation 13:18 and A Scroll from Murabba'at," *Bulletin of the American Schools of Oriental Research* 170 (April, 1963): 65.

21. Marcus Jastrow, *A Dictionary of the Targumim, the Talmud Babli and Yerushalmi, and the Midrashic Literature* (London: Judaica, 1903). See Charles, *Revelation* 1:367. P. Benoit, J. T. Milik, and R. deVaux, *Les Grottes de Muraba'at,* DJD 2 (Oxford: Clarendon, 1961).

22. B. C. Birch, "Number," in Geoffrey W. Bromiley, ed., *The International Standard Bible Encyclopedia,* 2nd ed. (Grand Rapids: Eerdmans, 1982), 3:561. See: Ralph P. Martin and Peter H. Davids, eds., *Dictionary of the Later New Testament & Its Developments* (Downers Grove, Ill.: InterVarsity Press, 1997), 909. Bruce M. Metzger and Michael D. Coogan, eds., *The Oxford Companion to the Bible* (New York: Oxford University Press, 1993), 700. Brent C. Butler, ed., *Holman Bible Dictionary* (Nashville: Holman, 1991), 1030–31. Allen C. Myers, ed., *The Eerdmans Bible Dictionary* (Grand Rapids: Eerdmans, 1987), 956. Schmitz in Brown, *New International Dictionary of New Testament Theology,* 2:684.

23. For an insightful and concise defense of critical texts over against the Textus Receptus, see: Daniel B. Wallace, "The Majority-Text Theory: History, Methods, and Critique," *Journal of the Evangelical Theological Society* 38:10 (Sept., 1993):185–216.

24. Bruce M. Metzger, *A Textual Commentary on the Greek New Testament* (London: United Bible Societies, 1971), 751–752.

25. Donald B. Guthrie, *New Testament Introduction,* 4th ed. (Downer's Grove, Ill.: InterVarsity, 1990), 960.

26. Metzger, *Textual Commentary,* 752. See also: David E. Aune, *Revelation 6–16* (Nashville: Thomas Nelson, 1998), 770–71 and Gerhard Kittel, ed., *Theological Dictionary of the New Testament* (Grand Rapids: Eerdmans, 1964), 1:462-63.

27. Morris, *Revelation,* 169. William Hendriksen, *More Than Conquerors* (Grand Rapids: Baker, 1967), 182. Thomas Torrance, *Apocalyptic Today* (Grand Rapids: Eerdmans, 1959), 86.

28. Irenaeus, *Against Heresies* 5:30:3. See details in Aune, *Revelation 6–16,* 770.

29. This objection, however, would apply to *any* modern exposition of the name, for no modern commentator adopts Irenaeus's suggestions!

30. *Against Heresies* 5:30:3.

31. Robert L. Thomas, *Revelation 8–22: An Exegetical Commentary* (Chicago: Moody, 1995), 185.

32. G. K. Beale, *The Book of Revelation* (NIGTC) (Grand Rapids: Eerdmans, 1999), 719. G. B. Caird, *The Revelation of Saint John* (Peabody, Mass.: Hendrikson, 1966), 175. George Eldon Ladd, *A Commentary on the Revelation of John* (Grand Rapids: Eerdmans, 1972), 186.

33. "The Apocalypse contains more OT references than any other NT book." Beale, *Revelation,* 77.

34. Charles, *Revelation* 1:cxvii, cxlii.

35. Charles, *Revelation.,* cxliii.

36. David E. Aune, *Revelation 1–5* (Dallas: Word, 1997), clx–ccxi.

37. J. P. M. Sweet, *Revelation* (Philadelphia: Westminster, 1979), 16. Beale virtually lifts Sweet's text into his own, when he writes: "It seems that his grammatical 'howlers' are deliberate attempts to express Semitisms and Septuagintalisms in his Greek." Beale, *Revelation,* 96.

38. Charles C. Torrey, *The Apocalypse of John* (New Haven: Yale University Press, 1958), 27–58.

39. James S. Jeffers, *The Greco-Roman World of the New Testament Era: Exploring the Background of Early Christianity* (Downers Grove, Ill.: InterVarsity, 1999), 213. See also: Swete, *Revelation,* lxvi.

40. Mireille Hadas-Lebel, *Flavius Josephus: Eyewitness to Rome's First-Century Conquest of Judea,* trans. by Richard Miller (New York: Macmillan, 1993), 54–55.

41. Michael Grant, *The Jews in the Roman World* (New York: Barnes & Noble, 1973), vii.

4

The Character of the Beast

And the beast which I saw was like a leopard, and his feet were like
those of a bear, and his mouth like the mouth of a lion. And the
dragon gave him his power and his throne and great authority
Rev. 13:1-2

In Revelation 13 the one behind the 666 riddle is specifically designated a "beast." The word for "beast" in Greek is *therion*, a term frequently used of "wild animals," of "dangerous animals."[1] *Therion* is often used of the wild, carnivorous animals employed in the cruel Roman arenas.[2] Because of its natural association, the term is quite aptly used figuratively of persons with "a 'bestial' nature, *beast, monster.*"[3]

Not only is the name "Beast" employed by John in this passage, but he even symbolically represents this fearsome being with horrible, beastly imagery. This Beast is a compound of such feared and destructive carnivores as the leopard, bear, and lion. Almost all commentators agree that this vision of the Beast reflects Daniel's vision of the Four Beasts (Dan. 7). John's Beast even has ten horns like Daniel's fourth beast (Dan. 7:7; Rev. 13:1). Daniel emphasizes the fearsome terror of his beast: "After this I kept looking in the night visions, and behold, a fourth beast, dreadful and terrifying and extremely strong; and it had large iron teeth. It devoured and crushed, and trampled down the remainder with its feet" (Dan. 7:7). John, however, unites the lion, bear and leopard—three of Daniel's beasts—into one grotesque hybrid.

The Pagan Evidence of Nero's Nature

Scholars almost universally agree that Nero was possessed of a "bestial nature."[4] Nero was even feared and hated by his own countrymen. A perusal of the ancient literature demonstrates that Nero "was of a cruel and unrestrained brutality."[5]

We discover Nero's bestial conduct in the writings of the Roman historian Suetonius (A.D. 70–160), who speaks of Nero's "cruelty of disposition" evidencing itself at an early age.[6] He documents Nero's political evil, and states: "neither discrimination nor moderation [were employed] in putting to death whosoever he pleased on any pretext whatever."[7] Suetonius notes that Nero "compelled four hundred senators and six hundred Roman knights, some of whom were well to do and of unblemished reputation, to fight in the arena."[8] He also mentions that Nero was a sodomist, who is said to have castrated a boy named Sporus and married him.[9] He enjoyed homosexual rape and torture.[10] He ruthlessly killed his mother, brother, wife, aunt, and many others close to him and of high station in Rome.[11]

Roman historian Tacitus (A.D. 55–117) spoke of Nero's "cruel nature" that "put to death so many innocent men."[12] Roman naturalist Pliny the Elder (A.D. 23–79) described Nero as "the destroyer of the human race" and "the poison of the world."[13] Roman satirist Juvenal (A.D. 60–140) lamented "Nero's cruel and bloody tyranny."[14] Elsewhere he called Nero a "cruel tyrant."[15]

Nero so affected the imagination that the pagan writer Apollonius of Tyana (*ca.* 4 B.C.–A.D. 96) specifically designated Nero a "beast" (Gk. *therion*):

> In my travels, which have been wider than ever man yet accomplished, I have seen many, many wild beasts of Arabia and India; but this beast, that is commonly called a Tyrant, I know not how many heads it has, nor if it be crooked of claw, and armed with horrible fangs. . . . And of wild beasts you cannot say that they were ever known to eat their own mother, but Nero has gorged himself on this diet.[16]

The Sibylline Oracles agree with Apollonius. The fifth book of the Oracles (*ca.* A.D. 80–130) refers to Nero as "a destructive beast."[17] The eighth book (*ca.* A.D. 175) calls him "the great beast."[18] Other samples of beast designations for Nero include: Lactantius' (A.D. 240–320) calling him a "noxious wild beast"[19] and Severus' (A.D. 360–420) declaring he was worse than "even the wild beasts."[20]

Among the ancient pagan written traditions exhibiting a hatred and mockery of Nero are those by such Roman and Greek writers as: the writer of *The Octavia,* Pliny the Younger, Martial, Statius, Marcus Aurelius, Aulus Persius Flaccus, Vulcacius, Epictetus, Marcus Annaeus Lucan, and Herodian.[21] Nero scholar Miriam T. Griffin analyzes the presentation of Nero in the ancient tragedy *The Octavia:* "Nero is, in fact, the proverbial tyrant, robbed of any personal characteristics, a mere incarnation of the will to evil, unaffected by advice or influence."[22]

In the Jewish *Sibylline Oracles* Nero is spoken of as a "terrible snake, breathing out grievous war. . . . He will also cut the mountain between two seas and defile it with gore. But even when he disappears he will be destructive. Then he will return declaring himself equal to God."[23] Later it speaks of him as a notoriously "savage-minded mighty man, much-bloodied, raving nonsense."[24] Another of the *Sibylline Oracles* mentions him as "terrible and frightful"and "a terrible snake."[25]

Many of the early Christians remembered Nero with loathing. I will list just a few.

• Clement of Rome (A.D. 30–100) speaks of Nero's persecution as one which claimed "a vast multitude of the elect ... through many indignities and tortures."[26]

• Book 8 of the Christian *Sibylline Oracles* (A.D. 175) fearfully designates Nero a "great beast."[27]

• Tertullian (A.D. 160–220) satirically states: "We glory in having our condemnation hallowed by the hostility of such a wretch."[28]

• Eusebius (A.D. 260–340) echoes this hatred of Nero when he speaks of Nero's "depravity," "the coarseness of the man's extraordinary madness, under the influence of which ... [he] accomplished the destruction of so many myriads without any reason" and his being "the first of the emperors who showed himself an enemy of the divine religion."[29]

• Lactantius (A.D. 240–320) observes of Nero: "He it was who first persecuted the servants of God ... and therefore the tyrant, bereaved of authority, and precipitated from the height of empire, suddenly disappeared."[30] Lactantius also speaks of Nero as "an execrable and pernicious tyrant."[31]

• Sulpicius Severus (A.D. 360–420) writes that Nero was "the basest of all men, and even of wild beasts," that "he showed himself in every way most abominable and cruel," and that "he first attempted to abolish the name of Christian."[32] He even associates Nero with the prophecy of Revelation: "It was accordingly believed that, even if he did put an end to himself with a sword, his wound was cured, and his life preserved, according to that which was written regarding him,—'And his mortal wound was healed,' [Rev. 13:3]—to be sent forth again near the end of the world, in order that he may practice the mystery of iniquity."[33]

Nero and Modern Historians

From such evidence as presented above, many modern historians feel the terror and dread among the early Christians. Noted church historian John Laurence von Mosheim writes of Nero:

> Foremost in the rank of those emperors, on whom the church looks back with horror as her persecutors, stands Nero, a prince whose conduct towards the Christians admits of no palliation, but was to the last degree unprincipled and inhuman. The dreadful persecution which took place by order of this tyrant, commenced at Rome about the middle of November, in the year of our Lord 64.
>
> This dreadful state of persecution ceased with the death of Nero. The empire, it is well known, was not delivered from the tyranny of this monster until A.D. 68, when he put an end to his own life.[34]

B. W. Henderson notes that Nero was especially feared by Christians:

> An early Church tradition identified St Paul's "man of sin" and "son of perdition" and "mystery of iniquity" with the Emperor Nero; and of St Augustine's contemporaries some believed that he was still alive in the vigour of his age, others that he would rise again and come as Antichrist. Lactantius, St Chrysostom, St Jerome, and other Christian writers accept and repeat the theory that Nero is the Antichrist to come. The horrors of the first martyrdoms combined with the Nero-legend to produce the Christian tradition, and I doubt if the belief is any more dead to-day than in the eleventh century, though it cannot now as then obtain a Pope's sanction. Nero, after Judas, becomes the most accursed of the human race. "The first persecutor of the Church must needs be the last, reserved by God for a final and a more awful vengeance."

Thus Nero became a Type, the type of inconceivable wickedness and unnatural horror.[35]

Miriam Griffin observes that "the picture of him as the incarnation of evil triumphed as Christianity triumphed." She speaks at length of Nero's infamy:

> Commenting on the unanimity of opinion about the Emperor Nero that prevails among the ancient authorities, the historian Charles Merivale wrote, "With some allowance only for extravagance of colouring, we must accept in the main the verisimilitude of the picture they have left us of this arch-tyrant, the last and the most detestable of the Caesarean family. . . . Nero was the first Princeps to be declared a public enemy by the Senate."[36]
>
> * * * *
>
> In European literature Nero has served as the stock example of unnatural cruelty, a matricide in Shakespeare's *Hamlet,* a fratricide in Racine's *Britannicus.* The hero of the Marquis de Sade, he has fascinated decadent writers as the *incredibilium cupitor* longing to overcome human limits through extremes of luxury, cruelty and depravity. . . . Certainly no serious historian has been tempted to whitewash the tyrant.[37]

Conclusion

The Beast arises fearsomely within Revelation as a being possessed of an incredibly wicked character. Nero well fits the requirements, being one of the most evil of the Roman emperors. He "was a vicious and unbalanced man,"[38] "a moral monstrosity."[39] Interestingly, Nero was as destructive and terrifying as such carnivores as leopards, lions, and bears, which were used in the cruel Roman arenas and which John compounded in his imagery of the Beast. Surely Nero is the Beast of Revelation, specifically considered.

I will close this chapter with one last reference from Suetonius's history. The following quotation reinforces the aptness of applying the

Beast imagery to Nero. Speaking of Nero, Suetonius relates the following story:

> He so prostituted his own chastity that after defiling almost every part of his body, he at last devised a kind of game, in which, covered with the skin of some wild animal, he was let loose from a cage and attacked the private parts of men and women, who were bound to stakes, and when he had sated his mad lust, was dispatched by his freedman Doryphorus.[40]

The beasts of the arena were imitated by the Beast of Revelation, Nero Caesar.

Notes

1. F. Wilbur Gingrich and Frederick W. Danker, *A Greek-English Lexicon of the New Testament and Other Early Christian Literature,* 2nd ed. (Chicago: University of Chicago Press, 1979), 361. In Leviticus 26:6 the beasts of the land are symbolic of evil; in Leviticus 26:22 God promises their return to plague Israel and to bereave her of her children if she is unfaithful to the covenant. Messianic blessedness vanquishes the evil beasts (Isa. 11:6–9; Ezek. 34:25).

2. Josephus, *The Wars of the Jews* 7:2:1; 7:3:1; *Martyrdom of Polycarp* 2:4; 3ff.; 11:1ff. Ignatius, *Romans* 4:1ff.; 5:3; *Smyrnaens* 4:2; *Diognetus* 7:7; Hermas, *Visions* 3:2:1. Josephus' account of the Jewish captives in *Wars* 7:8:7 is most cruel: "Some have been half devoured by wild beasts, and yet have been reserved alive to be devoured by them a second time, in order to afford laughter and sport to our enemies."

3. Gingrich-Danker, *Lexicon,* 361.

4. Perhaps alone among historians, Arthur Weigall attempted to defend Nero in his *Nero, Emperor of Rome* (1930).

5. Sir Paul Harvey, *The Oxford Companion to Classical Literature* (Oxford: Clarendon Press, 1937), 287. See my Chapter 1 above for additional information.

6. Suetonius, *Nero* 7:1.

7. Suetonius, *Nero* 27:1.

8. Suetonius, *Nero* 12:1.

9. Suetonius, *Nero* 28, 29.

10. Suetonius, *Nero* 28, 29.

11. Suetonius, *Nero* 33–35. See also Dio, *Roman History* 61:1:2; *Ascension of Isaiah* 4:1; *Sibylline Oracles* 5:30; 12:82.

12. *Histories* 4:7; 4:8.

13. Pliny, *Natural History* 7:45; 22:92.

14. Juvenal, *Satire* 7:225.

15. *Satire* 10:306ff

16. Philostratus, *Life of Apollonius* 4:38.

17. *Sibylline Oracles* 5:343. An accessible and authoritative version of the *Sibylline Oracles* complete with critical notes and introduction, may be found in James H. Charlesworth, *Old Testament Pseudepigrapha: Apocalyptic Literature and Testaments,* vol. 1 (Garden City, N.Y.: Doubleday, 1983).

18. *Sibylline Oracles. Or.* 8:157.

19. Lactantius, *On the Death of the Persecutors* 2:2.

20. Sulpicius Severus, *Sacred Hsitory* 2:28.

21. Suetonius, *Domitian* 14; *The Octavia;* Pliny the Younger, *Panegyricus* 53; Juvenal, 4:38; Martial, *Epigrams* 7:21; 2 1:33; Martial, *Book of Spectacles* 2; Statius, *Silvae* 2:7; Marcus Aurelius, 3:16; Aulus Persius Flaccus in Suetonius's *On Poets—Aulus Persius Flaccus;* Vulcacius, *Life of Cassius* 8:4; *Capitolinus* 28:10; Epictetus, 4:5,17; Marcus Annaeus Lucan in Suetonius's *On Poets—Lucan;* Herodian, 3:4, *Historia Augusta.*

22. Miriam T. Griffin, *Nero: The End of a Dynasty* (New Haven: Yale, 1984), 100.

23. *Sibylline Oracles* 5:29, 33–35.

24. *Sibylline Oracles* 5:96.

25. *Sibylline Oracles* 12:79, 81.

26. *1 Clement 6:l.*

27. *Sibylline Oracles* 8:157.

28. Tertullian, *Apology* 5:3; cp. *To the Nations* 1:7.

29. Eusebius, *Ecclesiastical History* 2:25:2, 3.

30. *On the Death of the Persecutors* 2:2.

31. *On the Death of the Persecutors* 2:2.

32. Sulpicius Severus, *Sacred History* 2:28.

33. *Sacred History* 2:29. Although he asserts that John wrote Revelation under Domitian, 2:3 1.

34. John L. von Mosheim, *History of Christianity in the First Three Centuries* (New York: Converse, 1854) 1:138, 139.

35. B. W. Henderson, *The Life and Principate of the Emperor Nero* (London: Methuen, 1903), 420-421.

36. Griffin, *Nero,* 15.

37. Griffin, *Nero* 16. Griffin is mistaken when she suspects no historian has painted a favorable picture of Nero. See: Weigall, *Nero* (1930). See more tolerant views of Nero: Richard Holland, *Nero: The Man Behind the Myth* (Glouschester: Sutton, 2000) and Jas Elsner and Jamie Masters, eds., *Reflections of Nero* (London, 1994).

38. E. M. Blailock, 'Nero," in Merrill C. Tenney and Steven Barabas eds., *The Zondervan Pictorial Encyclopedia of the Bible*, vol. 4 (Grand Rapids: Zondervan, 1976), 412.

39. H. Cowan, "Nero," in James Hastings, ed., *A Dictionary of the Bible*, vol.3 (Peabody, Mass.: Hendrikson, [1898] 1988), 518.

40. Suetonius, *Nero* 29.

5

The War of the Beast

And there was given to him a mouth speaking arrogant words and
blasphemies; and authority to act for forty-two months was given
to him.... And it was given to him to make war with the saints and
to overcome them; and authority over every tribe and people and
tongue and nation was given to him
Rev. 13:5, 7

In this chapter I will consider the prophecy that the Beast strives to
"make war with the saints and to overcome them" (Rev. 13:7). According to John, such blasphemous warfare will last for a specific period of
time: forty-two months (13:5). If the Beast is Nero it will be necessary
to show that: (1) he did, in fact, make war with (or persecute) Christians, (2) he persecuted them *as Christians* ("saints"), and (3) this state
of persecutional threat hung over them for a period of forty-two months.

It seems clear enough to most commentators that Revelation evidences the fact that cruel imperial persecution against the faith has already begun as John writes.[1] In addition to the statement here in Revelation 13 which indicates persecution, several other passages point in
this direction. Particularly significant in this regard is a verse taken from
John's opening statement: Revelation 1:9.

In Revelation 1:9 we learn that John is writing Revelation while banished for his faith: "I, John your brother and fellow-partaker in the tribulation and kingdom and perseverance which are in Jesus, was on the island called Patmos, because of the word of God and the testimony of Jesus." This reflects the *present* experience of persecution for he informs his original audience that he is their "brother and fellow-partaker in the tribulation" (Rev. 1:9a). And since only Rome had the power to banish someone and since Patmos was an island used by Rome as a penal settlement,[2] this must indicate Roman involvement. Most probably this persecution is in its earliest stages, for (1) it is only beginning to be felt in Asia Minor (Rev. 2:10; 3:10) and (2) John points out that it will continue only for a brief period of forty-two months (Rev. 13:5).

Let us consider the suitability of the Neronic persecution as the proper historical eventuation of the Beast's "war against the saints." This will serve as strong evidence for identifying the Beast as Nero.

The Horror of the Neronic Persecution

As I have noted John and his Christian readers are entering what John himself designates as "tribulation" (Rev. 1:9). The Neronic persecution is tremendously significant to the history and development of early Christianity. For a number of reasons it necessarily leaves a lasting impression upon later Christianity.

The Significance of Nero's Persecution

First, this persecution, which was initiated by Nero in A.D. 64, was the first ever *Roman* assault on Christianity. Earlier Paul had safely appealed to Nero Caesar (Acts 25:11–12; 28:19) and in A.D. 62 had been acquitted and released.[3] Christianity was not being persecuted by Rome at that time. Furthermore, this A.D. 64 persecution was specifically directed against Christians as Christians. As Eusebius (A.D. 260–340) notes of Nero, he was famous for being the first imperial persecutor of Christianity: "Nero was the *first* of the emperors who showed himself an enemy of the divine religion."[4] Sulpicius Severus (A.D. 360–420) concurs: "He *first* attempted to abolish the name of Christian."[5]

As an imperial persecution (as opposed to the *Jewish* persecutions witnessed in Acts) it effectively removes early Christianity's protected status as a *religio licita*. Until this time Christianity is considered a sect of Judaism and thus protected under the umbrella of Judaism as a "legal religion." In his classic study on persecution, Workman confidently asserts that:

> we can date with some certainty this distinction in the official mind between Jew and Christian as first becoming clear in the summer of 64. The acquittal of St. Paul in 61 or 62—an event we may fairly assume as probable—is proof that in that year Christianity, a distinct name for which was only slowly coming into use, could still claim that it was a *Religio licita* ... still recognized as a branch of Judaism. . . . At any rate, both Nero and Rome now [in A.D. 64] clearly distinguished between the *religio licita* of Judaism and the new sect. . . . The destruction of Jerusalem would remove the last elements of confusion.[6]

This providential protected status during Christianity's infancy was vitally important in giving apostolic Christianity time to spread and gain a solid footing in the Empire. From the time of the Neronic persecution, however, Christianity is beginning to be distinguished from Judaism and will be exposed to the unprovoked cruelty of Rome. According to Judge, "what was disastrous for the Christians was that Nero's action had left a legal precedent for translating this popular odium into official action."[7] Thus, with Nero "the active persecution of the Christian Church began."[8] What is more, "the promptings of orthodox Jews in the capitol had something to do with it."[9]

That this persecution was against *Christians* as such may be proved not only from Christian but pagan sources. In his *Annals* Roman historian Tacitus (A.D. 56–117) points to those who were persecuted as "those who. . . were vulgarly called Christians."[10] Roman historian Suetonius (A.D. 70–160) concurs, for in a list of the few "positive" contributions of Nero as emperor, he includes the fact that Nero persecuted Christians: "During his reign many abuses were severely punished and put down, and no fewer new laws were made. . . . Punishment was inflicted on the Christians, a class of men given to a new and mischievous superstition."[11]

No imperial persecution other than the very first would be more important to establishing the durability of the faith. No imperial persecution more urgently required a word of exhortation and consolation to the beleaguered faith, a word such as that John offers in Revelation.

> To all appearance, at Rome, the Christian Church was drowning in its own blood in Nero's reign. We must consider the feeling of the ordinary Christian—the man in the street, so to speak—and look at it from his point of view. In later persecutions men had got to know that the Church could survive the furious edicts of Rome. But that was just the doubt which presented itself to the mind of the average Christian man in Nero's time.[12]

Thus the Beast's "war with the saints"—i.e., the Neronic persecution—was: (1) the first such "war," (2) contemporary with John's life, (3) relevant to the first century Christians, and (4) dramatically significant to the nascent faith.

The Severity of Nero's Persecution

Second, in addition to being the first imperial persecution, which set the stage for later persecutions by establishing the legal precedent,[13] the Neronic assault on Christianity was arguably her severest. Noted church historian Philip Schaff comments that the Neronian persecution was "the most cruel that ever occurred."[14] In his *Sacred History,* Christian writer Sulpicius Severus (A.D. 360–420) reserves two chapters for considering Nero's reign, and only three sentences for Domitian's alleged persecution. Severus extols the sainted life of Martin of Tours by noting that even though he did not suffer martyrdom, he would gladly have done so. He then chooses two of the worst persecutors of the Church to exalt Martin's willingness: "But if he had been permitted, in the times of Nero and of Decius, to take part in the struggle which then went on, I take to witness the God of heaven and earth that he would freely have submitted."[15]

We find the earliest evidence for Nero's persecuting wrath upon the Christians in an epistle from the first century Christian leader Clement of Rome (A.D. 30–100). His letter was written to the Corinthians and is designated *1 Clement.* Not only is his letter very early evidence for the persecution, but it comes from one who lived in Rome and who knew many of those who were slain by Nero. In *1 Clement* 6 Clement tells us that under Nero Christians suffered "through *many indignities and tortures"* and endured "cruel and unholy insults."

Tacitus gives a detailed and terrifying account of the beginning of the persecution. His account deserves recitation:

> But by no human contrivance, whether lavish distributions of money or of offerings to appease the gods, could Nero rid himself of the ugly rumor that the fire was due to his orders. So to dispel the report, he substituted as the guilty persons and inflicted unheard-of punishments on those who, detested for their abominable crimes, were vulgarly called Christians.
>
> So those who first confessed were hurried to the trial, and then, on their showing, an immense number were involved in the same fate, not so much on the charge of incendiaries as from hatred of the human race. And their death was aggravated with

mockeries, insomuch that, wrapped in the hides of wild beasts, they were torn to pieces by dogs, or fastened to crosses to be set on fire, that when the darkness fell they might be burned to illuminate the night. Nero had offered his own gardens for the spectacle, and exhibited a circus show, mingling with the crowd, himself dressed as a charioteer or riding in a chariot. Whence it came about that, though the victims were guilty and deserved the most exemplary punishment, a sense of pity was aroused by the feeling that they were sacrificed not on the altar of public interest, but to satisfy the cruelty of one man.[16]

Thus, we learn from both pagan and Christian sources that Christians were punished in huge numbers. Tacitus speaks of an "immense number";[17] Clement a "vast multitude of the elect."[18] Regarding Tacitus's observation that the spectacle ultimately elicited pity from the Roman populace, William M. Ramsay notes that: "It can have been no inconsiderable number and no short period which brought satiety to a populace accustomed to find their greatest amusement in public butcheries, frequently recurring on a colossal scale."[19]

The Impact of Nero's Persecution

Third, it was under the reign of Nero and during this state of siege that Christianity lost two of its greatest leaders, Peter and Paul,[20] and had another, John, banished.[21] From a human perspective, this would certainly strike a crippling blow to the young faith. As such, it would intensify the dreadful impact of the assault against the Church.

In fact, "the action of Nero inaugurates a new era in the relation of the Empire towards Christianity. . . . After 64 A.D. the example set by the Emperor necessarily guided the action of all Roman officials towards the Christians."[22] Blailock observes that "it may certainly be said that it was in Nero's principate that the suppression of the Church became state policy."[23] According to Angus and Renwick: "Christianity was permanently proscribed as a result of Nero's persecutions." They further note that "the emperor's example in Rome would have greatly influenced the provinces; the persecutions established a precedent of great importance in the imperial policy toward Christianity."[24]

The Length of the Neronic Persecution

Remarkably, the Neronic danger lasted almost precisely the length of time mentioned in Revelation 13:5. The persecution erupted after the destructive burning of Rome, which began on July 19, A.D. 64.[25] Soon after Rome's near destruction rumors began circulating that Nero himself intentionally caused the fires.[26]

Although Nero's unsuccessful efforts to dispel the rumors by his frantic largess must have taken a little time, he could not afford to wait for an extensive period of time to quell the politically damaging accusations. So in the latter part of November, A.D. 64, furious persecution broke out upon the innocent church.[27] Though the main brunt of Nero's crushing blow was absorbed within the first few months, a virtual state of persecution hung as an ominous cloud over the church until his death. Ultimately, lightning from that dark cloud claimed the lives of Peter and Paul in either A.D. 67 or 68.[28] According to Ellis, "sometime in the following months of AD 67–68 and clearly before the suicide of Nero 9 June 68, [Paul] was executed."[29] In fact, Ellis (citing Mommsen and referring to Suetonius, *1 Clement*, Acts of Peter, and Jerome) strongly asserts that the Neronian persecution "continued to be official policy until Nero's death on 9 June 68."[30]

This state of siege finally ended with the death of Nero on the ninth of June, A.D. 68.[31] Neither Vespasian nor Titus would molest or even threaten the church over the next decade. In fact, as I will note later (Chapter 15) neither does Domitian during his lengthy reign: "There is no solid evidence that Christians suffered persecution by the Roman state under Vespasian and his two sons, Titus and Domitian."[32]

Noted church historian Mosheim wrote of Nero's persecution:

> Foremost in the rank of those emperors, on whom the church
> looks back with horror as her persecutors, stands Nero, a prince
> whose conduct towards the Christians admits of no palliation,
> but was to the last degree unprincipled and inhuman. The dread-
> ful persecution which took place by order of this tyrant, com-
> menced at Rome about the middle of November, in the year of
> our Lord 64. . . . This dreadful persecution ceased but with the
> death of Nero. The empire, it is well known, was not delivered
> from the tyranny of this monster until the year 68, when he put
> an end to his own life.[33]

By June A.D. 68 the Empire was embroiled in civil war and could not
afford to be distracted by the Christians.

From November 64 until June 68 represents, but for a few days, a
period of forty-two months. How significant. Not only does Nero's
name fit the number of the Beast, but his state of war against Christianity lasted the very time required by the Beast's "war with the saints."

A Common Objection

Most commentators agree that Revelation definitely breathes the
atmosphere of violent persecution. But the question arises: Which persecution? The Neronic or the Domitianic? Although a number of commentators argue that the persecution background of Revelation is that
of Domitian, this view is not supported by the evidence.

Unfortunately for those who claim a Domitianic persecution background for Revelation, most historians now doubt whether Domitian
even persecuted Christians.[34] George E. Ladd is a capable New Testament scholar who believes Revelation was written during Domitian's
reign. Nevertheless, he warns against the use of evidence drawn from
the persecution motif for proving that John wrote the book under

Domitian: "The problem with this theory is that there is no evidence that during the last decade of the first century there occurred any open and systematic persecution of the church."[35]

Other late-date advocates recognize the paucity of evidence for a Domitianic persecution:

- Reginald H. Fuller (re: the evidence in Revelation): "there is otherwise no evidence for the persecution of Christians in Asia Minor" under Domitian.[36]
- Leon Morris: "While later Christians sometimes speak of a persecution under Domitian the evidence is not easy to find."[37]
- Guthrie: "data about the Domitianic persecutions tend to be elusive."[38]
- Carson, Moo, and Morris: "many scholars have exaggerated the evidence for a persecution of Christians under Domitian."[39]
- Michael Grant: a Christian persecution by Domitian does "not appear to be well-founded."[40]
- Beale exercises caution in employing the alleged Domitianic persecution as evidence for the late-date of Revelation, although he ultimately allows it.[41]

Many scholars understand Domitian's violent conduct in A.D. 95 as a paranoid outburst. It seems not to have been directed against Christians, but rather against "selected individuals whom he suspected of undermining his authority."[42] A major problem with the evidence for a "persecution" under Domitian is that it proceeds solely from Christian (and perhaps biased) sources—sources somewhat later than the events. A Domitianic "persecution" is not mentioned by *any* secular historian of the era. Furthermore, it is remarkable that though Roman historian Suetonius praises Nero for the persecution of Christians, he makes no mention at all of Domitian's alleged persecution.[43] It would seem that since he viewed the punishment of Christians as praiseworthy under Nero, any general persecution of them under Domitian would have deserved comment.

Thus, the evidence for the persecution of Christianity under Domitian is questionable. Such is not the case, however, with the persecution under Nero. As I have shown, the evidence for the Neronic persecution is overwhelming and is documented from heathen, as well as Christian, sources.

Conclusion

The paradigmatic role, extreme cruelty, and forty-two month length of Nero's persecution of Christianity fit well the role required in Revelation for the Beast. Nero did wage "war with the saints" to "overcome them" (Rev. 13:7). And he is the only Roman emperor of the first century to have waged such a war. Surely Nero looms before us in Revelation 13 as the specific manifestation of the Beast.

Notes

1. Not *all* commentators agree, however. See: Leonard L. Thompson, *The Book of Revelation: Apocalypse and Empire* (New York: Oxford, 1990). J. Ramsey Michaels, *Revelation* (Downers Grove, Ill.: InterVarsity Press, 1997).

2. Pliny (A.D. 23.79), *Natural History* 12:4–13, 23; Tacitus, *Annals* 3:68; 4:30; 15:71.

3. Richard L. Niswonger, *New Testament History* (Grand Rapids: Zondervan, 1988), 245–46; J. N. D. Kelly, *A Commentary on the Pastoral Epistles* (London: Harper, 1963), 6ff.; William Hendriksen, *I–II Timothy and Titus* (Grand Rapids: Baker, 1957), 39ff.

4. Eusebius, *Ecclesiastical History* 2:25:3.

5. Sulpicius Severus, *Sacred History* 2:28. See also Tertullian (A.D. 160–220), *On the Mantle* 4; *Apology* 5; Paulus Orosius (A.D. 385–415), *The Seven Books of History Against the Pagans* 7:7.

6. Herbert B. Workman, *Persecution in the Early Church* (Oxford: Oxford University Press, [1906] 1980), 22.

7. E. A. Judge, "Nero," in J. D. Douglas and F. F. Bruce, eds., *New Bible Dictionary*, 2nd ed. (Downers Grove, Ill: InterVarsity, 1982), 827.

8. E. M. Blailock, "Nero," in Merrill C. Tenney and Steven Barabas, eds., *The Zondervan Pictorial Encyclopedia of the Bible*, vol. 4 (Grand Rapids: Zondervan, 1976), 411.

9. W. H. C. Frend, *The Rise of Christianity* (Philadelphia: Fortress, 1984), 109.

10. Tacitus, *Annals* 15:44.

11. Suetonius, *Nero* 13.

12. James J. L. Ratton, *The Apocalypse of St. John* (London: R. and T. Washbourne, 1912), 87.

13. "The precedent was set by Nero," which precedent "guided provincial governors." *Oxford Illustrated History of Christianity* (Oxford: Oxford University Press, 1990), 41.

14. Philip Schaff, *History of the Christian Church*, 3rd ed. (Grand Rapids: Eerdmans, 1910), 1:386.

15. Sulpicius Severus., *Letters* 3 (To Deacon Aerialist).

16. Tacitus, *Annals* 15:44.

17. *Annals* 15:44.

18. *1 Clement* 6.

19. William M. Ramsay, *The Church in the Roman Empire Before A.D. 170* (Grand Rapids: Baker, [1897] rep. 1979), 241.

20. Clement of Rome (A.D. 30–100), *1 Clement* 5; Tertullian (A.D. 160–220), *On the Exclusion of Heretics* 36; Lactantius (A.D. 240–320), *On the Death of the Persecutors* 2; Eusebius (A.D. 260–34), *Ecclesiastical History* 3:1:3.

21. See Revelation 1:9; the Syriac *History of John the Son of Zebedee*, the Syriac versions of Revelation. See also Chapter 13 below.

22. Ramsay, *The Church in the Roman Empire*, 251.

23. Blailock, "Nero," in *Zondervan Pictorial Encyclopedia of the Bible*, 4:411.

24. S. Angus and A. M. Renwick, "Nero," in Geoffrey W. Bromiley, ed., *The International Standard Bible Encyclopedia*, 2nd ed. (Grand Rapids: Eerdmans, 1982), 3:523.

25. Tacitus, *Annals* 15:41. See discussion in Schaff, *History* 1:379.

26. Tacitus, *Annals* 15:39; Suetonius, *Nero* 38.

27. John Laurence von Mosheim, *Historical Commentaries,* vol. 1, trans. Robert Studley Vidal (New York: S. Converse, 1854), 138; Moses Stuart, *Commentary on the Apocalypse,* 2 vols. (Andover, Allen, Morrill, and Wardwell, 1845) 2:279.

28. Niswonger, *New Testament History,* 267. E. Earle Ellis, "Paul," in Douglas and Bruce, *New Bible Dictionary,* 891. Merrill F. Unger, *Archaeology and the New Testament* (Grand Rapids: Zondervan, 1963), 323. See also A. T. Robertson, "Paul, the Apostle" in James Orr, ed., *The International Standard Bible Encyclopedia* (Grand Rapids: Eerdmans, 1956) 3:2287; Richard Longenecker, *The Ministry and Message of Paul* (Grand Rapids: Zondervan, 1971), 85–86; *Zondervan Pictorial Encyclopedia of the Bible,* 4:650, 654. *New Bible Dictionary,* 891.

29. E. Earle Ellis, *The Making of the New Testament Documents* (Boston: Brill, 1999), 284.

30. Ellis, *Making of the New Testament Documents,* 246

31. Stuart, *Apocalypse,* 2:469. See also Justo L. Gonzalez, *The Early Church to the Dawn of the Reformation* (San Francisco: Harper and Row, 1984), 36.

32. F. W. Beare, "Persecution," in George Arthur Buttrick, ed., *The Interpreter's Bible Dictionary,* 5 vols. (Nashville: Abingdon, 1962), 3:737.

33. von Mosheim, *Biblical Commentaries* 1:138, 139.

34. In fact, Thompson provides compelling evidence that Domitian was a relatively good emperor. Leonard L. Thompson, *The Book of Revelation,* 173, see also: 16, 95, 116, 131, 136, 172.

35. George Eldon Ladd, *A Commentary on the Revelation of John,* 2nd ed. (Grand Rapids: Eerdmans, 1987), 37.

36. Reginald H. Fuller, *A Critical Introduction to the New Testament* (Letchworth: Duckworth, 1971), 187.

37. Leon Morris, *The Revelation of St. John* (Grand Rapids: Eerdmans, 1969), 36–37.

38. Donald B. Guthrie, *New Testament Introduction,* 4th ed. (Downer's Grove, Ill.: InterVarsity Press, 1990), 951.

39. D. A. Carson, Douglas J. Moo, and Leon Morris, *An Introduction to the New Testament* (Grand Rapids: Zondervan, 1992), 474.

40. Michael Grant, *The Jews in the Roman World* (New York: Barnes & Noble, 1973), 227.

41. G. K. Beale, *The Book of Revelation* (NIGTC) (Grand Rapids: Eerdmans, 1999), 12–16

42. Glenn W. Barker, William L. Lane, and J. Ramsey Michaels, *The New Testament Speaks* (New York: Harper and Row, 1969), 368.

43. *Nero* 16.

6

The Worship of the Beast

And they worshiped the dragon, because he gave his authority to
the beast; and they worshiped the beast, saying, "Who is like the
beast, and who is able to wage war with him?"
Rev. 13:4

If Nero is indeed the personal incarnation of the Beast of Revelation, as I have been arguing, then he must have been worshiped. Revelation speaks frequently of the worship of the Beast: Revelation 13:4, 8, 12, 15; 14:9, 11; 16:2; 19:20; 20:4. The most noteworthy passage is Revelation 13 where worship of the Beast is spoken of repeatedly and is a compelled worship. Revelation 13:4, cited as the chapter heading above, will suffice as a sample.

The Early History of the Emperor Cult

The worship of the Roman emperor through what is known as "the emperor cult" is a familiar feature of Roman imperial history. I will briefly survey the origins and early history of emperor worship before we set forth the evidence for the worship of Nero.

Julius Caesar

Emperor worship had its roots in the reign of Julius Caesar, the first ruler of the Roman Empire.[1] As a matter of fact, Julius was granted by the Roman Senate the title "Jupiter Julius." This act put him on a level with Jupiter, the leading god among the Romans.[2]

Archaeologists have discovered an interesting inscription at Ephesus, one of the very cities to which Revelation is addressed. Julius was described in this inscription as "god manifest and common saviour of the life of man."[3] His statue was placed in the temple of Quirinius, and was inscribed: "To the invincible God."[4] Roman historian Suetonius notes in this regard that "he allowed honours to be bestowed on him which were too great for mortal man: temples, altars, and statues beside those of the gods; a special priest, an additional college of the Superci, and the calling of one of the months by his name."[5] The senate decreed that a special temple be built for the *dementia Caesaris*. "There Caesar and his divine *dementia* were to be set up and worshipped."[6]

After Julius's death the Roman Senate voted him into the company of the gods. From that time forth he began to be called *Divus Julius*, that is, "divine Julius."[7] In addition, a formal cult of *Divus Julius* was established and "an altar to him was erected in the forum."[8]

Suetonius records for us that "some write that three hundred men of both orders were selected from the prisoners of war and sacrificed on the Ides of March like so many victims at the altar raised to the Deified Julius."[9] Here we find at least this one occurrence of the slaying of men as altar victims for the deified Caesar.

After Julius's death, several men set up a twenty foot high marble column inscribed with "To the Father of his Country." Suetonius notes that "at the foot of this they continued for a long time to sacrifice, make vows, and settle some of their disputes by an oath in the name of Caesar."[10] He was said to have been accepted as a god not only by a formal decree of the senate, "but also in the conviction of the common people."[11]

Augustus Caesar

Although the Empire's second ruler, Augustus, forbad divine honors to himself in Rome,[12] the Roman historians Tacitus and Suetonius note that he sanctioned his worship and the erection of altars elsewhere.[13] Even as early as 29 B.C. Augustus allowed such, giving the annually elected high priest of the cult much dignity in the provinces.[14] In fact, about the same time the assembly offered a crown "for the person who devised the greatest honours for the god [*sc.* Augustus]."[15]

Scullard comments regarding Octavian (*i.e.*, Augustus):

> In one respect Octavian had long been unique: since 42 B.C. and the consecrations of Divus Julius he had been the son of a god, "Divi filius." After Actium his birthday was celebrated as a public holiday; libations were poured in his honour at public and private banquets; from 29 B.C. his name was added to those of the gods in hymns; two years later he received the title of Augustus; his Genius, perhaps in 12 B.C., was inserted in official oaths between the name's of Jupiter and the Di Penates; in A.D. 13 an altar was dedicated by Tiberius in Rome to the Numen Augusti.[16]

Grant comments on "Octavian's exploitation of this development" which "was displayed upon coins which show himself on one side, described as 'Caesar Son of a God,' and Julius Caesar on the other, named 'the God Julius.'"[17] Indeed, "Priests of Augustus were found in more than thirty cities of Asia Minor" to which John sends the Revelation.[18]

Beckwith notes that on his death the Senate voted Augustus among the gods and that a temple was erected in the Palatine area of Rome. Furthermore "his worship spread rapidly in both the Asian and western provinces, so that the Jewish philosopher Philo (20 B.C.–A.D. 50) could report that "everywhere honors were decreed to him equal to those of the Olympian gods."[19]

Archaeologists have in their possession a formal decree of the Synod of the Province of Asia, which is dated about 9 B.C. This decree is preserved in a letter of the proconsul to the cities of Asia:

> Whether the natal day of the most divine Caesar is to be observed most for the joy of it or for the profit of it — a day which one might justly regard as equivalent to the beginning of all things, equivalent, I say, if not in reality, at any rate in the benefits it has brought, seeing that there was nothing ruinous or that had fallen into a miserable appearance that he has not restored. He has given another aspect to the universe, which was only too ready to perish, had not Caesar— a blessing to the whole of mankind—been born. For which reason each individual may justly look upon this day as the beginning of his own life and physical being, because there can be no more of the feeling that life is a burden, now that he has been born.
>
> Resolved by the Greeks of the province of Asia, on the proposal of the High-priest Apollonius ... : Whereas the Providence which orders the whole human life has shown a special concern and zeal and conferred upon life its most perfect ornament by bestowing Augustus, whom it fitted for his beneficent work among mankind by filling him with virtue, sending him as a Savior, for us and for those who come after us, one who should cause wars to cease, who should set all things in fair order, and whereas Caesar, when he appeared, made the hopes of those who forecast a better future [look poor compared with the reality], in that he not only surpassed all previous benefactors, but left no chance for future ones to go beyond him, and the glad tidings which by his means went forth into the world took its rise in the birthday of the God.[20]

Tiberius Caesar

During the reign of the third ruler of the Empire, we discover an event in the ministry of Christ that highlights the presence of emperor worship and Tiberius's divine pretensions. Christ's remarks regarding the tribute money are telling evidence of emperor worship (Matt. 22: 15–22; Mark 12:13–17; Luke 20:20–26). Here Christ teaches that servants of the true God should "render unto God" those things which are God's (*i.e.*, worship), and only "render unto Caesar" those things which are rightfully his (*i.e.*, taxes). This is a tacit protest against emperor worship under Tiberius (ruled A.D. 14–37).[21]

At Tiberius's death "eleven cities of Asia struggled for the honour of erecting a temple to his memory."[22] The Senate finally awarded the temple to Smyrna,[23] one of the seven cities to which the Seven Letters in Revelation is written.

Gaius ("Caligula") Caesar

The fourth ruler of the Empire was Gaius Caesar, also known by his nickname "Caligula." Gaius was clearly a madman possessed with the conviction of his own deity. He placed the head of his own statue on that of Jupiter, had himself saluted as Jupiter, and had temples erected to himself.[24]

According to the Hellenistic Jewish philosopher Judeaus Philo, Caligula/Gaius:

> mounted up to and invaded the veneration and worship paid to those who are looked upon as greater than they, as the supreme deities of the world, Mercury, and Apollo, and Mars.[25]
>
> * * * *
>
> All others [beyond the Jews], all men, all women, all cities, all nations, and every country, and region of the earth, I had almost said the whole of the inhabited world, although groaning over what was taking place, did nevertheless flatter him, dignifying him above measure, and helping to increase his pride and arrogance; and some of them even introduced the barbaric custom into Italy of falling down in adoration before him.[26]
>
> * * * *

> Gaius puffed himself up with pride, not only saying, but
> actually thinking that he was a god.[27]

The Jewish historian Josephus records the deluded pretensions of
Gaius (here spelled: "Caius"): "All who were subject to the Roman empire built altars and temples to Caius, and in other regards universally
received him as they received the gods."[28] His infamous plan to have
his image erected in the temple at Jerusalem and the providential pre-
vention of it is well-known, thanks to Josephus and Philo.[29] Philo records
the Jewish alarm: "Our temple is destroyed. . . . Gaius has ordered a
colossal statue of himself to be erected in the holy of holies, having his
own name inscribed upon it with the title of Jupiter."[30] That attempt,
prevented by his death, would certainly have issued forth in war with
the Jews.

Grant notes that

> Caligula began to go farther than ever before, much farther
> than either of the two previous emperors, in authorizing his
> own deification—to take effect immediately, now while he was
> still alive. . . . What Caligula now arranged at Rome was some-
> thing quite unprecedented, the establishment of two temples of
> his own godhead, one erected from his own resources and the
> other at state expense by decree of the senate.[31]

Claudius Caesar

The fifth ruler, the immediate forerunner of Nero, was Claudius
Caesar. Suetonius and Tacitus both record the up and down position of
Claudius as a god. He was voted a god upon his death only to have his
enrollment among the gods annulled by Nero but later restored by
Vespasian.[32] Even during his life a temple was erected to him at
Colchester.[33] Grant observes of this action that "Claudius's new foun-
dation included a large and sumptuous temple dedicated to his own

divinity, as was customary at provincial capitals."[34] Grant continues: "writers were permitted to speak of his Sacred Hands and Duties, and even to describe him as 'our god Caesar.'"[35]

Summary

Church historian Kurt Aland comments: "In the first century of the Christian Era all the emperors claim this supreme achievement [*i.e.,* divinity] for themselves." He even remarks that "the emperors after Augustus especially promoted the cult of the emperor."[36] As a matter of fact, A. S. Peake notes that "the practice in its worst form, that is the worship of the living emperor, had been known in Asia as early as the reign of Augustus."[37] Indeed, Julius's actions effected the "official deification of the state."[38]

Thompson agrees:

> Christians living in the seven cities mentioned in the Book of Revelation probably found the imperial cult an objectionable social, religious institution, but it was just as objectionable under Claudius as under Domitian. Change in emperors throughout the first century did not affect the presence of the cult in Asia. . . . Five of the seven cities had imperial altars (all but Philadelphia and Laodicea), six had imperial temples (all but Thyatria), and five had imperial priests (all but Philadelphia and Laodicea).[39]
>
> * * * *
>
> The churches of the Book of Revelation were located geographically, organizationally, and culturally where the imperial cult was most heavily distributed.[40]

Clearly then, the emperor cult had a prominent role in the political and social life of the Roman empire. Let us now consider the matter from the perspective of Nero's reign in particular.

The Neronic History of the Emperor Cult

Nero was surely the most notorious Roman emperor of the first century, excelling both the insane Caligula and the paranoid Domitian in notoriety. He was also jealously vain in his proud appreciation of his own artistic talents.[41] How could such a vain character resist the glory afforded by the emperor cult? As a matter of historical record, he did not.

Nero's Deity

The Roman dramatist and statesman Seneca (4 B.C.–A.D. 65) was one of young Nero's tutors and a powerful influence in his early rule.[42] Seneca convinced Nero that he was destined to become the very revelation of the divine Augustus and of the god Apollo.[43] Speaking as Apollo, Seneca praised Nero:

> He is like me in much, in form and appearance, in his poetry and singing and playing. And as the red of morning drives away dark night, as neither haze nor mist endure before the sun's rays, as everything becomes bright when my chariot appears, so it is when Nero ascends the throne. . . . He restores to the world the golden age.[44]

Suetonius remarks of Nero that "since he was acclaimed as the equal of Apollo in music and of the Sun in driving a chariot, he had planned to emulate the exploits of Hercules as well."[45] An inscription from Athens speaks of him as "all powerful Nero Caesar Sebastos, a new Apollo."[46]

Nero's portrait appears on coins as Apollo playing the lyre. He appears with his head radiating the light of the sun on copper coins struck in Rome and at Lugdunum. One type has Genius (a Roman tutelary deity) sacrificing over an altar on the reverse side; another has

Apollo on the reverse. As Bo Reicke notes of Nero's Apollo fascination: "All this was more than pomp and show: Nero strove with deadly seriousness to play the role of Augustus and Apollo politically, the former primarily from 54 to 61, the latter from 62 to 68."[47] Remarkably, eastern provincial coins hailed Nero's mother (Agrippina) "as goddess and the parent of a god."[48]

As early in his reign as 55 the senate erected a huge statue of Nero in the Temple of Mars in Rome.[49] The statue was the same size as that of Mars in Mars's own Temple:

> [The] effigy of Nero, which stood between 110 and 120 feet high, was erected as the centre-piece for the vestibule of the palace (the rebuilt Domus Transitoria) where it probably stood within a central colonnaded court overlooking the Forum. The emperor's brow was crowned with rays, suggesting a comparison or identification with the Sun-god.[50]

Nero was also "equated with Jupiter, by Calpurnius Siculus, *Eclogues*, IV, 142, and on coins of Dioshieron in Lydia. The towns of Cyme and Synaus describe him in his lifetime as a god (*theos*)."[51]

Nero's Worship

Nero was actually worshiped, for inscriptions found in Ephesus call him "Almighty God" and "Savior."[52] Nero is referred to as "God and Savior" in an inscription at Salamis, Cyprus.[53] Indeed, "as his megalomania increased, the tendency to worship him as ruler of the world became stronger, and in Rome his features appeared on the colossus of the Sun near the Golden House, while his head was represented on the coinage with a radiate crown. Members of the imperial house also began to receive unheard of honours: "Nero deified his child by Poppaea and Poppaea herself after their deaths. All this was far removed from the modest attitude of Augustus."[54]

Regarding the imperial development of the emperor cult, Caligula (Gaius) and Nero "abandoned all reserve"[55] in promoting emperor worship. In fact, "Caligula and Nero, the only two of the Julio-Claudians who were direct descendants of Augustus, demanded divine honors while they were still alive."[56]

Perhaps this demand for worship by Nero is best exposed in the following incident. In A.D. 66 Tiridates, King of Armenia, approached Nero in devout and reverential worship, according to Roman historian Dio Cassius (A.D. 150–235):

> Indeed, the proceedings of the conference were not limited to mere conversations, but a lofty platform had been erected on which were set images of Nero, and in the presence of the Armenians, Parthians, and Romans Tiridates approached and paid them reverence; then, after sacrificing to them and calling them by laudatory names, he took off the diadem from his head and set it upon them.
>
> * * * *
>
> Tiridates publicly fell before Nero seated upon the rostra in the Forum: "Master, I am the descendant of Arsaces, brother of the kings Vologaesus and Pacorus, and thy slave. And I have come to thee, my god, to worship thee as I do Mithras. The destiny thou spinnest for me shall be mine; for thou art my Fortune and my Fate."[57]

By this action this king actually worshiped "the image of the Beast" (Rev. 13:15).

Dio Cassius notes also the fate of one senator who did not appreciate Nero's "divine" musical abilities: "Thrasaea was executed because he failed to appear regularly in the senate . . . and because he never would listen to the emperor's singing and lyre-playing, nor sacrifice to Nero's Divine Voice as did the rest."[58] This senator failed to worship the Beast and was executed. This reflects Revelation 13:15 which says "as many as do not worship the image of the beast" are "to be killed." In fact, Seneca puts these words in Nero's mouth:

> From out of all the host of mortal beings, have I been chosen and thought worthy to do the work of the gods upon the earth? I have been given the power of life and death over all the nations. To determine the condition and to control the destinies of every race and of every individual is my absolute prerogative.[59]

In A.D. 67 Nero went to Greece, where he remained for more than a year performing as a musician and an actor in the Grecian festivals. The response of the Greeks is given by Arthur Weigall, as he comments upon the history of Rome written by Dio Cassius:

> Soon Nero was actually deified by the Greeks as "Zeus, Our Liberator." On the altar of Zeus in the chief temple of the city they inscribed the words "to Zeus, our Liberator" namely Nero, for ever and ever; in the temple of Apollo they set up his statue; and they called him "The new Sun, illuminating the Hellenes," and "the one and only lover of the Greeks of all time."[60]

When Nero returned to Rome from Greece in A.D. 68, the triumphant praise of the city echoed in his ears as he entered the Palace and Apollo's Temple on the Palatine. Dio Cassius records the scene thus:

> The city was all decked with garlands, was ablaze with lights and reeking with incense, and the whole population, the senators themselves most of all, kept shouting in chorus: "Hail, Olympian Victor! Hail, Pythian Victor! Augustus! Augustus! Hail to Nero, our Hercules! Hail to Nero, our Apollo! The only Victor of the Grand Tour the only one from the beginning of time! Augustus! Augustus! O, Divine Voice! Blessed are they that hear thee."[61]

During the Roman Civil Wars, begun with the death of Nero in June A.D. 68, the emperor Vitellius even offered sacrifices to the spirit of the deceased Nero. To better secure his own emperorship, Emperor Vespasian, who overthrew Vitellius, had to make the effort to check this Nero cult.[62]

Conclusion

The presence of emperor worship in Revelation demonstrates that we are on the right track in specifying the Roman empire as the Beast, particularly as it is incarnate in Nero Caesar. Abundant testimony to emperor worship exists at various stages of development well before Nero. And Nero himself actually demanded such worship in a way unsurpassed by any previous emperor, except, perhaps, for Caligula.

Notes

1. Technically, Julius was not an "emperor." Augustus was the first emperor. Yet though Julius was not an emperor *de jure*, he certainly functioned as one *de facto*. Revelation uses the word "king."

2. H. H. Scullard, *From the Gracchi to Nero,* 2nd ed. (New York: Barnes and Noble, 1963), 152. Jupiter "becomes the chief of the Roman gods, Jupiter Optimus Maximus, 'Jupiter the best and greatest.'" Paul Harvey, *Oxford Companion to Classical Literature* (Oxford: Clarendon, 1937), 232.

3. Scullard, *From the Gracchi to Nero,* 152.

4. James J. L. Ratton, *The Apocalypse of St. John* (London: R. and T. Washbourne, 1912), 48. See Dio Cassius, 47:18:33.

5. Suetonius, *Julius* 76.

6. Ethelbert Stauffer, *Christ and the Caesars* (Philadelphia Westminster, 1955), 50.

7. See the Roman writers Cicero (*Philippi* 2:110), Suetonius (*Julius* 38), and Dio Cassius (*Roman History* 14:6:4).

8. Scullard, *Gracchi,* 152.

9. Suetonius, *Augustus* 15.

10. Seutonius, *Julius* 88.

11. Seutonius, *Julius* 88.

12. He disdained the title *"Dominius"* ("Lord") because he preferred to be known as the governor of free men rather than the master of slaves.

13. Suetonius, *Augustus* 52-53; Tacitus, *Annals* 1:10.

14. Edward Selwyn, *The Christian Prophets and the Prophetic Apocalypse* (London: Macmillan, 1900), 122–123. For a helpful study of the socio-political implications of the "genius" of Caesar, see R. J. Rushdoony, *The One and the Many* (Fairfax, Vir.: Thoburn, [1971] 1978), ch. 5.

15. Leonard L. Thompson, *The Book of Revelation: Apocalypse and Empire* (New York: Oxford University Press, 1990), 160.

16. Scullard, *Gracchi,* 242.

17. Michael Grant, *The Twelve Caesars* (New York: Barnes & Noble, [1975] 1996), 55.

18. Thompson, *The Book of Revelation,* 159.

19. Isbon T. Beckwith, *The Apocalypse of John: Studies in Introduction* (Grand Rapids: Baker, [1919] 1967), 199. See also: Grant, *The Twelve Caesars,* 88.

20. Howard Clark Kee, *The Origins of Christianity: Sources and Documents* (Englewood, N. J.: Prentice-Hall, 1973), 76. See also Stauffer, *Christ and the Caesars,* chs. 5–7.

21. See: Tertullian, *On Idolatry,* 15. For a helpful summary of this matter, see: Richard L. Niswonger, *New Testament History* (Grand Rapids: Zondervan, 1988), 163–65; and Craig S. Keener, *Matthew* (Downers Grove, Ill.: InterVarsity Press, 1997), 326–27. For more detail see: F. F. Bruce, "Render to Caesar," in E. Bammel and C. F. D. Moule, eds., *Jesus and the Politics of His Day* (Cambridge: Cambridge University Press, 1984), 249–63.

22. Herbert B. Workman, *Persecution in the Early Church* (Oxford: Oxford University Press, [1906] 1980), 39ff.

23. Edward C. Selwyn, *The Christian Prophets and the Prophetic Apocalypse* (London: Macmillan, 1900), 123.

24. Suetonius, *Caligula* 21.

25. Philo, *Embassy to Gaius*, 93.

26. Philo, *Embassy to Gaius*, 116.

27. Philo, *Embassy to Gaius*, 162.

28. *Antiquities* 18:8:1 See also Eusebius, *Ecclesiastical History* 2:5–6.

29. Josephus, *Antiquities* 18:8:2. Philo, *Embassy to Gaius*, 184ff.

30. Philo, *Embassy to Gaius*, 774.

31. Grant, *The Twelve Caesars*, 121–22.

32. Suetonius, *Claudius* 45; *Nero* 9; Tacitus, *Annals* 12:69.

33. Workman, *Persecution*, 40.

34. Grant, *Twelve Caesars*, 139.

35. Grant, *Twelve Caesars*, 139.

36. Kurt Aland, *A History of Christianity* (Philadelphia: Fortress, 1985) 1:18,

37. A. S. Peake, *The Revelation of St. John* (London: Joseph Johnson, 1919), 84.

38. Michael Grant, *The Army of the Caesars* (New York: Charles Scribner's, 1974), 34.

39. Thompson, *The Book of Revelation*, 159.

40. Thompson, *The Book of Revelation*, 160.

41. Miriam T. Griffin, *Nero: The End of a Dynasty* (New Haven: Yale University Press, 1984), chs. 9 and 10.

42. See Chapter 1 above.

43. Seneca, *On Clemency* 1:1:6; *Apocolocyntosis* (or *Pumpkinification)* 4:15–35.

44. Stauffer, *Christ and the Caesars*, 52.

45. Suetonius, *Nero* 53.

46. Mary E. Smallwood, *Documents Illustrating the Principates Gains Claudius and Nero* (Cambridge: University Press, 1967), 52 (entry #145).

47. Bo Reicke, *The New Testament Era: The World of the Bible from 500 B.C. to A.D. 100* (Philadelphia: Fortress, 1968), 70.

48. Michael Grant, *Nero* (New York: Dorest, 1970), 31.

49. See Tacitus, *Annals* 13:8:1.

50. Grant, *Nero*, 148–49. See also: Kenneth Wellesley, *The Year of the Four Emperors*, 3rd ed. (London: Routledge, 2000), 3.

51. Grant, *Nero*, 222.

52. Ratton, *Apocalypse*, 48.

53. Smallwood, *Documents Illustrating the Principates*, 142 (entry #142).

54. Scullard, *Gracchi*, 371.

55. Eduard Lohse, *The New Testament Environment*, trans. John E. Steely (Nashville: Abingdon, 1976), 220.

56. Joseph Ward Swain, *The Harper History of Civilization* (New York: Harper, 1958), 1:229.

57. Dio Cassius, *Roman History* 62:5:2.

58. Dio Cassius, *Roman History.* 62:26:3.

59. Seneca, *On Clemency,* 1, 2. Cited in Grant, *Twelve Caesars,* 154.

60. Arthur Weigall, *Nero: Emperor of Rome* (London: Thornton Butterworth, 1933), 276.

61. Dio Cassius, *Roman History* 62:20:5.

62. Dio Cassius, *Roman History* 65:4

7

The Revival of the Beast

And I saw one of his heads as if it had been slain, and his fatal
wound was healed. And the whole earth was amazed and followed
after the beast. ... And the beast which was and is not,
is himself also an eighth, and is one of the seven
Rev. 13:3; 17:11a

A most interesting and perplexing aspect of the Beast is that which indicates his death and revivification. The specific verses of Revelation which contain allusions to this phenomenon are Revelation 13:3, 14 and 17:8, 11. Two of these are cited at the heading of the present chapter.

The Death of the Beast

The manner of Nero's death corresponds with the prophecy of Revelation 13:10: "If anyone is destined for captivity, to captivity he goes; if any one kills with the sword, with the sword he must be killed." In the context of speaking of the Beast, John gives encouragement to those whom the Beast was presently afflicting: "Here is the perseverance and the faith of the saints," *i.e.* that the Beast who slays by the sword would also be slain by the sword. Revelation 13:14 also mentions his death by sword.

That Nero did in fact kill by the sword is well-attested fact. Paul, for example, is said to have died under Nero by decapitation by means of the sword. Tertullian credits "Nero's cruel sword"[1] as providing the martyr's blood as seed for the church.[2] He urges his Roman readers: "Consult your histories; you will there find that Nero was the first who assailed with the imperial sword the Christian sect."[3]

Just as well-attested is Nero's own death by sword. According to Suetonius, he "drove a dagger into his throat, aided by Epaphroditus, his private secretary."[4] He not only killed others by the sword, but himself—as Revelation prophesies.

This evidence alone cannot compel the conclusion that Nero is in mind; many emperors died by the sword, even Domitian. But it quite harmoniously lends its voice to the chorus of other evidences, both major and minor.

The Revival of the Beast

We now come to a most interesting aspect of Revelation, the revival of the Beast after his death. At first glance this detail regarding the Beast may seem fatal to my designating the Beast as Rome (corporately) and Nero Caesar (specifically). But looks are deceiving. As a matter of fact, this aspect of the Beast's function in Revelation confirms my argument in a surprising way. This confirmation, when properly understood, not only is historically verifiable but also inappropriate to any other time in Rome's history than that of the A.D. 60s, the imperial era dominated by Nero Caesar. Let us see how this is so.

The Beast's Two-fold Referent

As we consider the proper interpretation we must remember that John allows some shifting in his imagery of the Beast: The one Beast has seven heads (Rev. 13:1; 17:3), which at some places are seven kings collectively considered (17:9–10a), or seven kings who arise in chronological succession (cf. 17: 10b–11). Thus, the *Beast* is generically portrayed as a *kingdom.* But in the same contexts it is spoken of as an individual (he is a man with a specific name, 13:18) and one head among the seven (17:11). This unusual feature, as noted before, is recognized by a number of commentators.[5]

We must recognize at the outset that one of the heads receives a death blow: "And I saw one of his heads as if it had been slain, and his fatal wound was healed" (Rev. 13:3). I demonstrated earlier that Nero Caesar is the "head" which is in view here.[6] John prophesies that Nero will die by the sword (13:10, 14). Nero is the one mysteriously numbered "666" (13:18).

Recognizing these factors takes us a long way toward resolving the interpretive issue before us. The mortal sword wound to *one* of the heads is a wound that should have been fatal to the Beast, *generically* considered. This explains why after the wound was healed and *the Beast* continued alive, "the whole earth was amazed and followed after the beast" (Rev. 13:3b). The seven-headed Beast seems indestructible, for the cry goes up: "Who is like the beast, and who is able to wage war with him?" (13:4b).

Now how does all of this imagery have anything to do with Rome and Nero Caesar?

The Historical Fulfillment

At this point we must reflect upon a most significant series of historical events of the A.D. 60s. A perfectly reasonable and historical explanation of the revived Beast lies before the interpreter. Here is where so many faddish interpretations of Revelation go wrong. They forget the *original audience relevance* factor and, consequently, overlook the history of the era.

When Nero committed suicide on June 9, A.D. 68, two major inter-related historical situations presented themselves to the world. Both carried with them catastrophic consequences.

First, with the death of Nero the Julio-Claudian line of emperors perished from the earth. In other words, the Roman Empire's founding family vanished from rule, for "almost overnight, a hundred-year-old dynasty had vanished."[7] The blood line that had given birth to, extended, stabilized, brought prosperity to, and had received worship from the Roman Empire was suddenly cut off forever. In superstitious, pagan fashion Suetonius notes that "many portents" foreshadowed the tragedy that was to be, *i.e.* that "the race of the Caesars ended with Nero."[8] This was a grave and serious matter for the Roman Empire which must now undergo the trials of dynastic succession.

Second, catastrophe upon catastrophe followed the death of Nero and the extinction of the Julian line. Immediately, the Roman Empire was hurled into civil wars of great ferocity and dramatic proportions. In fact, the civil wars almost destroyed the empire, seriously threatening to reduce "eternal Rome" to dusty rubble. The peril the Empire faced and the upheaval that shook it were well known in that era. As Josephus notes of these Roman civil wars: "I have omitted to give an exact account of them, because they are well known by all, and they are described by a great number of Greek and Roman authors."[9]

These civil wars are tremendously important in first-century world history—and ecclesiastical history, as well. Since the book of Revelation was written during Nero's reign and regarding the Neronic evils, as the wealth of evidence demands,[10] we should expect that prophetic allusions to Rome's civil wars would appear. And they do.

In introducing the months following the death of Nero, Tacitus (A.D. 56–117) wrote:

> The history on which I am entering is that of a period rich
> in disasters, terrible: with battles, torn by civil struggles, hor-

rible even in peace. Four emperors felled by the sword;[11] there were three civil wars, more foreign wars and often both at the same time. There was success in the East,[12] misfortune in the West. Illyricum was disturbed, the Gallic provinces wavering, Britain subdued and immediately let go. The Sarmatae and Suebi rose against us; the Dacians won fame by defeats inflicted and suffered; even the Parthians were almost roused to arms through the trickery of a pretended Nero. Moreover, Italy was distressed by disasters unknown before or returning after the lapse of ages. Cities of the rich fertile shores of Campania were swallowed up or overwhelmed; Rome was devastated by conflagrations, in which her most ancient shrines were consumed and the very Capitol fired by citizens' hands. Sacred sites were defiled; there were adulteries in high places. The sea was filled with exiles, its cliffs made foul with the bodies of the dead. In Rome there was more awful cruelty.

Besides the manifold misfortunes that befell mankind, there were prodigies in the sky and on the earth, warnings given by thunderbolts, and prophecies of the future, both joyful and gloomy, uncertain and clear. For never was it more fully proved by awful disasters of the Roman people or by indubitable signs that gods care not for our safety, but for our punishment.[13]

Tacitus's detailed account of the despair settling over the Empire almost equals in psychological horror and cultural devastation that which overwhelmed Jerusalem during the Jewish War, as recorded by Josephus and Tacitus.[14] Tacitean scholar Kenneth Wellesley relates Galba's carefully conducted ritual upon entering office as consul on January 1, A.D. 69:

> No rational observer could possibly have suspected the anger of the gods. No one could have supposed that the great triple shrine on the hill towards which the company moved would in this year sink into ashes and rubble, a symbol no longer of Rome's eternity but of its seemingly imminent extinction. That Italy should be twice invaded by Roman armies, that its cities

and capital should be taken by storm, that three successive emperors should die by assassination, suicide or lynching, and that the whole empire, from Wales to Assouan and from the Caucasus to Morocco, should be convulsed and disarrayed, were matters beyond imagination or surmise.... The long and single year now beginning [A.D. 69] would provide a spectacle of calamity, endurance and survival without parallel, so far, in Rome's history.[15]

The Roman civil wars were the firstfruits of Nero's death.

These civil wars would, to all appearance, strike the citizens, subjects, neighbors, and enemies of the vast empire as being the *very death throes of the Empire,* the Beast generically considered. Indeed, in Tacitus's estimation it very nearly was so: "This was the condition of the Roman state when Serius Galba, chosen consul for the second time, and his colleague Titus Vinius entered upon the year that was to be for Galba his last and *for the state almost the end."*[16]

Before the world's startled eyes, the seven headed Beast (Rome) was toppling to its death as its sixth head (Nero) was mortally wounded with the sword. As Suetonius viewed the long months immediately following Nero's death, the empire "for a long time had been unsettled, and as it were, drifting, through the usurpation and violent death of three emperors."[17]

Josephus records the matter as perceived by the Roman generals Vespasian and Titus, while they were engaged in the Jewish War in A.D. 69: "And now they were both in suspense about the public affairs, the Roman empire being then in a fluctuating condition, and did not go on with their expedition against the Jews, but thought that to make any attack upon foreigners was now unseasonable, on account of the solicitude they were in for their own country."[18] The reports of the destruction and rapine were so horrible that it is reported of General Vespasian: "And as this sorrow of his was violent, he was not able to support the torments he was under, nor to apply himself further in other wars when his native country was laid waste."[19]

According to the pseudo (after-the-fact) prophecy of *4 Ezra* 12:16–19, written around A.D. 100, the Empire was in danger of falling: "In the midst of the time of that kingdom great struggles shall arise, and it shall be in danger of falling; nevertheless it shall not fall then, but shall regain its former power."[20]

Josephus agrees that during this time Rome was brought near to utter "ruin."[21] He notes that "about this time it was that heavy calamities came about Rome on all sides."[22] Josephus writes elsewhere that "the Roman government [was] in a great internal disorder, by the continual changes of its rulers, and [the Germans] understood that every part of the habitable earth under them was in an unsettled and tottering condition."[23] Men everywhere understood that "the state of the Romans was so ill."[24] Formerly stable Rome experienced the Year of the Four Emperors—Galba (rule ended Jan. 15, 69), Otho (Jan. 15, 69—Apr. 16, 69), Vitellius (Apr. 69—July 1, 69), and Vespasian (began July 1, 69).[25] And quite naturally "the year of conflict after Nero's death—in which Galba, Otho, and Vitellius one after another laid claim to the throne—left the Roman treasury bankrupt by the time Vespasian came to power."[26]

But what eventually occurred at the end of these death throes? The rest of Suetonius's quotation begun above informs us that "the empire, which for a long time had been unsettled and, as it were, drifting through the usurpation and violent death of three emperors, was at last taken in hand and given stability by the Flavian family."[27] Josephus agrees when he writes, "So upon this confirmation of Vespasian's entire government, which was now settled, and upon *the unexpected deliverance of the public affairs of the Romans from ruin,* Vespasian turned his thoughts to what remained unsubdued in Judea."[28] Thus, after a time of grievous civil wars, the Empire was revived by the ascending of Vespasian to the purple.

James Moffatt states the matter well when he writes regarding Revelation 13:3:

> The allusion is . . . to the terrible convulsions which in 69
> A.D. shook the empire to its foundations (Tac. *Hist.* i. 11). Nero's
> death with the bloody interregnum after it, was a wound to the
> State, from which it only recovered under Vespasian. It fulfilled the
> tradition of the wounded head. . . . The vitality of the pagan em-
> pire, shown in this power of righting itself after the revolution, only
> added to its prestige.[29]

The relevant verses in Revelation reflect the death and revivification
of the Beast, that is, the earth-shaking historical events of the late 60s
wherein Rome died (A.D. 68), as it were, and returned again to life (A.D.
69). In light of John's original audience (Rev. 1:4, 11), his call for their
careful consideration (1:3; 13:9), and his contemporary expectation (1:1,
3), we must wonder why commentators search the distant future seeking
some other fulfillment of these events. All the evidence heretofore dove-
tails nicely with this revivification factor. In fact, the evidence I present
herein was compelling enough to convince dispensationalists C. Marvin
Pate and Calvin B. Haines to agree with my argument in the first edition
of the present book—though they attempted to argue for a double fulfillment of the prophecies.[30]

An Objection Considered

The reference to the "eighth" king in Revelation 17:11 has caused
some commentators to stumble here.[31] There we read: "And the beast
which was and is not, is himself also an eighth, and is one of the seven."
In response to a view such as I am presenting, some commentators note
that the eighth emperor of Rome was actually Otho, the second of the
rulers during Rome's awful civil wars. Thus, they point out, this head
does not refer to Vespasian. Given the interpretive approach presented
above, it would appear that the eighth head (according to my calculation)
is one of the *destroying* elements of Rome, not one who actually stabilized
the Empire, causing its revival. Consequently, the supposed imagery fails.

This problem does not, however, undermine the view I have presented. In an important sense the revival of the Empire under Vespasian, was a revival under "an eighth," who is, nevertheless, "of the seven." The *same* Roman Empire is coming back to life from the death of the civil wars—not some new empire. John's concern particularly regards the contemporaneous events: the Roman civil wars that occurred within the compass of the reign of the seven kings. The eighth is beyond his most pressing and immediate concern (although it is not unimportant) and thus is not specified and detailed.

Consulting the Greek text alleviates any apparent tension in this understanding. Exegetically, the chronological line of heads/kings is spoken of with careful exactness by use of the definite article, "the." That is, if we translate John with exact literalness, he writes of the "kings" (emperors) in Revelation 17:10 as follows: *"the* five fell, *the* one is, *the* other not yet come, and whenever he comes a little [while] him it behooves to remain."[32]

But John conspicuously (in the Greek) drops the definite article when he mentions the eighth head/king in Revelation 17:11: "And the beast which was and is not, even he *an* eighth is."[33] The definite article that clearly and repetitively defined the chronological series of head/kings ("*the* five," "*the* one," "*the* one to come") vanishes before the eighth is mentioned. Thus, this eighth king is *"an* eighth," *i.e.* it refers not to any one particular individual, but to the revival of the Empire itself under one who is outside of the originally specified seven kings. The Roman Empire is arising from ruin.

In addition, the number eight appears to be the number of resurrection.[34] The *eighth* day is the beginning of a new week. Thus, Jesus was resurrected on the first or eighth day (John 20:1). Eight people were saved on the ark to "resurrect" the human race (1 Pet. 3:20).[35] In that leprosy was "regarded as a decomposition of the vital juices, and as putrefaction in a living body, [it] was an image of death."[36] Thus, the leper was not re-admitted back into the holy community as alive again until his eighth day sacrifice (Lev. 14:10, 23). The menstruous woman was unclean for seven days, then cleansed on the eighth day when she offered a sacrifice (Lev. 15:29), which cleansing was necessary "unless they die in their uncleanness" (Lev. 15:31).

Here in Revelation 17, John originally sees "seven" heads, but suddenly an "eighth" appears. The eighth head is something *new*, in that the original vision only presents seven kings. This reestablishment of the Roman Empire under Vespasian offers a new beginning (the Julio-Claudian line was gone; the Flavian line established) and a revival of the Roman Empire, which had been through death throes. That recovery will come shortly after the demise of *the* original seven when *an* eighth arises.

Conclusion

Despite the pervasive view among many evangelicals today, Revelation was a crucially relevant book to the apostolic era church. We have seen how many roads lead to the Rome/Nero view of the Beast. Perhaps the most difficult piece of prophetic material for the Rome/ Nero view of the Beast is that which speaks of the Beast's death and revival. Yet again, however, an understanding of the circumstances of the first century is immensely helpful to our interpretation.

With the death of Nero and the ensuing civil wars which plagued Rome, the world witnessed what surely seemed the final demise of mighty Rome. But to the surprise of friend and foe alike, Rome arose anew under Vespasian to assert its vitality and to demonstrate its power. Beginning with Vespasian Christianity would be left in peace for almost forty years, until the reign of Trajan (A.D. 98–117). John clearly spoke of the events of his era as a true prophet of God and as one concerned for his "fellow-partakers in the tribulation" (Rev. 1:9). He did not overlook the earth-shaking events of his own era; he spoke directly to them.

He did not taunt his original readers by referring to events centuries distant; he ministered to them in their current circumstances.

Notes

1. Eusebius, *Ecclesiastical History* 2:25:5; Tertullian, *The Exclusion of Heretics* 36; the Syriac *The Teaching of the Apostles.*

2. Tertullian, *Exclusion* 21.

3. Tertullian, *Apology* 5.

4. *Nero* 49.

5. See discussion in Chapter 1 *supra.*

6. See Chapter 3. More discussion of this may be found in Chapter 10 below.

7. Kenneth Wellesley, *The Year of the Four Emperors*, 3rd ed. (London: Routledge, 2000), 4

8. Suetonius, *Galba* 1.

9. Josephus, *The Wars of the Jews* 4:9:2.

10. See Part 2 of the present work for a popular summation of the pre-A.D. 70 composition of Revelation. For a more rigorous treatment see my doctoral dissertation, published under the title: *Before Jerusalem Fell: Dating the Book of Revelation*, 3rd ed. (Atlanta: American Vision, 1998). For additional information, see: John A. T. Robinson, *Redating the New Testament* (Philadelphia: Westminster, 1976), 221–53; and E. Earle Ellis, *The Making of the New Testament Documents* (Boston: Brill, 1999), 210–16.

11. Nero died June 9, A.D. 68; Galba was murdered January 15, A.D. 69; Otho committed suicide April 16, A.D. 69; and Vitellius was slain on December 20, A.D. 69.

12. The Jewish War, which ended with the destruction of the Temple in A.D. 70.

13. Tacitus, *Histories* 1:2–3.

14. Josephus, *Wars*, and Tacitus, *Histories* 5: 10ff. See also Eusebius, *Ecclesiastical History,* 3:5:8.

15. Wellesley, *The Year of the Four Emperors*, 1. The barbarity of the assassination of the emperors and their supporters was grotesque: "The bodies of Galba, Piso and Vinius were decapitated, and the heads carried to the barracks to be displayed to Otho. They were then impaled and paraded round the square in a grisly procession backed by the cohort standards of the Praetorians and the legionary eagle of the marine legion" (p. 29).

16. Tacitus, *Histories* 1:11. Emphasis added.

17. Suetonius, *Vespasian* 1.

18. Josephus, *Wars* 4:9:2.

19. *Wars* 4:10:2.

20. For an excellent analysis of 4 *Ezra*, see Bruce M. Metzger, "The Fourth Book of Ezra," in James H. Charlesworth, ed., *The Old Testament Pseudepigrapha,* 2 vols. (Garden City: Doubleday, 1983) 2:517ff.

21. Josephus, *Wars* 4:11:5.

22. *Wars* 4:10:1.

23. *Wars* 7:4:2.

24. *Wars* 7:4:2.

25. The classic study of this fateful year is Wellsley, *The Year of the Four Emperors.* See also: P. A. L. Greenhalgh, *The Year of the Four Emperors* (London: Weidenfeld and Nicolson, 1975. A helpful summary appears in Mark Reasoner, "Emperor, Emperor Cult," in Ralph P. Martin

and Peter H. Davids, eds., *Dictionary of the Later New Testament & Its Developments* (Downers Grove, Ill.: InterVarsity Press, 1997), 321.

26. Leonard L. Thompson, *The Book of Revelation: Apocalypse and Empire* (New York: Oxford, 1990), 72. Even prior to the Year of the Four Emperors: "The state treasury was empty.... Nero had squandered enormous sums on acting, architecture, and athletics." Wellesley, *The Year of the Four Emperors*, 8.

27. *Vespasian* 1.

28. *Wars* 4:11:5. Emphasis added.

29. James Moffatt, *The Revelation of St. John the Divine*, vol. 5 in W. Robertson Nicoll, ed., *The Expositor's Greek Testament* (Grand Rapids: Eerdmans, rep. 1980), 430.

30. C. Marvin Pate and Calvin B. Haines, Jr., *Doomsday Delusions: What's Wrong with Predictions About the End of the World* (Downer's Grove, Ill.: InterVarsity Press, 1995). See also: Pate's contribution to C. Marvin Pate, ed., *Four Views on the Book of Revelation* (Grand Rapids: Zondervan, 1998), 133–76.

31. Responding to me in particular is: Robert L. Thomas, "Theonomy and the Dating of Revelation," *The Master's Seminary Journal*, 5:2 (Fall 1994): 189–90. For my response to Thomas's rebuttal, see: Kenneth L. Gentry, Jr., *Before Jerusalem Fell: Dating the Book of Revelation* (rev. ed.: Atlanta: American Vision, 1998), xxix-xxxii.

32. Literal translation taken from Alfred Marshall, *The Interlinear Greek-English New Testament*, 2nd ed. (Grand Rapids: Zondervan, 1959), 1007.

33. Marshall, *Interlinear Greek-English New Testament*, ibid.

34. Gary North, The *Dominion Covenant: Genesis*, 2nd ed. (Tyler, Tex.: Institute for Christian Economics, 1987), ch. 5; E. W Bullinger, *Number in Scripture* (London: Eyre and Spottiswoode, n.d.).

35. See Justin Martyr, *Dialogue with Trypho*, 138:1.

36. C. F. Keil and F. Delitzsch, *Commentary on the Old Testament: The Pentateuch*, trans. by James Martin (Grand Rapids: Eerdmans, rep. 1975), 2:384.

Part Two
When Was Revelation Written?

8

The Importance of the Date of Revelation

I, John, your brother and fellow-partaker in the tribulation and kingdom
and perseverance which are in Jesus, was on the island called Patmos,
because of the word of God and the testimony of Jesus
Rev. 1:9

The Issue

The present section of this book will analyze the vitally important
question of the date of the composition of Revelation, which was written while John was banished to Patmos. The reader should recall that in
the Introduction I noted that this matter is a major difficulty confront-
ing the student of Revelation. The position one takes on this issue has a
great bearing on the interpretive possibilities available. Indeed, the view
of the Beast presented heretofore could well be affected by the question
we now approach.

The Debate

Unfortunately, much lively debate rages over the question of the date of Revelation. In fact, scholarly opinion has shifted back and forth between two major viewpoints. The two leading views held by New Testament scholars are: (1) The early date view, which holds that John wrote Revelation prior to the August-September, A.D. 70, destruction of the temple. (2) The late-date view, which proposes that John composed his work around A.D. 95–96, in the last days of the principate of Domitian Caesar, who was assassinated September 18, A.D. 96.

My Position

The position I will defend in the following pages is the early date before A.D. 70,[1] somewhere in the time-frame of late-A.D. 64 (after the initial outbreak of the Neronic persecution around November) to early in A.D. 67 (prior to the formal imperial engagement of the Jewish War with Rome in February[2]). For too long, popular commentaries have brushed aside the evidence for the early date for Revelation. Despite the majority opinion of current scholarship, the evidence for an early date for Revelation is clear and compelling.

Almost invariably the major reason for the dismissal of the early date for Revelation is due to a statement by an early church father named Irenaeus. Other supportive evidences for a late-date are brought into the discussion later. *Initially,* however, almost all commentators begin with and depend upon Irenaeus's statement in his late second century worked entitled *Against Heresies.*[3] Pick a Revelation commentary off your shelves and see for yourself.

One particularly frustrating aspect of the debate presents itself to early date advocates. Affirming a date for Revelation prior to the destruction of the temple, produces a too-predictable response: "Aren't you aware that all scholars agree it was written at the end of the first century?" Or, if talking with a seminarian, the reply might be: "Don't you realize Irenaeus clearly settled this question?" In such encounters the early date proponent is deemed intellectually naive and historically misinformed. He is thought to be throwing objective evidence and assured conclusions out the window on the basis of sheer presumption or theological bias.

But not all Revelation scholars are as committed to the late-date as many students think. Alan F. Johnson even goes so far as to state: "Though the slender historical evidence on the whole favors the later date (81–96), in the light of the present studies, the question as to when Revelation was written must be left open."[4] Competent late-date advocate J. P. M. Sweet concurs: "the evidence is far from conclusive."[5] Beale concurs, even citing Sweet.[6]

Early Date Advocates

Holding an early date for Revelation is not, however, a denial of "historical facts." This should be evident in the list of scholars who have held to an early date. An appeal to venerated scholarship (an *argumentum ad verecundiam*) cannot settle the issue, to be sure. But the very fact that a good (and growing) number of astute biblical scholars hold to a minority position should at least forestall too hasty a dismissal of that position.

I herewith list a number of noted scholars who have discounted the late-date for Revelation in favor of an earlier date. Some of the following are noted liberal scholars, some orthodox. The historical facts of the matter are not necessarily determined by a particular school of thought. In fact, that some of the scholars are liberals is quite remarkable in that the liberal view usually tends to push the dates of biblical books to a later, not an earlier, period.

We list these names in alphabetical, rather than chronological, order: Jay E. Adams, Luis de Alcazar, Karl August Auberlen, Greg L. Bahnsen, Arthur S. Barnes, James Vernon Bartlet, F. C. Baur, Albert A.

Bell Jr., K. Berger, Willibald Beyshclag, Charles Bigg, Friedrich Bleek, Heinrich Bohmer, Wilhelm Bousset, F. F. Bruce, Rudolf Bultmann, W. Boyd Carpenter, David Chilton, P. L. Couchoud, Adam Clarke, William Newton Clarke, Henry Cowles, Berry Stewart Crebs, Samuel Davidson, Edmund De Pressense, P. S. Desprez, W. M. L. De Wette, Friedrich Düsterdieck, K. A. Eckhardt, Alfred Edersheim, George Edmundson, Johann Gottfried Eichhorn, E. Earle Ellis, G. H. A. Ewald, F. W. Farrar, Grenville, Field, A. J. P. Garrow, George P. Fisher, J. A. Fitzmeyer, J. Massyngberde Ford, Hermann Gebhardt, James Glasgow, R. M. Grant, James Comper Gray, Samuel G. Green, Heinrich Ernst Ferdinand Guerike, Henry Melville Gwatkin, Henry Hammond, H. G. Hartwig, Karl August von Hase, B. W. Henderson, Johann Gottfried von Herder, Adolf Hilgenfeld, David Hill, F. J. A. Hort, H. J. Holtzmann, John Leonhard Hug, William Hurte, A. Immer, B. W. Jones, Theodor Keim, Theodor Koppe, Max Krenkel, Johann Heinrich Kurtz, Victor Lechier, Francis Nigel Lee, John Lightfoot, Gottfried C. F. Lucke, Christoph Ernst Luthardt, James M. Macdonald, Frederick Denison Maurice, Charles Pettit M'Ilvaine, John David Michaelis, Theodor Mommsen, A. D. Momigliano, Charles Herbert Morgan, C. F. D. Moule, John Augustus Wilhelm Neander, Bishop Thomas Newton, A. Niernieyer, J. Borton Payne, Alfred Plummer, Edward Hayes Plumtree, T. Randell, James J. L. Ratton, Ernest Renan, Eduard Wilhelm Eugen Reuss, Jean Reville, Edward Robinson, John A. T. Robinson, Christopher Rowland, J. Stuart Russell, William Sanday, Philip Schaff, Johann Friedrich Schleusner, J. H. Scholten, Albert Schwegler, J. J. Scott, Edward Condon Selwyn, Henry C. Sheldon, William Henry Simcox, Robert B. Sloan, S. S. Smalley, D. Moody Smith, R. C. Sproul, Arthur Penrhyn Stanley, Edward Rudolf Stier, Moses Stuart, Milton S. Terry, Friedrich August Gottreu Tholuck, Charles Cutler Torrey, Cornelis Vanderwaal, Gustav Volkmar, Arthur Weigall, Bernhard Weiss,

Brookes Fost Westcott, J. J. Wetstein, Karl Wieseler, J. C. Wilson, Charles Wordsworth, Herbert B. Workman, Robert Young, C. F. J. Züllig.[7]

Can it be that these scholars are intellectually careless and historically naive?

My Approach

Since I have already begun swimming against the tide of contemporary opinion on this point, why not continue the swim? Whereas most approaches to the question of Revelation's date begin with the evidence from *church tradition* (often called "external evidence"), I will begin with evidence drawn from Revelation's *self-witness* (usually called "internal evidence"). Holding to an unshakable conviction regarding Scripture's divine inspiration, I also affirm its inherent authority, infallibility, and inerrancy. Hence, I am convinced the self-witness is the superior and determinative evidence. I will turn to the evidence from tradition in due time, however.

The reader should note that this part of the book is a condensation and popularization of a fuller, more technical doctoral dissertation.[8] The larger work contains much fuller exegetical and historical argumentation, as well as bibliographical documentation.

The Significance of the Issue

If we adopt the earlier date for Revelation, an interesting result presents itself: Most of the judgment visions in Revelation (chs. 4-19) could easily foreshadow the historical turmoil which came to a head shortly after John wrote. The majority of its prophecies would then apply to the very *beginning* of Christianity, rather than to its *conclusion*. Contained in Revelation might be prophetic allusions to the first Roman persecution of Christianity (A.D. 64–68), the Jewish War with Rome (A.D. 67–70), the death of Christianity's first persecutor (Nero

Caesar, d. A.D. 68), the Roman Civil Wars (A.D. 68–69), and the destruction of Jerusalem and the temple (A.D. 70).[9]

Certainly the "war with Rome was one of the most significant events in Jewish history. The fall of the temple in A.D. 70 marks a watershed that affects all aspects of Jewish history, whether political or religious."[10] In fact, Michael Grant observes regarding the impact of the Jewish War: "The rebellion continues to this day to exert a profound influence on the politics of the middle east."[11] The centuries old Daily Sacrifice at the Temple ceased permanently and was mourned by the Jews annually by fasting. In the Mishnah "Days of Fasting" we read: "Five things befell our fathers . . . on the ninth of Ab. . . . On the ninth of Ab it was decreed against our fathers that they should not enter into the Land, and the Temple was destroyed the first and the second time, and Beth'-Tor was captured and the City ploughed up. When Ab comes in, gladness must be diminished."[12] Since "temple life was . . . an extremely important facet of Jewish identity,"[13] its permanent loss was enormous. "With the destruction of the Jewish cult the keeping of the Torah in all its details became impossible."[14]

If Revelation refers to such dramatic events then many of its prophecies could easily be documented from history.[15] Furthermore, the book would then be intensely relevant to the suffering churches to which John addressed it (Rev. 1:4, 11; chs. 2–3; 22:16). Revelation's original pastoral purpose would have been to stabilize infant Christianity against the tribulational storms into which it was entering (Rev. 1:9; cp. 2:10, 22; 3:10; 6:9–11). In addition, John would also be explaining to the early Christians (and to us) the spiritual and historical significance of the destruction of Jerusalem and the temple and the demise of Bible-based Judaism. Such preparing of first-century Christianity would be immensely practical and spiritually important: For apostolic Christianity focused around Jerusalem and the temple (Luke 24:47; Acts 1:8, 12; 3:1, 2, 11; 5:12–16, 42; 8:1; 11:1, 2; 15:1, 2) and the early converts to Christianity were predominantly from Judaism (Acts 2:14, 41, 47; 4:1–4).

If the late-date of around A.D. 95–96 is accepted, a wholly different situation would prevail. The events of the mid- and late 60s of the first century would be *absolutely excluded* as possible fulfillments. The prophecies within Revelation would be opened to an endless series of speculative scenarios, which could be extrapolated into the indefinite future. Revelation might outline the course of Church history according to any number of outlines[16] or to certain general principles.[17] Or it might focus exclusively on the end of history, which would begin approaching thousands of years after John's time, either before, after, or during the tribulation or the millennium.[18]

The purpose of Revelation would then be to show early Christians that things will get worse, that history will be a time of constant and increased suffering for the Church.[19] This understanding, of course, would be tempered by references within Revelation to the spiritual reality of heaven above to which the martyrs go upon departing this life. And, in the case of premillennial systems, the latter chapters would hold forth the ultimate hope of Christ's intervention in the course of history to impose his triumphant kingdom over the agelong harriers of the Church.

Conclusion

The impact or the question of the dating of Revelation is of great significance to evangelical theology. Though the majority of current scholars calls for a Domitianic date for Revelation (A.D. 95–96), we are witnessing a growing movement toward the more conservative Neronic dating which predominated in the late 1800s. I trust that this section of the present study will be used in some small way to interest Christians in the important debate. Even more: I hope that the evidence rehearsed below will draw many to the early date view of the writing of Revelation.

Notes

1. I would like to thank Dr. George W. Knight III for his suggestions on the following order of arrangement, which differs from my dissertation's order.

2. "Vespasian's appointment to Judaea [was in] February 67." Kenneth Wellesley, *The Year of the Four Emperors,* 3rd ed. (London: Routledge, 2000), 45. "In February of the following year [*i.e.,* A.D. 67] he was appointed governor of Judaea with the task of suppressing the First Jewish Revolt, known to the Jews as the First Roman War." Michael Grant, *The Twelve Caesars* (New York: Barnes & Noble, [1975] 1996), 211.

3. Two notable exceptions are: Leon Morris in his *The Revelation of St. John,* 2nd ed. (Grand Rapids: Eerdmans, 1987), 35ff. G. K. Beale, *The Book of Revelation* (Grand Rapids: Eerdmans, 1999), 5.

4. "Revelation," in Frank E. Gaebelein, ed., *The Expositor's Bible Commentary* (Grand Rapids: Zondervan, 1991), 12:406.

5. J. P. M. Sweet, *Revelation* (Philadelphia: Westminster, 1979), 21.

6. Beale, *The Book of Revelation,* 27.

7. For source documentation, see: Kenneth L. Gentry, Jr., *Before Jerusalem Fell: Dating the Book of Revelation,* 3rd ed. (Atlanta: American Vision, 1998). See also: E. Earle Ellis, *The Making of the New Testament Documents* (Boston: Brill, 1999), 210–16.

8. Gentry, *Before Jerusalem Fell.*

9. Adherents to this view include: David Chilton, *The Days of Vengeance: An Exposition of the Book of Revelation* (Fort Worth, Tex.: Dominion Press, 1987); Cornelis Vanderwaal, *Search the Scriptures,* trans. Theodore Plantinga, 10 vols. (St. Catherines, Ontario: Paideia Press, 1978), vol. 10; and Philip Schaff *History of the Christian Church,* 3rd ed. (Grand Rapids: Eerdmans, 1910), vol. 1.

10. L. L. Grabbe, "Jewish History: Roman Period," in Craig A. Evans and Stanley E. Porter, eds., *Dictionary of New Testament Background* (Downers Grove, Ill.: InterVarsity, 2000), 579.

11. Michael Grant, *The Ancient Historians* (New York: Charles Scribner's, 1970), 245.

12. Taanith 4:6.

13. Jacob Neusner, ed., *Dictionary of Judaism in the Biblical Period* (Peabody, Mass.: Hendrickson, 1996), 623.

14. Crispin H. T. Fletcher-Louis, "The Destruction of the Temple and the Revitalization of the Old Covenant," in Kent E. Brower and Mark W. Elliott, eds., *Eschatology in Bible & Theology: Evangelical Essays at the Dawn of a New Millennium* (Downers Grove, Ill.: InterVarsity, 1997), 163. See also: C. A. Evans, "Judaism, Post-A.D. 70 in Ralph P. Martin and Peter H. Davids, eds., *Dictionary of the Later New Testament & Its Developments* (Downers Grove, Ill.: InterVarsity Press, 1997), 605ff.

15. One dispensationalist complains that my historical documentation is basically a variant of newspaper exegesis. In my debate book with Thomas Ice he writes: "In accordance with this belief, they search first century 'newspapers' for an event that comprises the closest fit to the passage and usually cite it as a fulfillment of the biblical text in discussion." Thomas Ice and Kenneth L. Gentry, Jr., *The Great Tribulation: Past or Future?* (Grand Rapids: Kregel, 1999), 108. This is a remarkable charge in that: (1) Dispensationalists have for *decades* claimed

contemporary world events are evidences of the fulfillment of biblical prophecy, and have always been proven wrong. (2) Dispensationalist newspaper exegesis is contrary to their own theological foundation, which demands that the "prophetic time-clock is on hold" and that no prophecy remains to be fulfilled until the Rapture. (3) The very nature of preterism *requires* historical documentation: if we claim the events of Revelation have already been fulfilled, we must show *when* and *where* they were accomplished. (4) Referring to historically significant documents in antiquity is a common scholarly practice when dealing with biblical events.

16. Adherents to this outline-of-history view (i.e., historicism) include: Albert S. Barnes, *Barnes' Notes on the New Testament* (Grand Rapids: Kregel, rep. 1962); and W. Boyd Carpenter, "The Revelation of St. John," in John C. Ellicott, *Ellicott's Commentary on the Whole Bible* (Grand Rapids: Zondervan, rep. n.d.).

17. Representatives of idealism: G. K. Beale, *The Book of Revelation* (Grand Rapids: Eerdmans, 1999). Vern S. Poythress, *The Returning King: A Guide to the Book of Revelation* (Phillipsburg, N.J.: P & R, 2000). William Hendriksen, *More Than Conquerors* (Grand Rapids: Baker, 1967). Simon J. Kistemaker, "The Temple in the Apocalypse," in *Journal of the Evangelical Theological Society* 43:3 (Sept. 2000): 433–442. Sam Hamstra, "Idealist," in C. Marvin Pate, ed., *Four Views on the Book of Revelation* (Grand Rapids: Zondervan, 1998).

18. For example: Robert L. Thomas, *Revelation 1–7* (Chicago: Moody, 1992); Herman Hoeksema, *Behold, He Cometh!* (Grand Rapids: Kregel, 1969); and Robert H. Mounce, *The Book of Revelation*, 2nd ed. (Grand Rapids: Eerdmans, 1998).

19. For the necessity of Christian suffering in history, see: Richard Gaffin, "Theonomy and Eschatology: Reflections on Postmillennialism," in Will S. Barker and W. Robert Godfrey, *Theonomy: An Informed Critique* (Grand Rapids: Zondervan, 1990), 197–226. For my response, see: Kenneth L. Gentry, Jr., "Whose Victory in History?" in Gary North, *Theonomy: An Informed Response* (Tyler, Tex.: Institute for Christian Economics, 1991), 207–30. See also: Gentry, "Agony, Irony, and the Postmillennialist," *Westminster Theological Journal* (2002) and Gentry, "The Victory is the Lord's," P. Andrew Sandlin, ed., *Chalcedon Symposium Series* (Vallecito, Calif.: Chalcedon Foundation, 2002).

9

The Thematic Evidence

Behold, He is coming with the clouds, and every eye will see Him,
even those who pierced Him; and all the tribes of the earth will
mourn over Him. Even so. Amen
Rev. 1:7

As should be obvious, an author's stated theme is fundamentally
important for understanding his message. Fortunately, we have a broad
consensus among commentators regarding the location of the *theme
verse* in Revelation. Determining Revelation's theme holds much potential value for our inquiry into its date. Nevertheless, though the *fact*
of Revelation's theme is widely agreed upon, the *nature* of its fulfillment
is not.

Determination of the Theme

We discover the theme of Revelation in its introduction at Revelation 1:7 (cited above): Christ's coming in judgment. A great number of
scholars concur in identifying this verse as John's thematic statement.
Among them we could list older and newer commentators, as well as

critical and conservative: Moses Stuart, Friedrich Düsterdieck, Bernhard Weiss, Justin A. Smith, Milton S. Terry, J. Stuart Russell, T. D. Bernard, Donald W. Richardson, George E. Ladd, Charles C. Ryrie, G. R. Beasley-Murray, David Chilton, and G. K. Beale.[1]

The coming of Christ presented here is Revelation's theme as is evident in the emphasis placed on it. It serves as a constant refrain in the personal letters to the Seven Churches (Rev. 2:5, 16, 25; 3:3, 11, 20) and elsewhere (16:15; 22:7, 12, 20). The theme, introduced dramatically with a "Behold!" not only introduces Revelation (1:7), but closes it as well (22:20).

Clearly John expects this event, an event of tremendous import. But exactly what does he expect? And how does it assist in our determining the date of Revelation?

Explication of the Theme

The event prophesied in Revelation 1:7 is a "cloud-coming" of Christ: "Behold! He is coming with the clouds." Here we must remember that the Old Testament is the rich vein from which John's imagery is extracted (see Ch. 3). Old Testamental imagery suggests an interpretation of this verse that has escaped the notice of many students of Revelation.

In the Old Testament clouds are frequently emblems of divine wrath and judgment. This is because God is surrounded with thick, foreboding clouds due to his unapproachable holiness and glory (Gen. 15:17; Ex. 13:21–22; 14:19–20; 19:9, 16–19; Deut. 4:11; Job 22:14; Pss. 18:8ff; 97:2; 104:3; Isa. 19:1; Ezek. 32:7–8). Thus, Scripture poetically portrays God as *coming in clouds* in historical judgments upon men (Pss. 18:7–15; 104:3; Isa. 19:1; Joel 2:1, 2; Nah. 1:2ff.; Zeph. 1:14, 15). Likewise, the New Testament speaks of Christ's coming in clouds of judgment (Matt. 24:3; 26:64) and at his Second Coming at the end of world history (Acts 1:11; 1 Thess. 4:15–17).

According to our theme, Christ's cloud-coming is a judgment which causes men to "mourn." But upon whom does this cloud coming fall? And when? And how?

Fortunately, clues appear within the theme text itself, as well as in the other New Testament reference to this conflation of Daniel 7:13 and Zechariah 12:10. Along with these clues we may surmise the objects of his wrath: The passage clearly states that Christ will come to and cause mourning among "those who pierced Him," even upon "all the tribes of the earth." I am convinced that this reference speaks directly of the first century Jews regarding the A.D. 70 holocaust. Let me lay before the judicious reader the following evidence in this regard.

"Those Who Pierced Him"

First, Christ's crucifixion is here blamed on the *nation* of Israel. Of course, the Romans were responsible for physically nailing Christ to the cross (John 18:30–31).[2] Nevertheless, when *covenantally* and *biblically* considered the onus of the divine curse falls squarely upon those who instigated and demanded it: the Jews. The biblical record is quite clear and most emphatic: the *Jews* sought his death (John 11:53; Matt. 26:4; 27:1), paid for his capture (Matt. 26:14–15, 47; 27:3–9), brought false witnesses against him (Matt. 27:59–62), initially convicted him (Matt. 27:65–66), turned him over to Roman civil authority (Matt. 27:2, 11, 12; Acts 3:13), and even called down his blood upon their own heads (Matt. 27:24–25). The biblical record is so obvious that on this basis many liberal scholars decry the New Testament as "anti-Semitic."[3]

John even informs us in his Gospel that the Roman procurator, Pontius Pilate, sought to free Jesus, finding no fault in him (John 18:38; 19:12; cp. Acts 3:13). But the Jews demanded that the robber Barabbas be released instead (John 18:39–40), and that Christ be immediately crucified (John 19:6, 15). They even threatened Pilate's tenuous Roman procuratorship by affirming "we have no king but Caesar" (John 19:14–15), suggesting that Pilate was allowing Christ to supplant Caesar.[4] Jesus himself points out to Pilate that "he who delivered Me up to you has the greater sin" (John 19:11). This should settle the matter of culpability, but there is more.

Peter's Pentecost sermon at Jerusalem (recorded in Acts 2) lays the blame wholly upon Israel: "Men of Israel, listen to these words: Jesus the Nazarene . . . *you nailed to a cross* by the hands of godless men and put Him to death. . . . Therefore let all the house of Israel know for certain that God has made Him both Lord and Christ—this Jesus whom *you crucified*" (Acts 2:22–23, 36). He does the same in his next sermon in Acts 3:1 3–15a: "The God of Abraham, Isaac, and Jacob, the God of our fathers, has glorified his servant Jesus, the one whom *you* delivered up, and disowned in the presence of Pilate, when he had decided to release Him. But *you* disowned the Holy and Righteous One, and asked for a murderer to be granted to you, but put to death the Prince of life." He repeats this to the Jews in Acts 5:30 where he proclaims: "The God of our fathers raised up Jesus, whom *you* had *put to death* by hanging Him on a cross." And again in Acts 10:39: "And we are witnesses of all the things He did both in the land of the Jews and in Jerusalem. And they also put Him to death by hanging Him on a cross."

In Acts 7:52 Stephen makes the same accusation: the Jews were the "betrayers and murderers" of Christ. Paul concurs in 1 Thessalonians 2:14–15 when he speaks of "the *Jews, who both killed the Lord Jesus* and the prophets, and drove us out."

This consistent and constant witness against the Jews in the canon of the New Testament continues into post-apostolic Church history. I will list a few quotations from the early fathers to illustrate the matter.

- Ignatius (A.D. 50–115) quite frequently drives home the point of Jewish culpability regarding Christ's death when he refers to the Jews as "Christ-killing Jews,"[5] "those murderers of the Lord,"[6] and "the Jews fighting against Christ."[7]

• Justin Martyr (A.D. 100–165) plays the same theme of Jewish liability when he writes: "Jesus Christ stretched forth his hands, being crucified by the Jews,"[8] "all these things happened to Christ at the hands of the Jews,"[9] and "the Jews deliberated about the Christ Himself, to crucify and put him to death."[10]

• Irenaeus (A.D. 130–202) concurs when he says of the Jews: "[God] sent in Jesus, whom they crucified and God raised up,"[11] and "to the Jews, indeed, they proclaimed that the Jesus who was crucified by them was the Son of God."[12]

Other church fathers who return to this theme include: Melito of Sardis (d. A.D. 190), Tertullian[13] (A.D. 160–220), Hippolytus[14] (A.D. 170–236), Cyprian[15] (A.D. 200–258), Lactantius[16] (A.D. 240–320), to name but a few.[17]

Thus, we see that Revelation 1:7 focuses the prophetic judgments upon those responsible for Christ's crucifixion, the first century Jews. And judgment certainly overwhelmed them in the catastrophic events culminating in A.D. 70.

"The Tribes of the Earth"

Second, divine judgment falls upon the *tribes* of Israel. Revelation 1:7 speaks of the mourning of "the tribes of the earth." The Greek word for "tribe" is *phule,* which in Scripture most frequently refers to the Jewish tribes. In fact, the Septuagint "with few exceptions . . . has *phule,* so that this becomes a fixed term for the tribal system of Israel."[18] The word for "tribe" is a common designation of the twelve-fold division of Israel,[19] even in the New Testament.[20] The New Testament often names particular "tribes" of Israel: Asher (Luke 2:36); Benjamin (Act 13:21; Rom 11:1; Phil 3:5); Judah (Rev. 5:5; Heb 7:14). The "tribes" found their home in Palestine; these are "the tribes of the Land" Revelation 1:7 mentions.

The reference to the "tribe of Judah" in Revelation 5:5 clearly refers to the tribal division among racial Jews. The term "tribe" obviously has that racial import in Revelation 7:4–8 (where it is used of each of the specifically named Twelve Tribes) and in Revelation 21:12 (where John refers to "the twelve tribes of the children of Israel"). Of course, "tribe" can refer to non-Jews in Revelation—when the term is found connected with "every kindred, tribe, tongue, and nation" (cf. Rev. 5:9; 7:9; 11:9; 13:7; 14:6). In fact, John attaches "every" to the term elsewhere, and multiplies sociological divisions (kindred, tongue, etc.) in those references to distinguish those "tribes" from the common Judaic usage of the term. But no such qualifications occur in Revelation 1:7; contextually "the tribes" must refer to racial Jews.

"The Earth, or Land"

Third, Revelation focuses on the *land* of Israel. The Greek word for "earth" in Revelation 1:7 is *ge*.[21] This common word, which appears over eighty times in Revelation, has numerous related meanings in Scripture.[22] Two of its most basic meanings are: (1) "earth," i.e., the world; and (2) "land," a particular region. It is used in both senses in the New Testament, as well as in Revelation.

In a number of places in the New Testament this word speaks either of the Promised Land as a whole, or some portion of it. In those places we find it in such phrases as "the land of Judah" (Matt. 2:6), "the land of Judea" (John 3:22), "the land of Israel" (Matt. 2:20, 21), "the land of Zebulun" (Matt. 4:15), "the land of Naphtali" (Matt. 4:15), and "the land of the Jews" (Acts 10:39). It can be used with the definite article alone and without any modifiers. In these cases it means simply "the land" (Greek: *he ge*), signifying the famous Promised Land. This usage is found in Matthew 27:45; Mark 15:33; Luke 4:25; 21:23

(see v. 21); Romans 9:28 (see v. 27); and James 5: 17. Thus, upon purely lexical considerations, the term can be understood as designating the Promised Land.

The significance of this translation of *he ge* may be discerned from religio-cultural situations, such as noted of the ancient Rabbis by Edersheim: "For, to the Rabbis the precise limits of Palestine were chiefly interesting so far as they affected the religious obligations cr privileges of a district. . . . Indeed, viewing the question from this point, Palestine was to the Rabbis simply 'the land,' all other countries being summed up under the designation of 'outside the land.'"[23] The Jews were so attached to their land that it may be stated of Jerusalem: "To the Jew this was the true home of his soul, the centre of his inmost life, the longing of his heart."[24]

Allison well notes the significance of "the land" for the Jews: "The land of Israel belonged to Judaism's understanding of itself."[25] Indeed:

> The importance of and veneration for the land appear from a number of legends about Palestine: it was protected during Noah's flood and remained dry (Pseudo-Philo *Bib. Ant.* 7:4; *b. Zedah.* 113a); it lies at the center of the earth (*Jub.* 8:19; *Sib. Or.* 5:250); it is holier than any other land (*m. Kelim* 1:6-9); to leave it for a foreign country is to lose the merits of the fathers (*b. B. Bat.* 91a); in the great tribulation at the end of time those within its borders will be spared affliction (*2 Apoc. Bar.* 29:2; 40:2; 71:1; cf. Joel 2:32); at the resurrection of the dead the just outside the land will roll through underground tunnels until they emerge from a cleft Mount of Olives, in the middle of—to use a term found already in Zechariah 1:12—"the holy land" (*b. Ketub.* 111a [which also records the opinion that those who die outside the land will not rise from the dead]; *Tb.* Cant 8:5; *Gen. Rob.* 96:5). This glorification of the land is especially strong in the rabbinic sources.[26]

As a matter or fact, literal translations of the Scripture lean in this direction, with such translations as: "Lo, he doth come with the clouds, and see him shall every eye, even those who did pierce him, and wail because of him shall all the tribes of the land. Yes! Amen!"[27] and "Behold he comes with the clouds, and will see him every eye and [those] who him pierced, and will wail over him all the tribes of the land. Yes, amen."[28]

In addition, that such is the referent of *he ge* in Revelation 1:7 seems indicated in that the verse is a blending of Daniel 7:13 and Zechariah 12:10.[29] The Zechariah 12:10 passage indisputably refers to the land of Israel:

> And I will pour out on the house of David and on the inhabitants of Jerusalem, the Spirit of grace and of supplication, so that they will look on Me whom they have pierced; and they will mourn for Him, as one mourns for an only son, and they will weep bitterly over Him, like the bitter weeping over a firstborn. In that day there will be great mourning in Jerusalem, like the mourning of Hadadrimmon in the plain of Megiddo. And the land will mourn, every family by itself.

Christ's use of the compound phrases (as found in Rev. 1:7) ties the prophecy to Palestine, when he warns believers in *Jerusalem* and *Judea* to flee (Matt. 24:30, cp. 24:16) because of the approaching destruction of the temple (24:2–3).

Gospel Confirmation

That these phrases in Revelation 1:7 speak of *the Promised Land of the first century* is evident in Jesus' teaching. There we find a recurring emphasis upon the culpability of the generation of Jews *then living*—those who actually crucified the Messiah, the Lord of Glory. In Matthew 23 Jesus calls down a seven-fold woe upon the scribes and Pharisees, those who "sit in the chair of Moses" (Matt. 23:2). In this woe-filled passage Jesus distinctly and clearly warns: *"Upon you* [will] *fall the guilt of all the righteous blood shed on earth* [or: "on the land"]. . . . *Truly I say to you, all these things shall come upon this generation.* O Jerusalem, Jerusalem, who kills the prophets and stones those who are sent to her! How often I wanted to gather your children together, the way a hen gathers her chicks under her wings, and you were unwilling. Behold, your house is being left to you desolate!" (23:35–38).

Christ then describes the desolation of Israel's "house" (temple) in Matthew 24. In Matthew 24:1-2 Jesus clearly and distinctly refers to the destruction of the first-century temple. And in the following context he expands on this as involving the "abomination of desolation" in the temple (v. 15) and the "great tribulation" (v. 21), which signify "the Son of Man coming on the clouds of the sky with power and great glory" (v. 30). And according to Christ, these events are coming upon "this generation" (v. 34), i.e., *the very generation which rejected and "pierced" him.* The crucifixion took place in Israel in its very capital, Jerusalem (Malt 20:17–19; Luke 9:31; 13:33–34; 18:31; 24:18–20). Indisputably, *that generation* was to be destroyed in his judgment-coming.[30]

The destruction of Jerusalem was absolutely catastrophic. Grant notes the enormity of the devastation:

> Damage to the land had been severe, partly owing to the scorched earth policy of the rebels themselves. . . . As for Jerusalem, it was a wreck of its former self. Half of the buildings had been destroyed, and only a small part of the wall was still standing; a mere forty thousand inhabitants remained. The city had to wait until the nineteenth century to become the largest Jewish centre in the country once again. The Temple had gone, and resumption of its worship was forbidden. Furthermore, the high priesthood itself was abolished, and so was the Council . . . .

And so the year AD 70 marked the end of the nation's life in Israel until its restoration in 1948. [31]

The horrible instance of teknophagia (child eating) during the siege becomes a stark symbol for the holocaust for generations of Christian writers. [32]

Objections

Despite the strength of the evidence for this interpretation of Revelation 1:7, many are not convinced. Beale specifically complains against my exposition on the following grounds: (1) "Zechariah 12 does not prophesy Israel's judgment but Israel's redemption." He urges that John "typically adheres to and consistently develops the contextual ideas of his OT references." (2) The Zechariah citation is combined with Dan. 7:13, which also refers to the eschatological deliverance, not judgment, of Israel." (3) "'Tribes of the earth' never refers to Israelite tribes; 'all the tribes of the earth' refers to all nations in every one of its Septuagint occurrences (*pasai hai phulai tes ges*, Gen. 12:3; 28:14; Ps 71 [72]: 17; Zech. 14:17)." [33]

Regarding Beale's argument about Zechariah 12 and Israel's redemption: (1) Certainly we must agree that Zechariah 12:10 speaks of repentance unto salvation. But the question arises: Is John *prophetically interpreting* this prophecy in Revelation 1:7? Or is he *adapting and applying* it—according to his own requirements? Commentators debate this matter of John's use of the Old Testament. [34] In fact, Beale even admits: "There is unanimous consensus that John uses the OT with a high degree of liberty and creativity." [35] Not only so, but Beale's own statement that John "typically" does so, allows that Revelation 1:7 could be a rare *a*typical use of the Old Testament. [36] What is more, Beale writes: "Rev. 1:7 . . . refers to the peoples throughout the earth, although in Zech. 12:10 it is limited to the Israelite tribes." He then defends this by urging that "John creatively reworks the OT and changes its application" while retaining "significant points of correspondence with the OT context."[37] I would think a "significant point of correspondence" would be maintaining *who* the prophecy is about.

(2) The same merging of Zechariah 12:10 and Daniel 7:13 occurs most significantly in the Olivet Discourse (Matt. 24:30). There the passage is (a) expanding upon the woes upon *Israel's* desolate "house" (Matt. 23:38), (b) related to the destruction of the *then-existing* temple (Matt. 24:1–2), and (c) confined to the *first century* (Matt. 24:34). As an original hearer of Christ, John is surely employing the text as Christ did—as Beale allows.[38] This is especially likely since Revelation functions as John's version of the Olivet Discourse, a pattern that "a number of scholars have argued." [39]

Beale's second argument (really the second feature of his first) fails for the same reasons. Especially since Revelation 1:7 appears just a few verses after strong assertions of the temporal proximity of the events (Rev. 1:1, 3).

Regarding his third argument about the Septuagint use of "all the tribes of the earth" signifying universality: (1) As I have shown, Beale argues *both* that John's use of the Old Testament "typically" transports the original contextual meaning into Revelation *and* that sometimes it does not (John "transfers what is said of Israel in Zechariah 12 to the peoples of the earth, who now assume the role of Israel, repentant after having rejected God's messenger"[40]). His argument giveth and it taketh away. (2) And again, Christ's prior employment of this merged citation, seems clearly to refer to Israel (see above). (3) Neither Beale nor any other commentator of which I am aware argues that John is quoting the Old Testament with the phrase "all the tribes of the earth." Consequently, the Septuagintal references though interesting, are not determinative. (4) In Revelation, when John wants to universalize the "tribes," he adds other descriptors "kindred, nations, and tongues." Here in 1:7 he does not—even though he could easily have done so.

Thomas argues against me that "the 'cloud-coming' to which Revelation is devoted turns out to be *no* coming. It is obvious to most that Christ did not come in A.D. 70, so the hermeneutics used to conclude that He did come are suspect."[41] Unfortunately for Thomas, his argument could be as vigorously made against God's "coming" against Egypt in Isaiah 19:1, thereby exposing his error in assuming literality (or better, corporeality). Furthermore, many commentators agree that Matthew 21:40 prophesies A.D. 70—while using "coming" language.[42] And Thomas is still stuck with the thorny problem of John's near time indicators (1:1, 3).

Drawing Conclusions

With the several contextual indicators before us, it seems certain that the theme of Revelation deals with Christ's judgment-coming *upon the generation of those Jews who crucified him.* Clearly, the judgment-coming of Christ upon "those who pierced Him" was against the Jews, according to the repeated and uniform witness both of the New Testament and of early church history. As Chilton observes: Revelation 1:7 "announces the theme of the book, which is not the Second Coming of Christ, but rather the Coming of Christ in judgment upon Israel, in order to establish the Church as the new Kingdom."[43] Desprez notes of this theme verse in conjunction with the temporal expectations of the book "no scriptural statement is capable of more decided proof than that the coming of Christ is the destruction of Jerusalem, and the close of the Jewish dispensation."[44]

We know as a matter of indisputable historical fact that the temple was destroyed by Titus's August, A.D. 70, siege.[45] Hence, as Jesus bears his cross to Calvary he exhorts the "daughters of Jerusalem" to weep for themselves because of the coming judgment (Luke 23:28–31, cp. Rev. 6:16).

Thus, only a pre-A.D. 70 date fits the circumstances, for what events subsequent to the A.D. 70 destruction of the temple parallel the magnitude and covenantal significance of this event?[46] Surely the destruction of the Jewish temple (accomplished now for over 1900 years) and the gruesome Jewish War with Rome *must* be in view here. In terms of Jewish calamity and woe, what events near the reign of Domitian could equal those which transpired just after Nero's reign?

Revelation 1:7 must indicate that "the *Jewish people* are most evidently intended, and therefore the whole verse may be understood as predicting the destruction of the Jews; and is a presumptive proof that the Apocalypse was written *before* the final overthrow of the Jewish state."[47] Westminster divine and Talmudic scholar John Lightfoot holds that Revelation 1:7 speaks of "Christ's taking vengeance [on] that exceeding wicked nation" of Israel,[48] and argues that the "sending forth and execution of judgment against that nation is almost always called in the NT 'his coming in glory.'"[49] He even suggests (as I do) that Israel's judgment is Revelation's theme: "Nay, I may further add, that perhaps this observation might not a little help (if my eyes fail me not) in discovering the method of the author of the Book of the Revelation."[50] Of Revelation 1:7 he states elsewhere: it "especially referreth to the first most visible evidence of his power and dominion, in coming to destroy his enemies, the Jewish nation, and their city. And here is one reason that induceth me to suppose this book written, before that city was destroyed."[51]

As I press on with my case for a pre-A.D. 70 date for Revelation, I must consider Israel's condition as evidenced in Revelation. We will discover that her circumstances bespeak a time pre-A.D. 70.

Coming Judgment in the Land

With these observations before us, it would seem certain that the theme of Revelation deals with Christ's judgment-coming *upon the generation of those Jews who crucified him.* And it was a judgment-coming upon them, particularly as they dwelt in "the Land," the Promised Land God had given them. We might well expect that the theme would recur throughout Revelation—and so it does. I will cite just one illustration of the fact that Revelation looks to the Jewish War with Rome of A.D. 67–70.[52]

The Sealing of the Saints[53]

In Revelation 7:1–8 we find an interesting temporary divine protection of "the Land" where four angels are seen holding back the winds of destruction. I will translate the Greek words normally rendered "the earth" by the preferred translation "the Land":

> After this I saw four angels standing at the four corners of the Land,[54] holding back the four winds of the Land, so that no wind should blow on the Land or on the sea or on any tree. And I saw another angel ascending from the rising sun, having the seal of the living God; and he cried out with a loud voice to the four angels to whom it was granted to harm the Land and the sea, saying, "Do not harm the Land or the sea or the trees, until we have sealed the bond-servants of our God on their foreheads."

Then follows the sealing of the 144,000 from the Twelve Tribes of Israel.

Surely those who are sealed are *Christians.* This must be so in that: (1) God intervenes to protect them, and (2) they are called "bond-servants of our God." These cannot be unbelieving Jews (Rev. 2:9; 3:9). Furthermore, these would have to be Christian *Jews* for (1) they are from Israel's Twelve Tribes (7:4), (2) they are in "the Land" (7:1, 2), and (3) they are contrasted with the "great multitude" from "every nation" who praise God (7:9).

The "Twelve Tribes" is another common means by which John speaks of "the tribes of the Land" (cp. Rev. 1:7). Here, however, note that the entirety of the Twelve Tribes is not protected, the whole race of Israel, as such. Rather, only 144,000 of them: a perfect number[55] representing the "cream of the crop," *i.e.* those Jews who have converted to Christ. They are sealed "out of" or "from among" (Greek: *ek)* "every tribe of the sons of Israel" (7:4).

Why are these 144,000 solely from Jewish tribes? Because the pending "wind of destruction" was threatened against Judea, the land where the city of Jerusalem is found, in which the Lord was crucified (Rev. 11:1, 2, 8).

The Destruction in the Land

That an angel intervenes to prevent their being destroyed along with the Land surely indicates the era prior to the devastation of Israel in A.D. 70 (remember the expectation of soon occurrence that I noted in Chapter 2 above). Were "the Land" already destroyed (which occurred in August, A.D. 70), such a promised protection would have been painfully anachronistic.

In the Olivet Discourse Jesus speaks of the destruction of the very temple to which the disciples could physically point (Matt. 24:1–2). He warns his disciples that they should flee *Judea* (24:16) when it is time for these things to come to pass (i.e., A.D. 70). He adds further that they should accept his promise that these horrendous events would be cut short (24:22), and that he who endures to the end will be saved through it all (24:13). He also clearly taught that all of these things would happen to "this generation" (24:32). Indeed, this coming event will be "the great tribulation" (24:21).

The protection of Jewish Christians in Jerusalem is thus indicated in Revelation 7:1–7 via the symbolism of sealing. This refers to the providential protection of those Christians of Jewish lineage who were "in the Land."

An extremely interesting and famous piece of history informs us that the Jewish Christians in Jerusalem escaped the city before it was too late, possibly either at the outset of the War or during one of its providential lulls before the final siege. Church historian Eusebius (A.D. 260–340) records the situation thus:

> But the people of the church in Jerusalem had been com-
> manded by a revelation, vouchsafed to approved men there be-
> fore the war, to leave the city and to dwell in a certain town of
> Perea called Pella. And when those that believed in Christ had
> come thither from Jerusalem, then, as if the royal city of the
> Jews and the whole land of Judea were entirely destitute of holy
> men, the judgment of God at length overtook those who had
> committed such outrages against Christ and his apostles, and
> totally destroyed that generation of impious men.[56]

Thus, Revelation 7, which provides supplemental evidence to John's overarching theme, strongly indicates a pre-fall Judea. This must be so because after the Jewish War "Palestine was proclaimed a Roman province, and a great part of the land became the personal property of the emperor. But the country was in ruins, its once flourishing towns and villages almost without inhabitants, dogs and jackals prowling through the devastated streets and houses."[57]

Conclusion

The theme of Revelation is Christ's judgment upon first century Israel for her rejection of his Messianic kingship. This is evident from the various terms used in the thematic statement of Revelation 1:7: Christ is to come upon (1) those who pierced him, *i.e.* the Jews, (2) those who are of "the tribes," *i.e.* the Jews, and (3) those who dwell in "the Land," *i.e.* the Promised Land. All of this comes about as a fulfill-ment of his own prophecies in Matthew 21:33–45; 23:1ff; 24:1–34; Luke 21:5–28; 23:27–31; and elsewhere. And all of this was to come upon "this generation" (Matt. 23:36; 24:34)—or, employing John's ter-minology, these events were "near" (Rev. 1:3) and were to occur "shortly" (1:1; 22:6ff).

The events to which Christ and John point were those associated with the Jewish War with Rome in A.D. 67–70. Particularly in view is the de-struction of the temple, which was destroyed in August, A.D. 70. Conse-quently, Revelation must have been written prior to its destruction.

Notes

1. Moses Stuart, *Commentary on the Apocalypse,* 2 vols. (Andover: Allen, Morrill, and Wardwell, 1845), 1:273. Friedrich Düsterdieck, *Critical and Exegetical Handbook to the Revelation of John,* trans. Henry E. Jacobs, 3rd ed. (New York: Funk and Wagnalls, 1886), 28. Bernhard Weiss, *A Manual of Introduction to the New Testament,* 2 vols., trans. A. J. K. Davidson (New York: Funk and Wagnalls, 1889) 2:71. Justin A. Smith, *Commentary on the Revelation* in Alvah Hovey, ed., *An American Commentary on the New Testament* (Valley Forge: Judson, [1884] rep. n.d.), 18. Milton S. Terry, *Biblical Apocalyptics* (New York: Eaton and Mains, 1898), 280. J. Stuart Russell, *The Parousia: A Study of the New Testament Doctrine of Our Lord's Second Coming,* 2nd ed. (Grand Rapids: Baker [1887] 1983), 368. Thomas Dehany Bernard, *Progress of Doctrine in the New Testament* (Grand Rapids: Eerdmans, [1864] 1949), 213. Donald W Richardson, *The Revelation of Jesus Christ* (Richmond, Vir.: John Knox, 1964), 28. George Eldon Ladd, *A Commentary on the Revelation to John* (Grand Rapids: Eerdmans, 1972), 28. Charles C. Ryrie, *Revelation* (Chicago: Moody Press, 1968), 15. G. R. Beasley-Murray, *The Book of Revelation* (Grand Rapids: Eerdmans, 1978), 58. David Chilton, *The Days of Vengeance: An Exposition of the Book of Revelation* (Fort Worth, Tex.: Dominion Press, 1987), 64. G. K. Beale, *The Book of Revelation* (NIGTC) (Grand Rapids: Eerdmans, 1999), 25.

2. The very fact that Jesus died by crucifixion (a Roman punishment) and not stoning (a Jewish punishment) by itself indicates the physical involvement of the Roman judicial apparatus.

3. See: John Dominic Crossan, *Who Killed Jesus? Exposing the Roots of Anti-Semitism in the Gospel Story* (San Francisco: HarperSanFrancisco, 1995). Dan Cohn-Sherbok, *The Crucified Jew: Twenty Centuries of Anti-Semitism* (Grand Rapids: Eerdmans, 1992). Heinz Schreckenberg and Kurt Schubert, *Jewish Historiography and Iconography in Early and Medieval Christianity* (Minneapolis: Fortress, 1992). James Parkes, *The Conflict of the Church and the Synagogue* (London: Soncino, 1934). Rosemary Ruether, *Faith and Fratricide* (New York: Seabury, 1974). John G. Gage, *The Origins of Anti-Semitism: Attitudes Toward Judaism in Pagan and Christian Antiquity* (New York: Oxford University Press, 1983). Alan Davies, ed., *Antisemitism and the Foundations of Christianity* (New York: Paulist, 1979).

4. Apparently, this was a common means of despoiling the Christians, for we read of this tactic again in Acts 17:6–7.

5. *Epistle to the Magnesians* 11.

6. *Epistle to the Trallians* 11.

7. *Epistle to the Smyrnaeans* 2.

8. *First Apology* 35.

9. *First Apology,* 38.

10. *Dialogue with Trypho* 72.

11. *Against Heresies* 3:12:2.

12. *Against Heresies* 3:12:13.

13. *Apology* 21 and 56; *On Idolatry* 7; *An Answer to the Jews* 9 and 13; *Against Marcion* 3:6; 3:25; 5:15.

14. *Treatise on Christ and Antichrist* 30 and 57; *Expository Treatise Against the Jews* 1, 2, and 7; and *Against Noetus* 18.

15. *Treatises* 9:7; 10:5; Introduction to *Treatise* 12; 12:2:14; 12:2:20.

16. *Divine Institutes* 46; *Epitome of the Divine Institutes* 46; *On the Manner in which the Persecutors Died* 2.

17. Additional references can be found in my *Before Jerusalem Fell: Dating the Book of Revelation*, 3rd ed. (Atlanta: American Vision, 1998).

18. Christian Maurer, *"phule"* in *Theological Dictionary of the New Testament*, ed. Gerhard Kittle and Gerhard Friedrich, trans. Geoffrey W. Bromiley (Grand Rapids: Eerdmans, 1974) 9:246. See also Burton Scott Easton, "Tribe," in *The International Standard Bible Encyclopedia*, ed. James Orr (Grand Rapids: Eerdmans, 1956), 4:3010. It should be noted, in addition, that the Gingrich-Danker *Lexicon* (868) and the Thayer *Lexicon* (660) both list "tribe," as in Israel, as their first lexical entries.

19. For example: Genesis 49:28; Exodus 24:4; 28:21; 39:14; Numbers 1:4–49; 34:18–28; Joshua 3:12; 4:8; 1 Kings 18:31; Ezekiel 47:13.

20. See Revelation 5:5; 7:4–8; cp. Matthew 19:28; Luke 22:30; Acts 26:6, 7; Hebrews 7:13. For the "twelve tribes of Israel," see also: 1 Clement 43:2; Barnabas 8:3; Hermes 9:17:1; Diodorus Siculus 40:3:3; Josephus, *Antiquities* 5:5:1:22; 9:14:1; 11:5:2; *Life of Josephus* 1:1; Testament of Benjamin 9:2; and the Qumranian documents: 1QSa 1:15, 29; 1QM 2:2ff; 3:14ff.; 15:1.

21. See Gingrich-Danker, *Lexicon,* 157; Thayer, *Lexicon,* 114–115; Abbott-Smith, *Lexicon,* 91.

22. Horst Balz and Gerhard Schneider, eds., *Exegetical Dictionary of the New Testament* (Grand Rapids: Eerdmans, 1990), 1:246.

23. Alfred Edersheim, *Sketches of Jewish Social Life in the Days of Jesus* (Grand Rapids: Eerdmans, rep. 1970), 14. Edersheim's entire second chapter is helpful reading along these lines.

24. Edersheim, *Sketches of Jewish Social Life,* 63.

25. Ralph P. Martin and Peter H. Davids, eds., *Dictionary of the Later New Testament & Its Developments* (Downers Grove, Ill.: InterVarsity Press, 1997), 642.

26. Allison, in Martin and Davids, *Dictionary of the Later New Testament & Its Developments,* 643.

27. Robert Young, *Young's Literal Translation of the Holy Bible,* 2nd ed. (Grand Rapids: Baker: [1898] n.d.), 167.

28. Alfred Marshal, *The Interlinear Greek-English New Testament,* 2nd ed. (Grand Rapids: Zondervan, 1993), 701.

29. An early note should be recalled at this point. Daniel 7:13 originally refered to the ascension of Christ to glory. Here John is not interpreting Daniel 7:13, but merging it with Zechariah 12:10 in application to the theme of his prophecy: the judgment-coming upon Israel that resulted from the ascension-coming to the Father to take up his rule.

30. For more information see: Kenneth L. Gentry, Jr., *Perilous Times: A Study in Eschatological Evil* (Texarkana, Ark.: Covenant Media Press, 1999), chs. 2–3. Thomas Ice and Kenneth L. Gentry, Jr., *The Great Tribulation: Past or Future?* (Grand Rapids: Kregel, 1999). Gary DeMar, *Last Days Madness: Obsession of the Modern Church,* 4th ed. (Powder Springs, Ga.: American Vision, 1999).

31. Michael Grant, *The Jews in the Roman World* (New York: Barnes & Noble, 1973), 205. See discussion in Pliny the Elder, *Natural Histories,* 12:111-23.

32. See the liberal scholars: Schreckenberg and Schubert, *Jewish Historiography and Iconography in Early and Medieval Christianity*, ch. 3 "Josephus in Early Christian Texts."

33. G. K. Beale, *The Book of Revelation* (NIGTC) (Grand Rapids: Eerdmans, 1999), 25, 26.

34. Charles asserts that "not only does our text agree in combining Zech. xii. 30 and Dan. vii. 13, but also in transforming the original meaning of Zech. xii. 10." R. H. Charles, *The Revelation of St. John* (Edinburgh: T & T Clark, 1920), 1:17. Others holding that the text does not indicate repentance but despair include: Leon Morris, *Revelation*, 2nd ed. (Downers Grove, Ill.: InterVarsity Press, 1987), 50. Ramsey Michaels, *Revelation* (Downers Grove, Ill.: InterVarsity Press, 1997), 57.

35. Beale, *Revelation*, 81.

36. Besides, this same John in his Gospel applies the Zechariah text to first-century witnesses of the crucifixion—apparently a non-"typical" use by John: John 19:37.

37. Beale, *Revelation*, 92.

38. Beale, *Revelation*, 196.

39. C. Marvin Pate and Calvin B. Haines, Jr., *Doomsday Delusions: What's Wrong with Predictions About the End of the World* (Downers Grove, Ill.: InterVarsity, 1995), 37.

40. Beale, *Revelation*, 26.

41. Robert L. Thomas, *Revelation 1–7: An Exegetical Commentary* (Chicago: Moody, 1992), 20.

42. The Gospel evidence is so strongly focusing on A.D. 70 that liberal scholars even argue that such prophecies are *ex eventu*. Schrekenberg even suggests that Christians read Josephus first and only *then* began putting such prophecies in Christ's mouth. Schreckenberg and Schubert, *Jewish Historiography and Iconography in Early and Medieval Christianity*, ch. 3.

43. Chilton, *Days of Vengeance*, 64.

44. P. S. Desprez, *The Apocalypse Fulfilled*, 2nd ed. (London: Longman, Brown, Green, Longmans, 1878), 9.

45. Josephus, *Wars* 7:1:1.

46. The Bar-Kochba revolt of 132–35 was perhaps equally devastating militarily, but the Temple, the very heart of Israel and the Jews' central meaning was already gone.

47. Adam Clarke, *Clarke's Commentary on the Whole Bible* (Nashville: Abingdon, rep. n.d.) 6:971.

48. John Lightfoot, *Commentary on the New Testament from the Talmud and Hebraica*, 4 vols. (Peabody, Mass.: Hendrickson, [1674] rep. 1989), 2:319; cp. 422.

49. Lightfoot, *Commentary on the New Testament*, 2:202.

50. Lightfoot, *Commentary on the New Testament*, 3:210. This view also appears in Milton S. Terry, *Biblical Apocalyptics* (1898); Cornelis Vanderwaal, *Search the Scriptures*, vol. 10 (1979); David Chilton, *The Days of Vengeance* (1987).

51. John Lightfoot, *The Harmony, Chronicle, and Order, of the New Testament*, in *The Whole Works of the Rev. John Lightfoot*, ed. by John Rogers Pitman (London: J. F. Dove, [1654] 1822), 3:333.

52. For additional information in this regard, see my larger work, *Before Jerusalem Fell: Dating the Book of Revelation*. The Jewish revolt broke out in late 66 when the Jews revolt against the Roman procurator Gessius Florus. Shortly thereafter the Syrian governor Cestius Gallus descends upon Jerusalem to punish the Jews. He mysteriously retreats, giving the Jews

hope of victory. The *formal* imperial engagement begins with Nero's commissioning of Vespasian to take matters in hand: "Vespasian's appointment to Judaea [was in] February 67." Kenneth Wellesley, *The Year of the Four Emperors*, 3rd ed. (London: Routledge, 2000), 45.

53. See further discussion of Revelation 7 in ch. 12 below, under the heading "Revelation 7."

54. Ezekiel prophesies the end "coming on the four corners of the land" Eze. 7:2).

55. The number 144,000 is derived from the number symbolic of quantitative fullness (10), which is trebled (10 x 10 x 10). This gloriously complete number is then multiplied by the number of tribes squared (12 x 12).

56. *Ecclesiastical History* 3:5:3. See also: Epiphanius, *Panarion* 29:7; 30:2; and *Weights and Measures* 15:2:5.

57. Rufus Learsi, *Israel: A History of the Jewish People* (New York: World, 1949), 178

10

The Political Evidence

Here is the mind which has wisdom. The seven heads are seven
mountains on which the woman sits, and the are seven kings; jive
have fallen, one is, tin other has not yet come; and when he
comes, he must remain a little while
Rev. 17:9-10

In this chapter I will present *the* leading objective evidence for
Revelation's date of composition: the list of "seven kings" in Revelation
17, which is cited above. Here we discover a concrete political statement of an historically datable quality that clearly establishes the outer
limits of the date of Revelation.[1] As I will show, that time-frame not
only precludes a Domitianic date for Revelation, but firmly establishes
a Neronic one.

The prominent features of the chapter bearing upon our inquiry
are: (1) The revelatory image itself: a Beast with seven heads (Rev. 17:3,
7, 9; cp. 13:2). (2) The angelic interpretation of the image: the seven
heads represent both seven mountains and seven kings (17:9, 10). (3)
The chronology of the image: of the seven kings, "five have fallen,"
"one is" reigning, and one is to come to rule for "a little while" (17:10).

Let us consider this evidence carefully to determine when Revelation was written.

The Line of Kings

In Chapter 1 I showed that the seven mountains represented by the seven heads reflect the distinctive geography of Rome. Rome was familiar to all of the ancient world as the "the city on Seven Hills." This geographical clue in the vision, coupled with temporal delimiters and audience relevance, necessarily limit us to the Roman Empire of the first century.[2]

But more particularly, Revelation confines us to the era demanded by the early date. I speak of the *political* implications of the line of the seven kings. John writes of the seven heads that they are not only "seven mountains" but: "They are seven kings; five have fallen, one is, the other has not yet come; and when he comes, he must remain a little while." Here he describes for us a sequence of "seven kings" of Rome. This statement, as we will see, closely fixes the time of composition. All we need do is determine the identity of these seven kings, and which one is ruling as John writes. I lay before the careful student the following evidences, supportive of the early date position.

First, prophetically the sixth king is alive and ruling as John writes. Clearly, the first five "have fallen," as the past tense indicates.[3] Therefore, the five that "have fallen" are *past* rulers. John continues by employing the present tense and noting the sixth king "is,"[4] that is, he is presently governing the kingdom. The seventh "has not yet come;[5] and when he comes, he must remain a little while" (Rev. 17:10). Thus, the seventh is not yet a present political reality.

Clearly then, this vision pictures a political succession in which five kings have come and gone, the sixth is currently reigning, and a seventh will eventually follow. Whoever these kings are, the sixth one is indisputably alive and in control *as John writes,* while in exile for his faith (cp. Rev. 1:9).

Second, politically Nero was the sixth ruler of the Roman Empire. Nero reigned in Rome from October 13, A.D. 54, to June 9, A.D. 68—well before the A.D. 90s required by the late-date theory. He was the sixth ruler to bear the name "Caesar." The list of the Caesars is as follows:

1. Julius Caesar (49–44 B.C.)
2. Augustus Caesar (31 B.C.–A.D. 14)
3. Tiberius Caesar (A.D. 14–37)
4. Gains Caesar, also called "Caligula" (A.D. 37–41)
5. Claudius Caesar (A.D. 41–54)
6. *Nero Caesar* (A.D. 54–68)

As Ehrman notes: "if we begin counting with Julius Caesar, Nero happens to have been the sixth ruler of Rome."[6] Nero fits the bill perfectly in terms of the enumeration of the emperors of Rome. But there is more.

Third, historically the next ruler of the Empire reigned only briefly. This fits perfectly the imagery of the seventh king who "has not yet come; and when he comes, he must remain a little while" (Rev. 17:10). Remarkably, upon Nero's death by suicide in June of A.D. 68, the empire collapsed into a seething cauldron of leadership struggle. The next ruler to appear after Nero was Galba, who reigned only seventh months: from June A.D. 68 until his treacherous murder on January 15 A.D. 69.

By almost any standard, Galba's brief rule of seven months was a "little while"—Nero's immediately preceding rule had exceeded thirteen years. The Greek term in Revelation 17:10 for "little" is *oligon.* We get our term "oligarchy" (which means "a rule by a few") from this word. When Galba's rule is compared to any of the preceding six emperors (see the listing above), it is obvious that his is the shortest imperial reign theretofore.

This evidence from Revelation 17 fits the reign of Nero, then, in more than one respect. The correspondence to the history of the era is perfect. But not all commentators accept this view. Let me survey the major objections against this position.

Objections to the Nero View

Several major objections have been raised against the view presented above. Initially these seem quite formidable. But careful analysis dispels any real force they may appear to have.

The Call for Wisdom

Some commentators point to the fact that Revelation is full of imagery that might not be so obvious. Regarding the present matter in particular, they argue that the text even cautions against too easy an interpretation. Immediately before our verse is the following statement: "here is the mind which has wisdom" (Rev. 17:9a). In this regard, John F. Walvoord writes: "The explanation of the beast introduced by the unusual phrase 'here is the mind which hath wisdom' anticipates the difficulty and complexity of the revelation to follow. The reader is warned that spiritual wisdom is required to understand that which is unfolded."[7]

Despite his observation, it appears that Walvoord is once again turning on its head a matter in Revelation (as I noted earlier regarding John's temporal expectation). The context of John's statement clearly suggests that this phrase is introducing an *elucidation* of the matter. It is not a warning about an additional difficulty to be added by verses 9 and 10. The angel who shows John the harlot seated on the seven-headed Beast, notes John's confusion about the vision (Rev. 17:1, 7a). So the angel interprets the matter for him: "Why do you wonder? I shall tell you the mystery of the woman and of the beast that carries her, which has the seven heads and the ten horns" (17:7). What follows is the angel's exposition of the vision. *He is not providing John with more diffi-*

cult material, but is explaining the confusing aspect of the vision. This experience is like the earlier one in which an "elder" (an angel of some sort) explains to John the vision of the "great multitude" in Revelation 7:9, 13, 14. In both Revelation 7 and 17 the angelic explanations provide *help* in understanding the visions.

The difficulty in the vision requiring "wisdom" is that it involves a *two-fold* referent. "The seven heads are [1] seven mountains on which the woman sits, *and* they are [2] seven kings" (Rev. 17:9–10a). This interpretation would doubtless escape the reader without the angelic explication. It would appear, therefore, that the expression "here is the mind which has wisdom" is introducing the *interpretation* of the vision. Consequently, he who follows the angelic interpretation "has wisdom."

Identifying the First King

Many scholars argue that the line of the emperors of Rome officially began with Augustus, whom I have as the *second* king. This is technically true in that Julius Caesar was not formally an emperor. But the historical evidence still points to the legitimacy of starting the count with Julius. As noteworthy a Revelation scholar (and late-date advocate) as Leonard Thompson provides a list of "emperors" beginning with Julius.[8] As Renwick observes: "In one sense Julius Caesar was the founder of the empire, and Augustus the founder of the principate."[9] Furthermore, the subsequent rulers of Rome, who were technically emperors, called themselves by the name "Caesar," indicating a continuity with Julius Caesar. "Caesar" was "the family name [that] became a mark of status" and "the title by which the NT refers to the emperors."[10]

But even more persuasively, Julius was commonly recognized as the first ruler of the empire, since he "first claimed the rights of Roman emperor."[11] Though he was not emperor *de jure*, he was *de facto*. Indeed, Suetonius notes that Julius "deserved assassination" in that "not only did he accept excessive honours, such as a life-consulship, a life-dictatorship, a perpetual Censorship, the title 'Imperator'[12] put before his name, and the title 'Father of his Country' appended to it."[13] The Roman biographer Suetonius (A.D. 70–160) entitles his famous biography of the emperors from the beginning up until his time, *Lives of the Twelve Caesars.* His work begins with Julius Caesar. Roman historian Dio Cassius (A.D. 150-235) also begins the count of the emperors with Julius.[14]

Other works from the same general era follow suit. Among the more prominent ones we could include *4 Ezra, The Epistle of Barnabas,* and various *Sibylline Oracles.*[15] In fact, the eleventh book of the *Oracles* has a vision that, according to Sibylline scholar J. J. Collins, refers to the "Roman kings, beginning with Julius Caesar and counting Galba, Otho, and Vitellius."[16] Theophilus of Antioch (A.D. 115–168[17]), a Christian writer praised by Eusebius for his pastoral fidelity,[18] is quite clear in his designation: "The annual magistrates ruled the Romans, as we say, for 453 years. Afterwards those who are called emperors began in this order: first, Caius Julius, who reigned 3 years 4 months 6 days; then Augustus, 56 years 4 months 1 day; Tiberius," and so on.[19]

Even more important, however, is the reckoning of the emperors by the Jewish historian Joseph ben Mathias, better known by his adoptive name Flavius Josephus. He holds Julius as the first emperor, in that he counts Augustus the second, and Tiberius the third.[20] Josephus is most significant in that he: (1) was a Palestinian Jew, as was John; (2) lived and wrote during John's lifetime (Josephus's dates are A.D. 37–101); (3) participated in the Jewish War, which seems to be the subject matter of much of Revelation; and (4) wrote his histories while at Rome and at the expense of the Flavian emperors.

In summary, while modern historians may often begin their count of the Roman emperors with Augustus, ancient writers often began with Julius. Consequently, we are justified in counting the emperors from Julius. The objection regarding the enumeration of the kings does not, therefore, overthrow our analysis.

Interestingly, however, even *if* we begin counting with Augustus, we would still end up in the era pre-A.D. 70. For in such a reckoning, Galba would be the sixth king, reigning until A.D. 69. The seventh king would then be Otho, who reigned an even shorter period of time (January 15 to April 16, A.D. 69). Still, the evidence requires that the count begin with Julius Caesar. And that evidence lands us in the era pre-A.D. 70, before Nero's death (June 9, A.D. 68).

The Civil War Emperors

Another objection comes from those who suggest that the three brief reigning emperors of the Roman Civil War—Galba, Otho, Vitellius—should not be counted. This would remove three kings in the enumeration. If we then started with Augustus we would have Vespasian (emperor from A.D. 69–79) as the sixth king.

This objection fails to overthrow the early date case, as well. I have already shown the improbability of starting the count from Augustus. And we should note that this counting still does not bring us to the late-date period of Domitian's rule (A.D. 95). Even Vespasian's reign begins before A.D. 70, in June 69.

In addition, this objection against the early-date is based on two grounds: (1) Roman biographer Suetonius speaks of the brief reigns of Galba, Otho, and Vitellius as but a "rebellion."[21] (2) The short reigns of these three would have been inconsequential to the far-flung provinces of the Roman Empire.[22] The ease with which we may dispose of these objections is surprising, in light of their widespread employment.

In regard to Suetonius's statement, it must not escape our notice that he does, nevertheless, list these three emperors in his *Lives of the Twelve Caesars*. In addition these three are recognized as emperors by Roman historian Tacitus, the pro-Roman, Jewish historian Josephus, the Christian pastor Theophilus of Antioch, the writer of 4 *Ezra,* and one of the *Sibylline Oracles*.[23]

In response to the notion that these three emperors would be inconsequential to the Roman provinces in Asia Minor, nothing could be more mistaken. These three emperors almost destroyed the city of Rome and nearly caused the collapse of the empire.[24] Inconsequential? Indeed, of Galba's brief rule, Grant observes:

> The brief reign of Galba was chiefly important because of the circumstances in which it came about. These were summed up by Tacitus in the introduction of his *Histories*: "A well-hidden secret of the principate had been revealed: it was possible, it now appeared, for an emperor to be chosen outside Rome." The revelation of this secret showed the provincial garrisons their own power, incited them to display it in armed conflict one against the other, and led the way to endless military rebellions and revolutions in the centuries that lay ahead.[25]

Emperors as "Kings"

Some might object to the interpretation I am defending on the grounds that John's vision designates these men "kings" (Gk., *basileus*), whereas the Roman imperial rulers were properly designated "emperors." Though formally correct, this complaint overlooks the ancient tendency to call the emperors "kings."

In non-biblical Christian writings and in pagan literature the emperors were often designated kings. The Roman poet Martial (A.D. 40–104) and Nero's court philosopher, Seneca (4 B.C.–A.D. 65), both call Nero "king."[26] The *Sibylline Oracles* of the first two centuries call various emperors "kings."[27] The early Christian writings entitled *The History of John the Son of Zebedee, The Giving Up of Pontius Pilate,* and *The Acts of the Holy Apostle and Evangelist John the Theologian,* and the fifth century Christian writer Sulpicius Severus[28] all call certain emperors "kings."

More importantly, in Scripture itself we find emperors called kings! In John 19:15 the priests reject Christ before Caesar by saying, "We have no king but Caesar." The accusers of Jason in Acts 17:7 warn of Jason's receiving Christians into their homes: "Jason has welcomed them, and they all act contrary to the decrees of Caesar, saying that there is another king, Jesus." In fact, we may safely speak of "the Jewish custom of referring to Caesar as a king (Jn. 19:12, 15). The dynastic family was from their point of view monarchical."[29] Clearly, this objection is without merit.

Conclusion

In light of all the evidence presented above, we may safely conclude that Revelation 17:9–10 provides objectively verifiable information supporting the early date for Revelation. The sixth king, who is presently reigning (Rev. 17:9), is Nero Caesar, whom I show in Part I of this work to be the specific identity of the Beast.[30] Thus, the latest possible date which we may ascribe to Revelation is before June, A.D. 68, the date of Nero's death.

Notes

1. I find it absolutely incredible that Leonard Thompson could write: "The author of the Book of Revelation does not give much of a clue about the particular time in which he is writing." But then, Thompson argues that John is writing to a church in comfort and in danger of complacency! Leonard L. Thompson, *The Book of Revelation: Apocalypse and Empire* (New York: Oxford, 1990), 13.

2. See Chapter 2.

3. The form of the Greek verb pipto ("fall") is the second aorist active indicative.

4. The Greek is the present indicative form of the verb eimi ("to be").

5. Here John uses the "prophetic second aorist active of erchomai" according to A. T. Robertson, *Word Pictures in the New Testament,* 6 vols. (Nashville: Broadman, 1933) 6:432.

6. Bart D. Ehrman, *The New Testament: A Historical Introduction to the Early Christian Writings* (New York: Oxford, 2000), 432.

7. John F. Walvoord, *The Revelation of Jesus Christ* (Chicago: Moody Press, 1966), 250. See also Henry B. Swete, *Commentary on Revelation* (Grand Rapids: Kregel, [1911] 1977), 219–220 and Alan F. Johnson, *Revelation* (Grand Rapids: Zondervan, 1983), 158.

8. Thompson, *The Book of Revelation,* xi, 14.

9. A. M. Renwick, "Roman Empire and Christianity," in Geoffrey W. Bromiley, ed., *The International Standard Bible Encyclopedia,* 2nd ed. (Grand Rapids: Eerdmans, 1982), 4:208.

10. Scott Nash, "Caesar," in David Noel Freedman, ed., *Eerdmans Dictionary of the Bible* (Grand Rapids: Eerdmans, 2000), 206. See: Matt. 22:17–21; Mark 12:14–17; Luke 2:1; 3:1; 20:22–25; 23:2; John 19:12, 15; Acts 17:7; 25:8, 10–12, 21; 26:32; 27:24; 28:19; Phil. 4:22

11. G. K. Beale, *The Book of Revelation* (NIGTC) (Grand Rapids: Eerdmans, 1999), 21.

12. "Imperator" is a general Latin term signifying conqueror, which later served as the root for "emperor." Cf. Josephus, *Antiquities* 14:10:2.

13. Suetonius, Julius 76.

14. Dio Cassius, *Roman History* 5.

15. 4 Ezra 11:13ff; 12:13ff, *Barnabas* 4:4; *Sibylline Oracles* 5:12; 8:135–138; 11:261ff.

16. Collins, "Sibylline Oracles," in James H. Charlesworth, *Old Testament Pseudepigrapha: Apocalyptic Literature and Testaments,* vol. 1 (Garden City, N.Y.: Doubleday, 1983), 421.

17. His dates are conjectural. I have followed the suggestion of Marcus Dods, which is found in Alexander Roberts and James Donaldson, eds., *The Ante-Nicene Fathers,* 10 vols. (Grand Rapids: Eerdmans, [n.d] rep. 1975) 2:87–88.

18. Eusebius, *Ecclesiastical History* 4:24.

19. Theophilus, *To Autolycus* 3:28.

20. Josephus, *Antiquities* 16:6:2; 18:2:2; 18:6:10.

21. Suetonius, *Vespasian 1.*

22. G. R. Beasley-Murray, *The Book of Revelation* (Grand Rapids: Eerdmans, 1978), 256–257; Robertson, *Word Pictures,* 5:432; James Moffatt, *The Revelation of St. John the Divine,* vol. 5 in W. Robertson Nicoll, ed., *The Expositor's Greek Testament* (Grand Rapids: Eerdmans, rep. 1980), 318.

23. Tacitus, *Histories* 1:1ff, 2:10; Theophilus, *To Autolycus* 2:28; Josephus, *Wars of the Jews* 4:9:2; *Sibylline Oracles* 5:35; and 4 *Ezra* 12:206.

24. See Chapter 7.

25. Michael Grant, *The Twelve Caesars* (New York: Barnes & Noble, [1975] rep. 1996), 178.

26. Seneca, *On Clemency* 2:12 (cited from Miriam T. Griffin, *Nero: The End of a Dynasty* [New Haven: Yale University Press, 1984], 95); and Martial, Book of Spectacles 2.

27. See *Sibylline Oracles* 4:119; 5:138ff 8:131ff 11:286; 12:25ff 13:15.

28. Sulpicius Severus, *Sacred History* 2:28.

29. E. A. Judge, "Caesar," in J. D. Douglas and F. F. Bruce, *New Bible Dictionary,* 2nd ed. (Downers Grove, Ill: InterVarsity Press, 1982), 155.

30. For a discussion of the eighth king. See chapter 7.

The Architectural Evidence

And there was given me a measuring rod like a staff and someone
said, "Rise and measure the temple of God, and the altar, and those
who worship in it. And leave out the court which is outside the
temple, and do not measure it, for it has been given to the nations;
and they will tread underfoot the holy city for forty-two months"
Rev. 11:1-2

We find another extremely helpful evidence for dating Revelation
in Revelation 11 (cited above), where we discover a reference to a temple
complex. If we can identify this temple, and if it exists in history, then
we should be able to point to it as hard evidence (no pun intended) for
a particular date for Revelation.

The initial question we must consider regards the *identity* of this
temple complex. Basically, three leading interpretations prevail: (1) It is
"a symbol of the true church that worships the triune God"[1]; (2) it is "a
literal temple that will exist in actuality during the future period just
before Christ returns"[2]; and (3) it is "the old temple of the earthly city,"
i.e., the earthly temple which existed during Jesus' day.[3] I believe the
evidence compellingly points to the last view.

The most natural identity of the temple is the literal temple in Jerusalem in Jesus' day. This temple, known as Herod's temple, was familiar to the readers of the New Testament and was the subject of several of Christ's prophecies.[4] Let us consider the merits of this view, while noting the deficiencies inherent in the other interpretations.

Herod's Temple

The Historical Location

First, Revelation's temple is located in Jerusalem. According to John, the temple complex is located in a "holy city" (11:2). This must speak of *historical Jerusalem* of the first century, which housed the famous temple of God. Jerusalem is called the "holy city" in both the Old and New Testaments (Isa. 48:2; 52:1; Neh. 11:1–18; Matt. 4:5; 27:53). What city other than Jerusalem had a just claim to be called "the holy city" — especially in Scripture itself? Jerusalem was historically known as the "city of God" (Pss. 46:4; 48:1, 8; 87:3), "my holy mountain" (Isa. 11:9; 56:7; 57:13: 65:11, 25), the "city of the Great King" (Pss. 48:2; Matt. 5:35), the center of the whole earth (Eze. 5:5; 38:12; *1 Enoch* 26:1; *Jub.* 8:11), and other such sacred and intimate designations in Scripture and in other ancient Jewish literature.

Certainly "the OT affirms that Yahweh specifically chose Jerusalem (Ps 78:68; 87:2; 102:16; 132:13) to be his special dwelling place (Ps 2:6; 9:11; 74:2; 87:2; 102:16). Jerusalem is thus considered to be a sacred place, a place of worship and celebration (2 Chron. 5:2; Ps 99:2; 137:1-3; 146:10; 147:12). OT writers consistently glorify the city by describing it in epic proportions."[5] Interestingly, coins minted during the Jewish War of A.D. 67–70 (the era of the early date's concern) bore the legend "Jerusalem the Holy."[6]

Moreover, contextual clues demand we understand this "holy city" to be literal, historical Jerusalem, rather than spiritual Jerusalem: (1) The flow of the action leading up to Revelation 11 has an angel "coming down out of heaven" to John (Rev. 10:1), i.e., to the earth. Chapter 11 is connected with Chapter 10 with a simple "and," indicating the same sphere of activity. (2) Revelation states that this city was to be trodden underfoot (11:2), which cannot refer to the heavenly Jerusalem. (3) This city was the place "where also their Lord was crucified" (11:8): "And their dead bodies will lie in the street of the great city which mystically is called Sodom and Egypt, where also their Lord was crucified." Jesus was crucified at Jerusalem (Matt. 16:21; Luke 13:33; 24:18). (4) *After* the destruction of the temple, we read that "the temple of God *which is in heaven* was opened" (11:19), indicating a change of focus from earth below to heaven above, from the earthly temple to the heavenly.

We should note also that the "holy city" becomes *mystically* "Sodom and Egypt" (Rev. 11:8). In the Old Testament we find precedent for rebellious Jerusalem's designation by the pagan name "Sodom" (Isa. 1:9–10; Ezek. 16:46–49). In Revelation John applies to Jerusalem the names of evil enemies of God, demonstrating that Jerusalem has become God's enemy. The greatest crime of all history was perpetrated in Jerusalem: the crucifixion of the Lord of glory (Matt. 16:21; Mark 8:31; 10:32–34; Luke 9:22; 13:32; 17:11; 19:28). Through spiritual metamorphosis the once "holy city" had been transformed into a mutant, unholy "Sodom and Egypt."

That the same city can be called "holy" in one verse and "Sodom and Egypt" in the following verse does not require that John be referring to two distinct cities. This is simply John's way of declaring that "the faithful city has become an harlot" (Isa. 1:22a).

Jerusalem of the *first century* also is demanded by the imminent expectation of John (Rev. 1:1, 3, 19; 3:10; 22:6ff). No Jerusalem in the distant future could be in view, in light of John's own stated temporal restrictions. In addition, John's referring to Jerusalem as the place where the Lord was crucified would seem more appropriate for the first century

Jerusalem than for a twenty-first-century (or later!) Jerusalem so distantly separated from that horrible event.

Since historical, first century Jerusalem is in view, we should expect that the prominent, historical feature of that city should be in view, as well: the Herodian temple complex.

The Thematic Demand

Second, the theme of the book. John's dramatic purpose demands Revelation 11:1–2 refer to the literal temple in Jerusalem. Revelation was written to warn that "those who pierced Him" (the Jews of the first century, see my Chapters 2 and 9) would experience his cloud-coming judgment (Rev. 1:7). Again, we must recall that the judgment would be soon (1:1, 3, 19; 3:10; 22:6ff.), not thousands of years later. Hence, the significance of the literal, historical temple—the place of Jewish worship—in this passage, which speaks of the place where the Lord was "pierced."

The Parallel Evidence

Third, the parallel with other Scriptures. Scriptures elsewhere relate the destruction of the historic temple of Jesus' day, and with language closely corresponding to Revelation 11. John uses the future tense when he speaks of the nations treading down the city ("they will tread," Rev. 11:2b). He is not reminiscing over a past event, but pondering a future expectation.

Revelation 11:1-2 establishes an "eyecatching" (Ellis[7]) parallel with the prophecy of Christ recorded in Luke 21:24. The prophecy in Luke 21 (like its parallels in Matt. 24 and Mark 13) is widely held to refer to the destruction of Jerusalem and the temple in A.D. 70. Indeed, this *must* be the case, for at least two reasons: (1) The very occasion of the prophetic discourse arises from the disciples' pointing out the beauty of the material, first century temple to Christ. (2) That very temple to which they pointed was destroyed in A.D. 70 in a manner which precisely fulfills the terms of the prophecy.

Note that in Luke 21:5–7a the disciples pointed out the actual features of that historical structure:

> And while some were talking about the temple, that it was adorned with beautiful stones and votive gifts, He said, "As for these things which you are looking at, the days will come in which there will not be left one stone upon another which will not be torn down." And they questioned Him, saying, "Teacher, when therefore will these things be?"

The prophecy that follows the disciples' remarks was definitely spoken by the Lord as the historical temple stood! In Luke's record of the Olivet Discourse, Christ specifically speaks of the dismantling of the temple and destruction of Jerusalem in terms which form the basis of those in Revelation 11.

A little further into the context, we read in Luke 21:24: "and they will fall by the edge of the sword, and will be led captive into all the nations; and *Jerusalem will be trampled underfoot by the Gentiles* until the times of the Gentiles be fulfilled." Compare this to Revelation 11:2b, which reads: "it has been given to the *nations;* and they will *tread underfoot* the *holy city* for forty-two months." In these two passages the correspondences are so strong, they surely bespeak historical identity, rather than mere accidental similarity:

$$Luke\ 21:24 = Revelation\ 11:2$$
$$Jerusalem = the\ holy\ city$$
$$Gentiles\ (ethne) = nations\ (ethnesin)$$
$$trampled\ underfoot\ (patoumene) = tread\ under\ foot\ (patesousin)$$

Evidently these verses in both John's Revelation and Luke's Gospel look to the same events.[8] And these events literally occur to historical institutions and structures. These events had not already occurred, but lay in the future for both Jesus (whose words Luke records) and John (in Revelation). The context of Luke demands a literal Jerusalem (Luke 21:20) and temple (21:5, 6) besieged by literal armies (21:20) in literal Judea (21:21). As a matter of indisputable historical record this occurred in the events leading up to A.D. 70, *not after.*

The Temporal Length of Treading

Revelation 11:2 informs us that "they will tread under foot the holy city for forty-two months," which fits remarkably well with the historical time-frame of the Jewish War. Obviously wars are invariably *evolving* processes brought on by various complicated socio-political circumstances, thus oftentimes difficult to date precisely. And the Jewish War is no exception, for the Jewish "revolt against Rome did not begin suddenly but was preceded by a long series of incidents"[9]

Various precursors to the full scale, formally engaged "Jewish War" include several revolutionary events in A.D. 66: Agrippa II's being driven from Jerusalem by an angry Jewish mob, the subsequent massacre of the Roman garrison,[10] Menahem's surprise conquering of the Roman fortress at Masada, the Greek massacre of Jews in Alexandria, and the Syrian governor Cestius Gallus' coming to Jerusalem with two legions to put down the uprising. The *formal* imperial engagement of the War, however, should be dated when Nero effects "Vespasian's appointment to Judea in February 67" to put down the Revolt, thereby elevating it a full scale War.[11] Grant notes of Vespasian, "in February of the following year [i.e., in A.D. 67] he was appointed governor of Judaea with the task of suppressing the First Jewish Revolt."[12] Mason states that "the war began in earnest only in March or April of 67, when Vespasian and his son Titus gathered their legions in Ptolemais."[13]

The Jewish War "ended in with the destruction of Jerusalem" in August-September, A.D. 70.[14] Thus, the actual Jewish War lasted from

February of A.D. 67 until August-September of A.D. 70, which happens to be a period of time virtually forty-two months in length. This provides additional evidence that the destruction of the Temple mentioned in Revelation 11 is referring to the events of the first century, and, therefore, suggests the Herodian Temple is in John's prophetic view.

Kistemaker suggests two problems indicate that "the length of time does not fit the record"[15] : (1) "The Jewish revolt against Rome began in the late spring of 66 and ended with the destruction of Jerusalem in August-September 70." I have already anticipated and rebutted that argument above: the counting begins when Nero formally commissions Vespasian to put down the *Revolt;* it only then becomes a full-scale *War.*

(2) "The trampling of the holy city by the Gentiles began after Jerusalem fell into the hands of the Romans." Of course, this occurs in the last few weeks of the Jewish War, when the Romans batter down the walls and enter the city. But this is only a problem if we demand that the prophetic statement be interpreted in a woodenly literal manner, requiring that the Roman hob-nail military sandals must actually be in contact with Jerusalem's paved streets. But surely it is not at all far-fetched to interpret the "treading under foot the holy city" as a figure-of-speech indicating the engagement of the Jewish War which ultimately results in the literal trampling of Jerusalem. In the ancient world military conquest was often expressed by images of putting one's enemy under his feet (2 Sam. 22:38–39; 1 Kgs. 5:3; Ps 18:38; 47:3; Lam 3:34), or making the enemy a footstool (Ps 110:1; Lk 20:43; Ac 2:25), or trampling him into the dust (Ps 7:5; 44:5; 56:1–2; 57:3; Is 10:6; 14:25). No one requires that an oppressed or conquered people must *literally* be thrown to the ground and trampled upon for the metaphorical reality of military foot-trampling to prevail (though for a dramatic symbol of total victory they *may* actually do so to defeated kings, Jos 10:24).

Furthermore, biblical statements commonly employ *prolepsis* for dramatic effect. Prolepsis is the anachronistic representing of something as existing before its proper or historical time. Prolepsis looks to the end result anticipated in the proleptic observation. The Scripture is replete with examples of prolepsis. For instance, in Judges 9:13 "wine" is spoken of as on the "vine," just as figs exist on the tree (cp. Jdgs. 9:10–12). But actually grapes appear as a solid fruit on the vine—though wine is the ultimate liquid drink produced from the grapes. In Isaiah 65:8 we find "new wine" (Heb. *tirosh*) "in the cluster." Jeremiah 40:10 speaks of "gathering in wine" (Heb. *tirosh*) as if the liquid drink itself were in the field on the vine.[16] In Revelation 11 the entire Jewish War is set forth proleptically as a treading down of the Holy City, which is its final, horrifying result.

Beale presents a common interpretation of the forty-two months: "The number of the 'forty-two months' is not literal but figurative for the eschatological period of tribulation repeatedly prophesied by Daniel (7:25; 9:27; 12:7, 11–12)."[17] In response, I would urge the following: (1) Due to the divine involvement and prophetic significance of the destruction of Jerusalem, the God of history can cause symbolic time-frames (forty-two months = three and one-half years = one-half of seven, i.e., a broken seven) to transpire in history, as well. Josephus wonders at God's providence in causing events to fall out according to a remarkable pattern. When reflecting upon the destruction of the temple, he writes: "However, one cannot but wonder at the accuracy of this period thereto relating; for the same month and day were now observed, as I said before, wherein the holy house was burnt formerly by the Babylonians" (*Wars* 6:4:8).[18] (2) Even Beale himself notes of Revelation 11 that it mirrors an actual time in history: "Another reason that a three and one-half year period is chosen to represent the church's witness [in Rev. 11] is that Christ's ministry lasted about that amount of time."[19] (3) Our suggested time-frame is one of many lines of evidence that correspond to the historical events that were "shortly to come to pass" in John's day. Why kick against the pricks?

The Natural Interpretation

The most natural interpretation of Revelation 11, then, suggests that John is referring to the literal temple, for in literal Jerusalem did God have his temple. In light of these factors certain questions arise.

Even recognizing that the part of the temple to be preserved has a spiritual referent (see discussion below): how could John be commanded to measure symbolically that which did not exist, with the idea of preserving (in some sense) a part and destroying the rest? If Revelation were written in the A.D. 90s, why did John not mention the first century temple's recent destruction, particularly in such a work as this which focuses on the divine judgment upon Judaism? Early, post-apostolic Christianity made much of the fact of the destruction of the temple as evidence of God's rejection of the Jew. Let me survey a few early Christian references to the destruction of the temple.[20]

The Epistle of Barnabas is dated between A.D. 75 and 100. In *Barnabas* 16:1ff we read: "Moreover I will tell you likewise concerning the temple how these wretched men being led astray set their hope on the building, and not on their God that made them, as being a house of God. . . . So it cometh to pass; for because they went to war it was pulled down by their enemies." It is indisputably clear that *Barnabas* makes much of Jerusalem's fall as an apologetic for Christianity.

Ignatius wrote around A.D. 107. And although he does not clearly and explicitly refer to Jerusalem's fall, he does seem to allude to the matter. In his *Epistle to the Magnesians* 10 we read: "It is absurd to speak of Jesus Christ with the tongue, and to cherish in the mind a Judaism which has now come to an end." With the demise of the temple, Judaism is incapable of worshiping in the manner prescribed in the Law of God; it "has now come to an end." This is used by Ignatius to enhance the role of Christianity against that of now defunct *Bible-based* Judaism.

Justin Martyr wrote his *The First Apology of Justin* about A.D. 147. In this work we read at Chapter 32: "For of all races of men there are some who look for Him who was crucified in Judea, and after whose crucifixion the land [i.e. Israel] was straightway surrendered to you as a spoil of war." In Chapter 53 he writes: "For with what reason should we believe of a crucified man that He is the first-born of the unbegotten God, and Himself will pass judgment on the whole human race, unless we had found testimonies concerning Him published before He came and was born as man, and unless we saw that things had happened accordingly—the devastation of the land of the Jews."

In the fragments of the works of Melito of Sardis (written about A.D. 160–180), we discover his words against the Jews: "Thou smotest thy Lord: thou also hast been smitten upon the earth. And thou indeed liest dead; but He is risen from the place of the dead, and ascended to the height of heaven."

Hegesippus, in the fragments of his *Commentaries on the Acts,* writes regarding the death of James, the Lord's brother (A.D. 170–175): "And so he suffered martyrdom; and they buried him on the spot, and the pillar erected to his memory still remains, close by the temple. This man was a true witness to both Jews and Greeks that Jesus is the Christ. And shortly after that Vespasian besieged Judaea, taking them captive." He ties in the persecution of Christ's apostle James to the destruction of Jerusalem.

Clearly, early Christianity made much of the fall of Jerusalem and the Jews. Furthermore, where in Revelation is there any reference to a rebuilding of the temple so that it could be again destroyed (as per the dispensationalist argument)? If John fails to mention a rebuilding of the temple, and if the book was written about A.D. 95, how could the readers make sense of its prophecies? John definitely speaks of the temple as still standing.

As a matter of indisputable historical record—confirmed in both archaeology and ancient literature—the temple in Jerusalem was destroyed in August, A.D. 70 by the Roman general Titus. And yet in Revelation 11:1–2 we read of the temple standing while John wrote. John looks to its *future* destruction. Hence, John must have written prior to A.D. 70.

We need to realize how obviously John is referring to Herod's temple. The conclusion is so strong that this passage has played prominently in the various liberal critical theories of Scripture. These (erroneous) liberal approaches view Revelation as a hodgepodge collection of older and newer traditions from both Jewish and Christian sources. These traditions, it is alleged, were strung together, rather disjointedly, by one or more editors. For instance, M. E. Boring writes: "The initial unit of this vision may be a traditional fragment of a previous prophecy. Many scholars have thought it likely that 11:1–2 originated as a Zealot prophecy during the last days of the war against Rome."[21]

Obviously the presence of this temple in Revelation 11 is remarkable, even if the liberals handle it wrongly. It indicates the early date for Revelation, not a patch-work view of Revelation's composition.

Objections

Several objections have been raised against the position outlined above. I will briefly mention and respond to these.

The Preservation of a Portion of the Temple

A major objection to our view is that Revelation seems to indicate that the temple in view will be partially preserved, while history shows clearly that the temple was leveled to the ground. How are we to understand the commands for John to measure the temple but not to measure its court? That is, how are we to understand this partial preservation of the temple (that which is "measured") in Revelation if the first-century temple is meant (since it was totally devastated)?

The proper understanding of the passage *requires* that we allow a mixing of the figurative and the literal, the symbolic and the historical. This is true in virtually every interpretive approach to the passage, even the attempted alleged literalistic hermeneutic of dispensationalism. This may be why dispensationalist John F. Walvoord is prone to agree that "careful students of the book of Revelation will probably agree with Alford that chapter 11 'is undoubtedly one of the most difficult in the whole Apocalypse.'"[22]

Introducing his comments on Revelation 11, Walvoord writes that "the guiding lines which govern the exposition to follow regard this chapter as a legitimate prophetic utterance in which the terms are taken normally."[23] By "normally" he means "literalistically." Interestingly, Walvoord is conspicuously silent on the matter of John's literally scaling the walls of the temple, with a physical reed in hand, and his gathering the worshipers together to measure them. And he fails to interpret verse 5 as demanding that literal fire issue forth from the mouths of the two witnesses.[24] Even fellow premillennialist (though non-dispensationalist) Robert Mounce notes: "The measuring of the temple is a symbolic way of declaring its preservation."[25]

Regarding Revelation 11:1–2, I propose that the unmeasured (and unprotected) outer courts of the temple represent the literal temple, which as a physical entity is external and transitory. Whereas the measured (and protected) inner temple portrays that which is essential and permanent, the true worship of God's holy name by his ongoing people. Dispensationalist Thomas warns: Gentry's method "involves a mixture of figurative-symbolic and literal-historical. . . . He wants a figurative and literal meaning for essentially the same terminology."[26] He also complains that I give "no attention to the possibility that this may be a future literal temple."[27]

Though such admittedly can be confusing, it is neither unwarranted nor unparalleled in Scripture. We must recognize that as apocalyptic literature Revelation allows a greater flexibility in its exegesis. Even Thomas admits "the fluidity of metaphorical language in Scripture is undeniable."[28] In fact, Revelation itself teaches us that (at least) one symbol may have a two-fold referent: The seven heads on the beast represent both seven mountains and seven kings (Rev. 17:9–10). Though this double-referent does not align spiritual and material realities, it is, nonetheless, painfully confusing (apart from the angel's explanation).

John's mixing of spiritual and literal realities here in comparing the spiritual people of God and the physical temple building is not unprecedented (e.g.: 2 Kgs 21:12, 13; Amos 7:8, 9; Isa. 34:11; Lam. 2:8). In fact, elsewhere John himself records Christ's words regarding eating bread (John 6:49–50). There he parallels the spiritual eating of Christ's body with the literal eating of the manna in the wilderness, which in turn parallels spiritual death and physical death: "Your forefathers ate the manna in the desert, yet they died. But here is the bread that comes down from heaven, which a man may eat and not die." The same words "eat" and "die" occur in both statements, but they carry different connotations.

Furthermore, Revelation 11:1–2 reflects back on Luke 21 (particularly v. 24). Yet nothing in Luke 21:24 suggests that any portion of the *physical* temple will be spared in any sense—indeed, "there will not be left one stone upon another which will not be torn down" (Luke 21:6; cp. 21:24). In Luke 21, however, Jesus clearly prophesies God's sparing his true people during the destruction of the temple, for not "a hair of your head will perish" (21:18), because they are to "flee to the mountains" (21:21). Revelation incorporates this glorious protective truth in his Revelation prophecy by means of dramatic imagery.

Remarkably, this mix of physical and spiritual is rooted in the very idea of the temple itself. For instance, in Hebrews 8:5a we read of an earthly "sanctuary that is a copy and shadow of what is in heaven." The earthly, external is a copy/shadow of the heavenly spiritual reality.

The "man-made sanctuary" is a "copy of the true one" (Heb. 9:24). In Revelation 11 God removes the shadow-copy so that the essential-real remains, which John here portrays as the worshipers in the heart of the temple.

Furthermore, contrary to Thomas, two reasons dissuade me from seeking a future rebuilt temple: (1) The events of Revelation are near (Rev. 1:1, 3; 22:6, 10). Thomas's rebuilt temple is at least 2000 years distant. (2) Revelation 11 is based on Luke 21:24, which, like Revelation, is in a context also confined to the first century. After all, Jesus warns that "when these things begin" then "your redemption is drawing *near*" (Luke 21:28); his disciples are to "know that summer is *near*" (vv. 29–30); the must understand that "when you see these things happening, you know that the kingdom of God is *near*" (v. 31); he emphatically declares: "*this generation* will certainly not pass away until all these things have happened" (v. 32). After all, Luke 21 is a prophecy of the destruction of the first century temple (Luke 21:5–6).

In Revelation 11, then, John is commanded to not "measure" the outer court of the temple. In fact, the outer court is to be "cast out." The Greek of Revelation 11:2a is *ekbale,* a stronger term than "leave out," as per the New American Standard Bible. The outer court is not destined for preservation, "for it has been given to the nations." Neither is Jerusalem to be protected, for the nations "will tread under foot the holy city for forty-two months" (Rev. 11:2b). The prior prophecy of Christ regarding the destiny of the temple (Luke 21:6, 24) absolutely prohibits any hope of even its partial, useable preservation.[29] Thus, John here reveals the prophetic certainty of the destruction of the external, material temple ("the court which is outside").

On the other hand, John's measuring is for the preservation of its innermost aspects: the inner temple (Greek: *naos),* altar, and worshipers within (Rev. 11:1). Here the portions of the temple measured symbolize the inner-spiritual idea of the temple. In the New Coveant era—the

Christian era—the spiritual inner-temple supercedes the material temple of the Old Covenant era.

John prophesies that judgment is about to be brought upon literal Jerusalem and the temple (the court is to be cast out and the city trodden down). Nevertheless, his prophecy assures the preservation of God's Church, the new inner-temple (Greek: *naos,* Eph. 2:19ff.; 1 Cor. 3:16; 6:19; 2 Cor. 6:16; 1 Pet. 2:5ff). In the Old Testament those who worshiped at the altar were priests (Ex. 28:43; 29:44). In Revelation John calls Christians "priests" (Rev. 1:6; 5:10) who offer prayers at the altar of incense (Rev. 5:8; 6:9–10; 8:3–4).

It is important to remember that the Christian Church (the spiritual inner-temple) had its birth in and was originally headquartered at historical Jerusalem (Luke 24:47; Acts 1:8, 12; 3:1, 2, 11; 5:12–16, 42; 8:1; 11:1–2; 15:1–2). Furthermore, the early converts to Christianity were predominantly from Jewish extraction (Acts 2:14, 41, 47; 4:1–4). Hence, the need for protecting the Church during the work of destruction.

Revelation 11:2 parallels the idea in Revelation 7:1–8. There Christian Jews are sealed for protection, before the destruction of the Land. As such, both of these prophecies—Revelation 7:1–8 and 11:1–2—teach the truth for Christians that was contained in Christ's prior prophecy: "Yet not a hair of your head will perish" in Jerusalem's destruction (Luke 21:18). Heeding Christ's command to "flee to the mountains" (21:21), Christians were protected from the destruction that fell upon Jerusalem. Early church history records that Christians fled to Pella and were spared.[30]

Also we should note that after the forty-two month treading down of Jerusalem, the altar is seen no longer in earthly Jerusalem, but in heaven (Rev. 11:18). This is significant because Christ's kingdom originates there (John 18:36; Heb. 1:3) and Christians have their ultimate citizenship there (Eph. 2:6; Col. 3:1–2; Heb. 12:22).

Although all sides recognize an obvious involvement of the symbolic in the passage, there surely must be some historical reality that forms the basis of the symbol. After all, the symbolic names "Egypt" and "Sodom" refer to the historical city Jerusalem (Rev. 11:8). If John wrote about literal Jerusalem ("where also their Lord was crucified") twenty-five years after the destruction of the literal temple (as per the evangelically formulated late-date argument), it would seem most improbable that he would speak of the temple as if it were still standing. The symbol would be confusing in its blatant anachronism. The temple's existence is required for the symbolic action of the vision to have any meaning.

The "Great City"

Many suspect that the phrase "the great city" (Rev. 11:8) indicates Rome, which actually authorized and performed the crucifixion of Christ. My designating historical Jerusalem as "the great city" may allow too grandiose a conception for this city "of modest size."[31] But it should not, however, surprise those aware of either the covenantal-redemptive significance of Jerusalem or its historical fame. Historically, even Roman historians speak of its magnificence: Tacitus calls it "a famous city,"[32] for it housed a temple which "was famous beyond all other works of men."[33] Pliny the Elder said of Jerusalem that it was "by far the most famous city of the ancient Orient."[34] Appian, a Roman lawyer and writer (ca. A.D. 160) calls it "the great city Jerusalem."[35] Truly, then, Jerusalem was one of the most famous cities of the civilized world at that time.[36]

More important, however, is the *covenantal* significance of Jerusalem in Scripture. The obvious role of Jerusalem in the history of the covenant should merit such a claim to greatness. The intense Jewish love of Jerusalem pictured it as of great stature among the famous cities of the nations: The Fifth Book of the *Sibylline Oracles* is a Jewish oracle written from Egypt in the A.D. 90s. There Jerusalem is spoken of in this way: "He seized the divinely built Temple and burned the citizens and peoples who went into it, men whom I rightly praised. For on his appearance the whole creation was shaken and kings perished, and those in whom sovereignty remained destroyed a *great city* and righteous people."[37] About three hundred lines later we read: "But now a certain insignificant and impious king has gone up, cast it down, and left it in ruins with a great horde of illustrious men. He himself perished at immortal hands when he left the land, and no such sign has yet been performed among men that others should think to sack a *great city*."[38]

Josephus sadly extols Jerusalem's lost glory after its destruction: "This was the end which Jerusalem came to by the madness of those that were for innovations; a city otherwise of *great magnificence, and of mighty fame* among all mankind."[39] A few paragraphs later we read: "And where is that *great city*, the metropolis of the Jewish nation, which was fortified by so many walls round about, which had so many fortresses and large towers to defend it, which could hardly contain the instruments prepared for the war, and which had so many ten thousands of men to fight for it? Where is this city that was believed to have God himself inhabiting therein? It is now demolished to the very foundations."[40]

Ezekiel's Visionary Temple

I have been arguing that John's measuring the temple to separate what will be destroyed from what will be preserved (Rev. 11:1) requires that it be presently intact, or else his prophecy would be anachronistic and confusing. Some respond to this argument by noting that Ezekiel's prophecy records a measuring of the temple (Eze. 43:10; 45:3; 47:18)—even though it had recently been destroyed by the Babylonians. Consequently, they aver, Revelation 11:1–2 cannot serve as evidence the temple is still standing.

In response I would note that a dramatic difference exists between Ezekiel and John's prophecies. Ezekiel clearly informs us that he is writing *after* Israel was sent into exile (Eze. 1:1), "*after* the city was taken"

(40:1), "*after* He came to destroy the city" (43:3). His vision clearly speaks of the temple's *re-building* in the future: "He said to me, 'Son of man, thus says the Lord God, "These are the statutes for the altar on the day it is built, to offer burnt offerings on it and to sprinkle blood on it"'" (43:18). *Nothing* in Revelation either assumes the temple is already destroyed or that it will be re-built. It simply refers to the temple as if it is still standing.

Clement of Rome

A number of evangelical scholars argue that the first-century writer Clement of Rome spoke of the temple as still standing, even though he (allegedly) wrote around A.D. 90. Clement's relevant statement is: "Not in every place, brethren, are the continual daily sacrifices offered, or the freewill offerings, or the sin offerings and the trespass offerings, but in Jerusalem alone. And even there the offering is not made in every place, but before the sanctuary in the court of the altar; and this too through the high-priest and the aforesaid ministers, after that the victim to be offered hath been inspected for blemishes."[41]

This language in the letter, however, opens the whole question of the actual date of *1 Clement* itself. Unfortunately, there is almost as serious a question over the dating of Clement's letter as with Revelation. One of Clement's translators, A. Cleveland Coxe, who himself opted for an A.D. 97 date for the letter, was quite cautious: "I have reluctantly adopted that his Epistle was written near the close of his life, and not just after the persecution of Nero."[42] Though J. B. Lightfoot accepted the late date of *1 Clement,* he recognized some unusual factors of the letter (which I will consider below) that are quite curious if the letter is late.[43] Four noteworthy scholars who have opted for an early (A.D. 69 or 70) date for Clement are historians Arthur S. Barnes and George Edmundston, and biblical exegetes John A. T. Robinson and E. Earle Ellis.[44] A brief summary of several of the leading early date evidences for *1 Clement* should easily demonstrate its early date.

First, the problematic *silence*. If the letter were written after A.D. 90—when Clement was appointed the bishop of Rome—then we must somehow account for an unusual ecclesiastical situation in the letter. Lightfoot was somewhat perplexed by the fact that there is absolutely no hint of a bishop at Rome.[45] Robinson is absolutely persuaded by the silence, noting that there is no appeal to episcopal authority in the letter and that the offices of bishop and elder are synonymous (42:4ff; 44:1ff.; 54:2; 57:1), as in New Testament times. If the offices *are* synonymous, it is remarkable that a radical transition could occur within a period of only two decades. The letters of Ignatius twenty years later clearly indicate a bishopric distinct from the eldership.[46] Robinson's point is well-taken. The evidence, such as it is, suggests a pre-bishopric rather than a later era.

Second, the more primitive Christian era represented. Edmundston noted that reference to Christ as the "child of God," the primitive form of Scripture quotations, the mention of the phoenix (which had been exhibited in Rome under Claudius's reign, A.D. 41–54), and other such matters, more readily lend themselves to the earlier period.[47] Barnes adds to these the mention of Fortunatus (a friend of Paul in A.D. 54, cf. 1 Cor. 16:17), the selection of Claudius and Valerius (who were of the household of Claudius the Emperor, according to Lightfoot) as messengers, and other such indications.[48]

Third, the recent deaths of the apostles. Clement refers to the deaths of "the good Apostles" in "our generation," suggesting a very recent occurrence quite compatible with a date around A.D. 69 or 70: "But to pass from the examples of ancient days, let us come to those champions who lived nearest our times. Let us set before us the noble examples which belong to our generation. By reason of jealously and envy the greatest and most righteous pillars of the church were persecuted, and contended even unto death. Let us set before our eyes the good Apostles" (*1 Clem.* 5:1). Clement thereupon mentions the deaths of Peter and Paul, which indisputably indicates he is referring to the Neronic persecution.

Furthermore, Clement specifically names some who died in the Neronian persecution. In *1 Clement* 5 he names Peter and Paul, but also in *1 Clement* 6 we read of the names of a couple of other martyrs now virtually unknown, Danaids and Dircae. It would be quite remarkable if he cited the names of those involved in the Neronian persecution (which allegedly occurred thirty years before), but was strangely silent about the names of those who died in the Domitianic persecution— even though they were supposed to be prominent members of his own congregation! In both chapters 5 and 6 of his letter Clement provides much history of the Neronian woes, while employing only ten words (in the Greek) for the (alleged) Domitianic persecution—the persecution through which he and many of his friends were allegedly passing! That reference reads: "by reason of the sudden and successive troubles and calamities which have befallen us."

If, however, the letter were written sometime near or in early A.D. 70, then the first, fifth, and sixth chapters would *all* speak of the Neronian persecution. In the course of its long history the city of Rome had never witnessed so many "sudden and successive troubles and calamities" among its population generally, and for the Christians particularly, than in Nero's rule. His era eventually issued forth in the chaotic and destructive Year of the Four Emperors (A.D. 69).

Tacitus introduces Rome's history after the death of Nero thus:

> The history on which I am entering is that of a period rich in disasters, terrible with battles, torn by civil struggles, horrible even in peace. Four emperors failed by the sword; there were three civil wars, more foreign wars and often both at the same time. There was success in the East, misfortune in the West. Illyricum was disturbed, the Gallic provinces wavering, Britain subdued and immediately let go. The Sarmatae and Suebi rose against us; the Dacians won fame by defeats inflicted and suffered; even the Parthians were almost roused to arms through

the trickery of a pretended Nero. Moreover, Italy was distressed by disasters unknown before or returning after the lapse of ages. Cities of the rich fertile shores of Campania were swallowed up or overwhelmed. Rome was devastated by conflagrations, in which her most ancient shrines were consumed and the very Capitol fired by citizens' hands. Sacred rites were defiled; there were adulteries in high places. The sea was filled with exiles, its cliffs made foul with the bodies of the dead. In Rome there was more awful cruelty.

Besides the manifold misfortunes that befell mankind, there were prodigies in the sky and on the earth, warnings given by thunderbolts, and prophecies of the future, both joyful and gloomy, uncertain and clear. For never was it more fully proved by awful disasters of the Roman people or by indubitable signs that gods care not for our safety, but for our punishment.[49]

Schaff commented on this period that "there is scarcely another period in history so full of vice, corruption, and disaster as the six years between the Neronian persecution and the destruction of Jerusalem."[50] Nothing approaching this chaos or even hinting at this level of upheaval was associated with Domitian's death. Combining the Neronian state of persecution begun in A.D. 64 with the Roman Civil Wars in A.D. 68–69, all becomes very clear.

Fourth, the temple reference in *1 Clement* 41 (cited above). All things considered, the reference to the temple services as if they were still being conducted is best construed as demanding a pre-August, A.D. 70 dating. Edmundson insists that "it is difficult to see how the evidential value of cxli. can be explained away."[51]

It would seem that at the very least the statement in *1 Clement* 41 cannot discount the possibility of our approach to Revelation 11, in that the date of *1 Clement* is in question. And as is probably the case, Clement did write his epistle prior to the temple's destruction.

Conclusion

The temple in Revelation is surely the famous Herodian Temple of Jerusalem to which Christ and the apostles could point. This temple is standing when Revelation was written (Rev. 11:1). The evidence is multiple and varied in this direction: (1) The temple is located in the "holy city," i.e., historical Jerusalem (11:2, 8). (2) The judgments on the temple and Jerusalem are justified by reference to Christ's crucifixion (11:8), which occurred in the first century and would more appropriately fall upon that generation. (3) The theme of Revelation directs the bulk of the judgment against the first-century Jews, "the tribes of the Land," who "pierced" Christ (1:7). (4) John's account parallels Luke's account in Luke 21, which definitely speaks of the A.D. 70 destruction of the physical temple to which the disciples actually pointed (Luke 21:5; cp. Matt. 24:1). (5) Revelation does not suggest the (allegedly) recently destroyed temple being rebuilt.

The appearance of the Jewish temple in this first century writing is impossible to account for if Revelation were written a quarter of a century after its destruction. Attempts to reduce its significance for dating fail in their purpose. But on the recognition of a pre-A.D. 70 date for Revelation, the temple's presence in Revelation is not only accounted for but even expected.

Notes

1. Simon J. Kistemaker, "The Temple in the Apocalypse," in *Journal of the Evangelical Theological Society* 43:3 (Sept., 2000): 435. See also: Peter W. L. Walker, *Jesus and the Holy City: New Testament Perspectives on Jerusalem* (Grand Rapids: Eerdmans, 1996), 247. G. K. Beale, *The Book of Revelation* (NIGTC) (Grand Rapids: Eerdmans, 1999), 558; cf. 559–565. Vern S. Poythress, *The Returning King: A Guide to the Book of Revelation* (Phillipsburg, N.J.: Presbyterian and Reformed, 2000). David Chilton, *The Days of Vengeance: An Exposition of the Book of Revelation* (Fort Worth: Dominion, 1987), 272–73.

2. Robert L. Thomas, *Revelation 8–22: An Exegetical Commentary* (Chicago: Moody, 1995), 82. See also: John F. Walvoord, *Prophecy Knowledge Handbook* (Wheaton, Ill.: Victor, 1990), 572–75. J. Dwight Pentecost, *Thy Kingdom Come* (Wheaton: Victor, 1990), Paul N. Benware, *Understanding End Times Prophecy: A Comprehensive Guide* (Chicago, Moody, 1995), 253–54.

3. John A. T. Robinson, *Redating the New Testament* (Philadelphia: Westminster, 1976), 239. See also: R. C. Sproul, *The Last Days According to Jesus: When Did Jesus Say He Would Return?* (Grand Rapids: Baker, 1998), 147. Keith A. Mathison, *Postmillennialism: An Eschatology of Hope* (Phillipsburg, N.J.: Presbyterian and Reformed, 1999), 151. Greg L. Bahnsen, *Victory in Jesus: The Bright Hope of Postmillennialism* (Texarkana, Ark.: Covenant Media Press, 1999), 14; David S. Clark, *The Message from Patmos* (Grand Rapids: Baker, rep. 1989 [1921]), 74–75. Jay E. Adams, *The Time Is Fulfilled* (Phillipsburg, N.J.: Presbyterian and Reformed, 1966), 68; Milton S. Terry, *Biblical Hermeneutics* (Grand Rapids: Zondervan, [1906] n.d.), 473ff.

4. "All four Gospels have Jesus making reference to a future destruction of the temple (Mt 24:2; Mk 13:2; Lk 21:6; cf. Mt 26:61; Mk 14:38; Jn 2:19)." Craig A. Evans and Stanley E. Porter, eds., *Dictionary of New Testament Background* (Downers Grove, Ill.: InterVarsity, 2000), 277. See my sections in Thomas Ice and Kenneth L. Gentry, Jr., *The Great Tribulation: Past or Future?* (Grand Rapids: Kregel, 1999). See also: Gary DeMar, *Last Days Madness: Obsession of the Modern Church,* 4th ed. (Atlanta: American Vision, 1999).

5. C. C. Newman, "Jerusalem, Zion, Holy City," in Ralph P. Martin and Peter H. Davids, eds., *Dictionary of the Later New Testament & Its Developments* (Downers Grove, Ill.: InterVarsity Press, 1997), 561. See also: J. D. Levenson, *Sinai and Zion: An Entry into the Jewish Bible* (Minneapolis: Winston, 1985).

6. George Adam Smith, *Jerusalem: The Topography, Economics, and History from the Earliest Times to A. D. 70* (London: Hodder and Stoughton, 1907), 1:270.

7. E. Earle Ellis, *The Making of the New Testament Documents* (Boston: Brill, 1999), 227.

8. This may explain why John's Gospel is the only Gospel which does not record Christ's Olivet Discourse, which pointed to the destruction of the Temple. See Matthew 24; Mark 13; Luke 21.

9. Evans and Porter, *Dictionary of New Testament Background,* 586.

10. September, A.D. 66, celebrated in the Jewish calendar (see: *Megillath Taanith,* 33).

11. Kenneth Wellesley, *The Year of the Four Emperors,* 3d. ed. (London: Routledge, 2000), 45.

12. Michael Grant, *The Twelve Caesars* (New York: Barnes & Noble, [1975] 1996), 211.

13. Steve Mason, *Josephus and the New Testament* (Peabody, Mass.: Hendrickson, 1992), 49.

14. J. D. Douglas and F. F. Bruce, *New Bible Dictionary*, 2nd ed. (Downers Grove, Ill: InterVarsity, 1982), 827. Cp. L. L. Grabbe, "Jewish Wars with Rome," in Evans and Porter, eds., *Dictionary of New Testament Background*, 586–87. Though Masada and a few small outposts remained for mopping up operations, the War was over with the fall of Jerusalem. Hence, Vespasian celebrates a Triumph in Rome upon Titus' return in 71 (*Wars* 7:5:3–7).

15. Kistemaker, "The Temple in the Apocalypse," 438.

16. For information, see my: *God Gave Wine* (Lincoln, Calif.: Oakdown, 2001).

17. Beale, *The Book of Revelation*, 565.

18. Previously Josephus had noted: "But as for that house, God had, for certain, long ago doomed it to the fire; and now that fatal day was come, according to the revolution of ages; it was the tenth day of the month Lous, upon which it was formerly burnt by the king of Babylon" (*Wars* 4:5:5).

19. Beale, *The Book of Revelation*, 567.

20. For more citations, see: Heinz Schreckenberg and Kurt Schubert, *Jewish Historiography and Iconography in Early and Medieval Christianity* (Minneapolis: Fortress, 1992), ch. 3.

21. M. Eugene Boring, *Revelation: Interpretation: A Bible Commentary for Teaching and Preaching* (Louisville: John Knox, 1989), 143.

22. Walvoord, *Revelation*, 175.

23. Walvoord, *Revelation*, 175.

24. Walvoord, *Revelation*, 180.

25. Robert Mounce, *The Book of Revelation* (Grand Rapids: Eerdmans, 1977), 219.

26. Thomas, "Theonomy and the Dating of Revelation," The Master's Seminary Journal, 5:2 (Fall 1994), 195, 196.

27. Thomas, "Theonomy and the Dating of Revelation," 195.

28. Thomas, *Revelation 8–22*, 372.

29. The remaining Western Wall or the "Wailing Wall" may actually be the remnants of a Roman edifice. See: Ernest L. Martin, *The Temples that Jerusalem Forgot* (Porthland, OR: ASK Publaicatiaons, 2000).

30. See the church history of Eusebius of the fourth century: *Ecclesiastical History* 3:5:3–5. Also see Eusebius's contemporary, Epiphanius, in his works: *De Mensuris* 15 and *Heresies* 29:7.

31. Martin and Davids, ed., *Dictionary of the Later New Testament and Its Development*, 561.

32. *Histories* 5:2.

33. *Fragments of the Histories*.

34. *Natural History* 5:14:70.

35. *The Syrian Wars* 50.

36. David Ben-Gurion, *The Jews in Their Land,* trans. Mordechai Nurock and Misha Louvish (Garden City, N.Y.: Doubleday, 1966), 152.

37. *Sibylline Oracles* 5:150–154. Emphasis added.

38. *Sibylline Oracles.* 5:408–413. Emphasis added.

39. Josephus, *Wars of the Jews* 7:1:1. Emphasis added.

40. *Wars* 7:8:7. Emphasis added.

41. *1 Clement* 41.

42. A. Cleveland Coxe, "Clement," in Alexander Roberts and James Donaldson, *The Ante-Nicene Fathers,* 10 vols. (Grand Rapids: Eerdmans, [1885] 1985) 1:1.

43. J. B. Lightfoot, *The Apostolic Fathers, Part I: S. Clement of Rome* (London: Macmillan, 1889), 52.

44. Arthur S. Barnes, Christianity at Rome *in the Apostolic Age* (Westport, Conn.: Greenwood, [1938] 1971), 209ff; George Edmundston, *The Church in Rome in the First Century* (London: Longman's, Green, 1913), 189ff.; Robinson, *Redating the New Testament,* 328ff; and Ellis, *The Making of the New Testament Documents,* 246n, 280n, 307ff. See also: H. E. Lona, *Clemensbrief* (Gottingen: 1998), 75ff and A. E Wilhelm-Hooijbergh, "A Different View of Clemens Romansu," *Heythrop Journal* 16 (1975): 266–288.

45. Lightfoot, *Apostolic Fathers,* 352.

46. Robinson, *Redating the New Testament,* 328.

47. Edmundston, *The Church in Rome,* 194ff.

48. Barnes, *The Church in Rome,* 213ff.

49. Tacitus, *Histories* 1:2-3.

50. Philip Schaff, *History of the Christian Church,* 7 vols., 3rd ed. (Grand Rapids: Eerdmans, 1910) 1:391.

51. Edmundston, *The Church in Rome,* 193.

12

The Ecclesiastical Evidence

Behold, I will cause those of the synagogue of Satan, who say that
they are Jews, and are not, but lie — behold, I will make them to
come and bow down at your feet, and to know
that I have loved you
Rev. 3:9

The final internal evidence I will consider for Revelation's early-date is the primitive nature of Christianity in John's prophecy. Strong indications suggest that the Church's stage of development indicates a pre-A.D. 70 era. But first, some brief background.

Early Christianity's Development

Regarding the origin of the Christian Church, New Testament scholars agree that "from the very beginning of the story in Acts this Christian group is marked as *Jewish* in its origins and background."[1] Indeed, "it may fairly be said at the outset that there is no Christianity in the NT that is not Jewish."[2] It is quite evident that Christianity gradually developed from Judaism through several stages of self-awareness and missionary outreach in the first-century of its existence.[3] Kruse well observes that "in the early years of the Christian church, Jewish Christians saw themselves as part of Judaism (Acts 2:46–3:1; 20:16; 21:17–26), though the relationship between Christians and Jews became increasingly tense as time went on."[4]

Christianity's earliest stage in Christ's ministry was almost wholly focused on racial Israel and religious Judaism. The Lord himself ministered first to "the lost sheep of Israel" (see Matt. 10:6ff.; 15:21ff; John 1:11; cp. Rom. 1:16). In fact, "earliest Christianity—that described by the opening chapters of Acts—was exclusively Jewish."[5] What careful reader of Scripture can deny this?

The second stage of development begins *in principle* toward the end of Christ's ministry, when Christ utters the Great Commission commanding worldwide outreach to *all nations* (Matt. 28:20ff; cp. Luke 24:47; Acts 1:8). This was, however, only dimly understood by the early original (Jewish) Christians. Their difficulty in accepting the full implications of the Great Commission is obvious in Acts 10:9–17, 28 (the necessity of a divine vision to overcome Peter's reluctance to interact with Gentiles), 11:1–3 (the Jerusalem church's concern over Peter's encounter with the gentile Cornelius), and 15:1–5 (the confusion regarding the Gentile Christian's freedom from Mosaic ritual, i.e., circumcision). Even in this early post-commission Christianity, the ministry continued to gravitate toward the Jews.

Furthermore, the earliest Christians even engaged in Jewish worship observances,[6] while focusing on and radiating their ministry from Jerusalem.[7] Not only so but they frequented the temple,[8] attended the synagogues,[9] and designated themselves as the true heirs of Judaism.[10] One modern writer discusses the matter of Jewish Christians worshiping as Jews and as Christians: Jesus' "disciples, however, were faithful at first in their observance of both, as Acts unobtrusively recounts . . . , so that their special teaching and customs offered no occasion for them not to be considered Jews. Indeed, they had not separated themselves publicly nearly as much as had the Essenes. Only after A.D. 70 did the requirements for membership in Judaism become more stringent."[11]

We should expect, then, that the earlier the date of a Christian book, the more Jewish it would appear. This phenomenon is blatantly obvious in one of the earliest epistles of the New Testament: The Epistle of James holds "little evidence of a developed or self-consciously Christian theology . . . which suggest an author writing at an early date in a Jewish context such as the Jerusalem church."[12] The interesting question then arises whether Revelation has a strongly Jewish cast to it. If it does, this may support a pre-A.D. 70 date, as opposed to a post-temple, A.D. 95 date.

The Jewish Character of Christianity in Revelation

As a matter of fact, in Revelation overwhelming evidence demands that the era in which John wrote was one in which Christianity was still largely affected by and strongly attached to the Jewish community. Let us survey a few aspects of Revelation indicating this.

Revelation 2 and 3

In Revelation 2:9 and 3:9 we discover some interesting evidence in this direction:

> I know your tribulation and your poverty (but you are rich), and the blasphemy by those who say they are Jews and are not, but are a synagogue of Satan (Rev. 2:9).
>
> Behold, I will cause those of the synagogue of Satan, who say that they are Jews, and are not, but lie—behold, I will make them to come and bow down at your feet, and to know that I have loved you (Rev. 3:9).

In these two passages John provides evidence that at least two of the seven churches (Smyrna and Philadelphia) are plagued by "those who say they are Jews," that is, by actual Jews themselves.[13]

We may reasonably assume that those who plagued them were *racial Jews* and undoubtedly of the Jewish faith. The Jews were not only (1) a distinctive race in the Empire, but (2) despised by the Romans and other Gentiles of the realm.

Jews were clearly distinguished from the Gentiles because they wore a distinctive cultic mark: circumcision. In one of his debates with a Jew, early church father Justin Martyr (A.D. 100–165) mentions the distinctiveness of the Jew in this regard: "For the circumcision according to the flesh, which is from Abraham, was given for a sign; that you may be separated from other nations, and from us; . . . For you are not recognised among the rest of men by any other mark than your fleshly circumcision."[14] Pagan Roman historian Tacitus (A.D. 56–117) wrote of the Jews: "They adopted circumcision to distinguish themselves from other peoples by this difference."[15] The Roman satirist Martial (A.D. 40–104) mocked them in that "they get themselves circumcised, and look down on Roman law."[16] The Roman historians even spoke contemptuously of the Jews as a "second race" of men, quite distinguished from the rest of the Roman empire in the second century.[17] The emperor Hadrian finally decreed "a total ban on circumcision."[18]

That the Jews were frequently despised is evident from various literary productions.[19] First Maccabees records that some Jews even "removed the marks of circumcision" (Macc. 1:15a) because of the "many disasters" that befell them at Gentile hands (Macc. 1:11b). Jewish historian Doron Mendels observes that we find:

> denigratory remarks such as the one found in Tacitus saying that the Jews were 'base and abominable' and that their religion was a 'superstition' . . ., and that they were an 'impious nation.' Claudius (the emperor who was himself a prolific scholar)

expressed a current idea that Jews might attempt to dominate the ecumene. And Philostratus, at the end of the second century C.E. and the beginning of the third, was of the opinion that 'the Jews have long been in revolt not only against the Romans but against humanity.' Cassius Dio also has terrible things to say about the Jews in relation to their revolt in Cyrene, Cyprus, and Egypt in 115–117 C.E.

* * * *

Ptolemy, a Greek from Alexandria, draws a detailed map of Palestine and describes the Jews alongside the inhabitants of Coele-Syria and Idumaea as being "bold, godless, and scheming."[20]

Roman statesman and orator Cicero (106–43 B.C.) called Judaism a "barbarous superstition."[21] The Syrian historian Diodorus Siculus (*ca.* 40 B.C.) despises the Jews because "they made the hatred of humanity into a tradition."[22] Roman statesman and philosopher Seneca (4 B.C.–A.D. 65) deems the Jews "that most criminal of races."[23] Grant comments on the Sibylline Oracles that "among these short poems of many epochs, one notable early example proclaims the widespread extent of the Dispersion—and its unpopularity as well: 'every sea and every land is full of you, and every one hates you, because of your ways . . . every man shall hold your ordinances in hatred.'"[24] He notes also that "even the light-hearted poet Martial, writing under the Flavian dynasty founded by Vespasian, delivers himself of a wide variety of sneers against the Jews."[25] Josephus defends Jews against Apollonius' charge that they are "the most witless of barbarians."[26]

Now the question naturally arises regarding the statements in Revelation 2:9 and 3:9: Who would array themselves against the Church, posing as racial Jews if they were not really racial Jews?[27]

Obviously, then, these two churches in Revelation were being persecuted by *Jews* in these two cities (Smyrna and Philadelphia); Christianity was very often persecuted by Jews in the first-century (Acts

4:18; 3:50; 5:40; 7:58–60; 14:2, 5, 19; 17:5; 18:12–17; 21; 30–32; 24:2–9). In fact, "down to A.D. 64 danger threatened the Christian Church from the Jews and the Jews alone."[28] Of the situation at Smyrna (Rev. 2:9), we should note that "Jews at Smyrna were both numerous and aggressively hostile."[29] Ignatius (*ca.* A.D. 107–08) even warns about the Jews when he writes the church at Philadelphia: "If anyone expounds Judaism to you, do not listen to him" (*Phila.* 6:1).

In writing to these churches, John derides these persecuting Jews as not really being Jews *in the true, spiritual sense of the word.* As another late-date advocate puts it: "Members of the local synagogue may claim to be Jews, but the very claim constitutes them liars."[30] Here, then, John follows the pattern of Paul's reproach in Romans 2:17–29, by distinguishing between the "true Jew" (the Christian who is a "Jew" inwardly and spiritually) and the "false Jew" (one who is a Jew racially and religiously, but not spiritually). These racial Jews had forsaken the truth of historic, God-given Judaism by not following after the Messiah and subscribing to the Christian faith.

Thus, John attributes a spiritual significance of the highest order to being a "Jew"—in the true sense of the word, *i.e.,* a Christian. In defying persecuting Judaism, the Christians *at this stage* were argumentatively presenting themselves as the true Jews.[31] This must be at an early stage of Christian development when Christianity still understood and presented itself as true Judaism.

Revelation 7

This primitive conception of Christianity is strongly reaffirmed later in Revelation. John speaks of Christians as the true Jews, the fullness of the Twelve Tribes of Israel (Rev. 7:4–8; 14:1ff; 21:12). Revelation 7:4–8 is particularly instructive:

> And I heard the number of those who were sealed, one hundred and forty-four thousand sealed from every tribe of the sons

of Israel: from the tribe of Judah, twelve thousand were sealed, from the tribe of Reuben twelve thousand, from the tribe of Gad twelve thousand, from the tribe of Asher twelve thousand, from the tribe of Naphthali twelve thousand, from the tribe of Manasseh twelve thousand, from the tribe of Simeon twelve thousand, from the tribe of Levi twelve thousand, from the tribe of Issachar twelve thousand, from the tribe of Zebulun twelve thousand, from the tribe of Joseph twelve thousand, from the tribe of Benjamin, twelve thousand were sealed.

Certainly we must understand an element of symbolism. If nothing else, the perfect rounding of numbers along with the exact and identical count in each of the tribes betray John's symbolic concern. Furthermore, the number "1000" is frequently used in Scripture as an indefinite, yet significantly large number (Ps. 90:4; Dan. 7:10; 2 Pet. 3:8; Heb. 12:22).

Despite the obvious symbolism, however, the symbols must be founded upon some historical designation—in that the "twelve tribes" are historically significant in forming "the basic constituent units of Israel" in history[32] and in Scripture (cf. Gen. 49:28).[33] In light of this, it would seem that two possible interpretations readily lend themselves to consideration: Either this body of 144,000 people represents the totality of the Christian Church as the fulfillment of the Jewish hope. Or it represents Christians of Jewish lineage. In either case the appearance of those 144,000 suggest the early date of Revelation. This is evidently due to Christianity in John's era being at a stage in which the Church at large was called by Jewish names and the bulk of Christians were Jewish.

The Grammar and Syntax of Revelation

Another indicator of the primitive Jewish stage of Christianity in Revelation is the (apparently intentional) style of language John uses.

A remarkable fact that has not escaped the notice of Greek scholars is that the language of Revelation is extremely Hebraic. Moses Stuart notes that "no book in all the New Testament is so Hebraistic as the Revelation."[34] R. H. Charles, E. C. A. Dougherty, David E. Aune and others have even developed special grammars for Revelation, based on its extremely Hebraic character.[35] Aune specifically notes: "The Greek of Revelation is the most peculiar Greek in the NT, in part because it exhibits interference from Semitic languages, perhaps both Hebrew and Aramaic."[36] Some, such as C. C. Torrey, have gone so far as to suggest that an Aramaic original was the forerunner of Revelation.[37]

John appears to be dramatically highlighting the Jew-Christian conflict not only by means of content but style. As Beale observes:

> A significant number of these irregularities occur in the midst of OT allusions. A number of expressions appear irregular because John is carrying over the exact grammatical forms of the allusions, often from the various versions of the Greek OT and sometimes from the Hebrew. He does not change the OT grammatical form to fit the immediate syntactical context in Revelation, so the OT expression sticks out like a sore thumb. This creates "syntactical dissonance." Just as often, the precise grammar of the OT passages is not retained, but stylistic Semitisms or Septuagintalisms are incorporated in order to create the dissonance.[38]

In addition, some words in Revelation are even translated into Hebrew. In Revelation 9:11 the "angel of the abyss" is given both Greek and Hebrew names. In Revelation 16:16 the place of a great battle is called by its Hebrew name: "the place which in Hebrew is called Har-Macedon."

Elsewhere, the Church is pictured under a symbol strongly expressive of a Judaistic Christianity: she is portrayed as a woman with a crown of twelve stars on her head (Rev. 12:1ff). Christians are represented as worshiping in the temple and ministering in Jerusalem (Rev. 11:1–8).

Interpreting the Evidence

In light of the various lines of evidence, we may conclude that Revelation surely belongs to the period in which Jews and Christians still lived together, even if uncomfortably so; the final breach of daughter from mother has not yet occurred. The looming catastrophe of A.D. 70 has yet to force its dramatic, irremediable breach between Christianity and Judaism.

Unfortunately, the significance of the destruction of Jerusalem and the temple is too often overlooked by many. But was not Christianity born in Jerusalem (Acts 2) in fulfillment of Christ's directive (Luke 24:44–53; Acts 1)? Was it not headquartered there in its earliest period (Acts 8:1; 11:2; 15:2; Gal. 1:17, 18; 2:1, 2)? Nevertheless, when the dust settles after the fall of Jerusalem, we no longer can discern any Christian focus on Jerusalem. In fact, we no longer find a dominant church community operating out of Jerusalem. Indeed, in A.D. 80 Jewish Rabbi Gamaliel II caused the Jewish daily prayer to include a curse on the Christians: "And may the Nazarenes [*sc.* Christian] and the heretics perish quickly."[39]

In *Barnabas,* a letter written by an early Christian after the fall of Jerusalem (*ca.* A.D. 100), we find evidence of this division. This epistle indicates a radical "us/them" distinction between Christians and Jews: "Let us see if this people [*i.e.,* Christians] is the heir, or the former [*i.e.,* the Jews], and if the covenant belongs to us or to them" (*Epistle of Barnabas* 13:1). Apostolic church father Ignatius also provides us early evidence in this direction. He writes (A.D. 107): "It is absurd to speak of Jesus Christ with the tongue, and to cherish in the mind a Judaism which has now come to an end. For where there is Christianity there cannot be Judaism" (*Epistle to the*

Magnesians 10). Both of these statements are in keeping with later, post-temple Christian practice.

Certainly the breach did not come overnight. From its very inception Christianity was persecuted almost exclusively by the Jews (see discussion above). This persecution continued throughout the entire period of early Christianity recorded in Acts. Yet many converts were being won from Judaism (Acts 2:41; 4:4; 18:8; 21:20–22; 28:23–24). The Christians, in fact, persistently and intentionally operated in Jewish circles. The non-Christian Jews refused to accept the legitimacy of Christianity as the fulfillment of Judaism and zealously persecuted the Christians as heretics.

Up until the era of the mid-A.D. 60s (but not after the outbreak of the Neronic persecution in late A.D. 64, nor especially after A.D. 70) the Romans were prone to identify Christianity as a sect of Judaism, intimately and necessarily bound up with it.[40] This was obviously due to: its object of worship (Christ, a Jew); its origin (Judea), leadership (Jewish apostles), the bulk of its membership (predominantly Jewish), and its practice (operating within the synagogue system). In addition, its self-designation ("the Israel of God" [Gal. 6:15], "seed of Abraham" [Gal. 3:29], "the circumcision" [Phil. 3:3] etc.); its message ("to the Jew first," Rom. 1:16); and its constant involvement in the religious life of the Jews, added to the difficulty for the Romans.

Church father Sulpicius Severus (A.D. 360–420) reported that Titus's war council conducted before the siege of the temple debated whether or not to destroy the temple:

> Titus is said, after calling a council, to have first deliberated whether he should destroy the temple, a structure of such extraordinary work. . . . Titus himself thought that the temple ought specially to be overthrown in order that the religion of the Jews and of the Christians might more thoroughly be subverted; for that these religions, though contrary to each other,

had nevertheless proceeded from the same authors; that the Christians had sprung up from among the Jews; and that, if the root were extirpated, the offshoot would speedily perish.[41]

Clearly the idea here involved the belief in Christianity's dependence upon the temple.

The early Christians were earnest in their concern to win Israel, even attempting to operate within the temple-synagogue structure of Judaism. Nevertheless, regarding the gradual chasm that grew between the Jew and Christianity, we should note that "the breach was no doubt clinched by political circumstance. In the disastrous war of A.D. 66–70, the 'Nazarenes' (a term by then applied to the Jewish Christians) refused to participate in the Jewish resistance movement, the Zealot insurrection. . . . The crisis of A.D. 66 decisively separated Jew from Christian."[42] "The destruction of the temple had a dramatic impact on Christianity as a whole. The distinctive character of the faith became more apparent. . . . Now without a temple building the church would be able to proclaim its independence, and the pagan people would not be so likely to consider it nothing more than a Judaistic sect."[43]

Conclusion

The matter is clear enough: When John writes Revelation, Christianity is still operating within Jewish circles and institutions to a very large extent. Historically this simply will no longer be true in the post-temple era beyond A.D. 70. The cleavage between Judaism and Christianity was too severe to heal from that time forth. Hence, the state of Christianity in Revelation indicates a pre-70 date for Revelation.

Notes

1. Joseph A. Fitzmeyer, *Essays on the Semitic Background of the New Testament* (London: Chapman, 1971), 274.

2. D. A. Hagner, "Jewish Christianity," in Ralph P. Martin and Peter H. Davids, eds., *Dictionary of the Later New Testament & Its Developments* (Downers Grove, Ill.: InterVarsity Press, 1997), 580.

3. My argument below will take into account only *orthodox* Christian issues, not the various heretical movements within it. "We know orthodox varieties of Jewish Christianity directly from a number of NT writings and the apostolic fathers," but there also existed "heterodox varieties of Jewish Christianity outside and later than the NT." Hagner, "Jewish Christianity," in *Dictionary of the Later New Testament & Its Developments*, 579. Nor does my presentation assume the Tübingen Hegelian dialectical framework of F. C. Baur. For helpful New Testament background studies, see: Paul Barnett, *Jesus & the Rise of Early Christianity: A History of New Testament Times* (Downers Grove, Ill.: InterVarsity Press, 1999) and James S. Jeffers, *The Greco-Roman World of the New Testament Era: Exploring the Background of Early Christianity* (Downers Grove, Ill.: InterVarsity Press, 1999).

4. C. G. Kruse, "Persecution," in Craig A. Evans and Stanley E. Porter, eds., *Dictionary of New Testament Background* (Downers Grove, Ill.: InterVarsity Press, 2000), 776.

5. Hagner, "Jewish Christianity," in *Dictionary of the Later New Testament & Its Developments*, 580.

6. Acts 2:1ff; 21:26; 24:11.

7. Acts 2–5.

8. Acts 2:46; 3:1ff.; 4:1; 5:21ff.; 21:26; 26:21.

9. Acts 13:5, 14; 14:1; 15:21; 17:1ff; 18:4, 7, 19, 26; 19:8; 22:19; 24:12; 26:11.

10. Galatians 3:27–29; 6:16; Philippians 3:3; Titus 2:14; 1 Peter 2:9.

11. Leonhard Goppelt, *Apostolic and Post-Apostolic Times,* trans. Robert A. Guelich (London: Adam and Charles Black, 1970), 26.

12. Duane F. Watson, "James, Letter of," in David Noel Freedman, ed., *Eerdmans Dictionary of the Bible* (Grand Rapids: Eerdmans, 2000), 670.

13. Albert A. Bell, Jr., *A Guide to the New Testament* World (Scottsdale, Penn.: Herald, 1994), 68.

14. *Dialogue with Trypho the Jew* 16.

15. *Histories* 5:5.

16. Martial, *Epigrams,* 14:99–100. In fact, he often mocked circumcision in his writings: *Epigrams,* 7:30, 35, 55, 82; 1:94.

17. See Tertullian, *To the Nations* 1:8.

18. Michael Grant, *The Jews in the Roman World* (New York: Barnes & Noble, 1973), 245.

19. For further study see: Hadas-Lebel's study "Anti-Judaism" in Mireille Hadas-Lebel, *Flavius Josephus: Eyewitness to Rome's First-Century Conquest of Judea,* trans. by Richard Miller (New York: Macmillan, 1993), 200-06. See also: "Pagan Anti-Judaism" in Dan Cohn-Sherbok, *The Crucified Jew: Twenty Centuries of Anti-Semitism* (Grand Rapids: Eerdmans, 1992), 1–4.

20. Doron Mendels, *The Rise and Fall of Jewish Nationalism: Jewish and Christian Ethnicity in Ancient Palestine* (Grand Rapids: Eerdmans, 1992), 396, 399.

21. Cicero, *Pro Flacco*, 69.

22. Didorus Siculus, *Bibliotheca Historica*, 34:1:2.

23. Seneca, *De Superstitione*, fragment 42.

24. Grant, *The Jews in the Roman World*, 36. Citing Sibylline Oracles 3:271–72.

25. Grant, *The Jews in the Roman World*, 222. See: Martial, *Epigrams*, 4:4:7; 7:55:7–8; 7:82:6; 12:57:13.

26. Josephus, *Antiquities* 2:14.

27. Interestingly for our thesis, in the two verses under consideration John uses the Hebrew word for the devil *(satanos)*, rather than the more common New Testament Greek term *(diabolos)*.

28. W. H. C. Frend, *The Early Church* (Philadelphia: Fortress, 1982), 29.

29. Henry B. Swete. *Commentary on Revelation* (Grand Rapids: Kregel, [1911] 1977), 31.

30. Robert Mounce *The Book of Revelation*, 2nd ed. (Grand Rapids: Eerdmans, 1998), 101.

31. Cp. Matthew 19:28; Luke 22:30; Galatians 6:16; James 1:1; 1 Peter 2:9.

32. "Tribes, twelve," in Jacob Neusner, ed., *Dictionary of Judaism in the Biblical Period* (Peabody, Mass.: Hendrickson, 1996), 649. See: *The Testaments of the Twelve Patriarchs*, Qumran's *Manual of Discipline*, 8; *The Temple Scroll*, *The War Scroll*, *The Testament of Moses* 3–4; and *The Testament of Abraham*.

33. See: Genesis 35:22ff; 46:8–11; 49:1–28; Exodus 1:1–2; Numbers 1:1–16; 2:1–32; 13:4–11; 26:4–50; 34:13–28; Deuteronomy 27:11ff; 33:6ff; Joshua 13–22; Judges 5; 1 Chronicles 2-8; 27:16ff; Ezekiel 48; Acts 26:7.

34. Moses Stuart, *Commentary on the Apocalypse,* 2 vols. (Andover: Allen, Morrill, and Wardwell, 1845) 1:229.

35. R. H. Charles, *A Critical and Exegetical Commentary on the Revelation of St. John,* 2 vols. (Edinburgh: T. and T. Clark, 1920) 1:cxvii ff. E. C. A. Dougherty, "The Syntax of the Apocalypse," Dissertation: Catholic University of America, 1990. David E. Aune, *Revelation 1–5* (Dallas: Word, 1997), clxii–ccxi.

36. David E. Aune, *Revelation 1–5* (Dallas: Word, 1997), clxii. See also: G. K. Beale, *The Book of Revelation* (Grand Rapids: Eerdmans, 1999), 100–107.

37. Charles C. Torrey, *The Apocalypse of John* (New Haven: Yale University Press, 1958), x. Also see my discussion in chapter 2.

38. Beale, *Revelation*, 101.

39. "The Jewish Daily Prayer and the Exclusion of Jewish Christians," Appendix in J. Julius Scott, Jr., *Jewish Backgrounds to the New Testament* (Grand Rapids: Baker, 1995), 366–67. Cp. Tertullian, *Dialogue with Trypho*, 96.

40. Tacitus, *Annals* 15:44; Sulpicius Severus, *Sacred History* 2:30. Grant observes the remarkable implication of Nero's pogrom: "One of the most significant aspects of these events lies in the evident ability of Nero's government, at this point of time, to assess the separate positions of the Christians and the Jews and discern that the two were no longer the same."

But he notes on the next page that this "heralded the eventual complete split between Judaism and Christianity"—effected permanently at A.D. 70. Grant, *The Jews in the Roman World,* 181, 182.

41. *Sacred History* 2:30. The importance of this statement lies in the fact that Severus had access to documents no longer available to us—and in his contradicting Josephus' account alleging that Titus did not want to destroy the temple (*Wars* 6:2:1, 3). Historians doubt Josephus' story of Titus' reluctance.

42. C. F. D. Moule, *The Birth of the New Testament,* 3rd ed. (New York: Harper and Row, 1982), 59.

43. Richard L. Niswonger, *New Testament History* (Grand Rapids: Zondervan, 1988), 267.

13

The Patristic Evidence

Give praise to our God, all you His bond-servants,
you who fear Him, the small and the great
Rev. 19:5

come finally to an analysis of the material generally called "external evidence." This material is "external" in that it comes from outside Revelation: it derives from church tradition. I will begin with those indications from tradition that support my contention for an early date for Revelation. In the next chapter I will analyze the witnesses generally enlisted to support the late date.

As I begin, the reader should be aware that the late-date camp frequently implies that the evidence from tradition is virtually unanimous in supporting the late date. For instance, J. P. M. Sweet comments: "To sum up, the earlier date *may* be right, but the internal evidence is not sufficient to outweigh the firm tradition stemming from Irenaeus" (Beale quotes Sweet as he concludes his brief study of the issue.[1]) Similarly, Andrè Feuillet writes: "The *traditional* setting of the Apocalypse in the reign of Domitian is too solidly established to be brought into question."[2] Henry B. Swete, one of the leading orthodox commentators on Revelation, insists that "early Christian tradition is almost unanimous in assigning the Apocalypse to the last years of Domitian."[3] In his monumental two-volume commentary on Revelation, R. H. Charles introduces the evidence from tradition as follows: "This evidence almost unanimously assigns [Revelation] to the last years of Domitian."[4]

These confident statements simply do not fit the facts, as I will show. Some of the evidence below is *directly* helpful to the debate, in that it speaks rather clearly to the matter. Other pieces are merely *suggestive* possibilities, being more subtle. I will survey them diachronically, rather than in order of significance.

The Shepherd of Hermas

A work little known among laymen today was once very important in early Christianity: *The Shepherd of Hermas*. Not only was it "widely popular in the second and third centuries"[5] but "Origin considered it inspired and identified its author with the Hermas of Rom. 16:14 (*Comm. on Romans, in loc.*). Though Eusebius rejected it, he admitted that it was widely quoted and read publicly in the churches, being considered especially valuable 'for those who need elementary instruction' (*HE* iii.3.6). Irenaeus' quotation of the elementary instruction in the first Mandate as 'Scripture' (*Adv. haer.* iv. 20) seems to support this."[6] *The Shepherd* contains three parts: *Vision, Mandates,* and *Similitudes.*

The Shepherd of Hermas indirectly suggests an early date for Revelation. Cautious employment of *The Shepherd* is demanded in light of both the nature of its usefulness (as indirect, circumstantial evidence) and the difficulty of its dating (see discussion below).

The Usefulness of the Shepherd

If written in the first century *The Shepherd of Hermas* may be helpful for discerning the date of Revelation. Many competent scholars detect evidence of Hermas's knowledge of Revelation: Moses Stuart, B. F. Westcott, H. B. Swete, and R. H. Charles. The editor of the classic series *The Ante-Nicene Fathers* states boldly that Revelation "is quoted in *Hermas* freely."[7] In more recent times noted critics have concurred in this assessment; we mention but a few. Patristics scholar Edgar J. Goodspeed states confidently that Hermas is "clearly acquainted with the Revelation of John."[8] John Lawson and M. H. Shepherd agree.[9] Even late-date advocates Donald B. Guthrie and Robert H. Mounce lean in this direction. Guthrie writes that "there are many common images in the two writers which are most naturally explained if Hermas knew our Apocalypse."[10]

But now: When was it written?

The Date of the Shepherd

Unfortunately, ascertaining the date of the composition of *The Shepherd* is difficult due to the question of its authorship. J. B. Lightfoot's analysis of the matter will guide our thinking.[11] Was it written by (1) the Hermas greeted by Paul in Romans 16:14, as Origen suggests? Or by (2) the brother of Pius I (A.D. 140–150), as the ancient Muratorian Canon teaches? Or by (3) some other own Hermas who lived in the time of the bishopric of Clement of Rome (A.D. 90–100), as a number of modern scholars propose? An assured conclusion on the matter may never be reached. Even Lightfoot, who prefers a date in the era of A.D. 140–50, acknowledges that the internal evidence strongly suggests a date in the span of A.D. 90–100.[12]

Church historian Philip Schaff decisively supports an earlier date for *The Shepherd,* arguing it was written by the very Hermas mentioned in Romans 16:14. He notes that the earlier date is suggested by its authoritative usage in the writings of Irenaeus, Clement of Alexandria, Origen, Eusebius, and Jerome.[13] We can add that early in his career, Tertullian seems to have agreed, although later he changed his opinion.[14] Because of its assumed early date and apostolic connection, *The Shepherd* tended to be used as if it were an inspired book. Interestingly, it is found in one of the earliest, complete Greek manuscripts of the Bible, the Codex Sinaiticus. This demonstrates *The Shepherd's* early and widespread respect as high authority, and even as Scripture by some.

Moreover, some argue for a date prior to A.D. 85. Arthur S. Barnes and John A. T. Robinson vigorously affirm this time-frame.[15] And the evidences they suggest are quite reasonable. Let us summarize them:

First, since the book is deemed at least quasi-scriptural by Irenaeus, Clement of Alexandria, Origen, (the early) Tertullian, Eusebius, and Jerome, we should expect a very early date. For a work to be accepted as inspired it would need to be written by an associate of the apostles, and probably very early, perhaps even pre-A.D. 80. In fact, a number of scholars agree that the late-date assigned to *The Shepherd* by the Muratorian Canon (see below) is designed to discredit it as canonical Scripture.[16]

Second, Irenaeus lived in Rome for awhile and just twenty years after Pius's death. It is highly unlikely he would have viewed *The Shepherd* as "Scripture" if written in his own era and location.

Third, after initially accepting it as scriptural, Tertullian (A.D. 160–220) later discredited the book. It seems likely he would have mentioned its recent authorship in his arguments against it had it been written in the era A.D. 140–150. But he does not.

Fourth, the Muratorian Canon's view (A.D. 170–200) cannot be right, for several reasons. (1) It identifies Hermas as the brother of bishop Pius of Rome. But as a foster child sold into slavery in Rome *(Vision 1:1:1)*, it is remarkable that *Hermas never mentions his alleged brother Pius, bishop of Rome.* (2) Nowhere in *The Shepherd* does it indicate the existence of a monarchical episcopate. Hermas speaks, instead, of "the elders that preside over the church" *(Vision* 2:4:3). (3) In *Vision* 2:4:2ff. Hermas is directed in his vision to write two books and to send one of them to Clement, who in turn "was to send it to foreign cities, for this is his duty." This implies Clement's role as a subordinate secretarial figure. Yet, in about A.D. 90 Clement was appointed Bishop of Rome.

The Significance of The Shepherd

If *The Shepherd* was written somewhere around A.D. 85 consider the following: Certain allusions in it show an awareness of Revelation. Thus, Revelation influenced the writing of *The Shepherd* in the late AD. 80s. Furthermore, *The Shepherd* was certainly written somewhere around Rome, for it mentions Clement of Rome *(Vision* 2:4). For John's Revelation to have been written, to have been copied (laboriously by hand), to have made its way to Rome by the 80s, and to have influenced the writing of *The Shepherd,* would strongly indicate that Revelation existed a good deal of time before A.D. 85+. It would, thus, be evidence against a date of *ca.* A.D. 95 and compatible with a pre-A.D. 70 date.

Papias of Hierapolis

Papias, Bishop of Hierapolis (A.D. 60–130), reportedly a disciple of the Apostle John and a friend of Polycarp. As such he would be an extremely early and valuable witness to historical matters of the sort with which we are dealing. Unfortunately, none of his books exist today. Nevertheless, an important piece of evidence purportedly from Papias is quite revealing.

Late-date advocate H. B. Swete deals with this evidence in his treatment of the Apostle John's extreme longevity. Swete notes that two ancient manuscripts, one from the seventh century and one from the ninth, cite a statement by Papias which says John the Apostle and his brother, James, were martyred by the Jews. Of this statement Swete observes:

> With this testimony before us it is not easy to doubt that Papias made some such statement. . . . But if Papias made it, the question remains whether he made it under some misapprehension, or merely by way of expressing his conviction that the prophecy of Mc. x. 39 had found a literal fulfillment. Neither explanation is very probable in view of the early date of Papias. He does not, however, affirm that the brothers suffered at the same time: the martyrdom of John at the hand of the Jews might have taken place at any date before the last days of Jerusalem.[17]

If these two pieces of data are in fact from Papias (as Swete, Lightfoot, and other competent scholars are inclined to believe), they provide fascinating evidence. For those holding Johannine authorship of Revelation, this would be strong external evidence for its pre-A.D. 70 composition.

The Muratorian Canon

Sometime between A.D. 170 and 200 someone drew up a list of canonical books. This list, known as the Muratorian Canon, is "the oldest Latin church document of Rome, and of very great importance for the history of the canon."[18] The witness of this manuscript, which is from the very era of Irenaeus and just prior to Clement of Alexandria, virtually demands the early date for Revelation. The relevant portion of the document states that "the blessed Apostle Paul, following the rule of his predecessor John, writes to no more than seven churches by name" and "John too, indeed, in the Apocalypse, although he writes to only seven churches, yet addresses all."[19]

The writer of the Canon clearly teaches that John *preceded* Paul in writing letters to seven churches. Yet, church historians are agreed that

Paul died before A.D. 70, either in A.D. 67 or 68.[20] This is clearly taught by Clement of Rome (ca. A.D. 100) in *1 Clement,* Section 5. Jerome certainly believed that Paul died in "the fourteenth year of Nero" (i.e., A.D. 68).[21] Whatever dates the writer of the Canon assigned to Paul's epistles, he could not have made them later than Paul's death! This is a most important piece of early evidence with which to reckon. It clearly teaches, then, that John wrote his seven letters in Revelation prior to A.D. 67/68.

Tertullian

Tertullian lived from A.D. 160–220. His era briefly overlaps Irenaeus's. We still today have many of Tertullian's writings. In his *Exclusion of Heretics* he makes a statement that is significant to our inquiry. Tertullian implies that John's banishment occurred at the same time Peter and Paul suffered martyrdom (about A.D. 67–68):

> But if thou art near to Italy, thou hast Rome, where we also have an authority close at hand. What a happy Church is that! on which the Apostles poured out all their doctrine, with their blood: where Peter had a like Passion with the Lord; where Paul hath for his crown the same death with John [the Baptist], where the Apostle John was plunged into boiling oil, and suffered nothing, and was afterwards banished to an island.[22]

In Jerome's *Against Jovinianum,* Jerome certainly understood Tertullian to state that John was banished by Nero.[23] In addition, when Tertullian speaks of Domitian's evil in the fifth chapter of his *Apology,* he does not mention anything about John's suffering under him. Such is quite strange if John actually suffered under Domitian.

It would seem that Tertullian's reference to an attempted oil martyrdom of John is quite plausible historically. This is due to the nature of the Neronic persecution of Christians in A.D. 64. Roman historian

Tacitus informs us that Christians were "fastened to crosses to be set on fire, that when the darkness fell they might be burned to illuminate the night."[24] Such a spectacle doubtless could have involved the dipping of the victims in oil to provide a lasting illumination of fire. As Schaff observed: "If there is some foundation for the early tradition of the oil-martyrdom of John at Rome, or at Ephesus, it would naturally point to the Neronian persecution, in which Christians were covered with inflammable material and burned as torches."[25]

Epiphanius of Salamis

Epiphanius (A.D. 315–403) was elected the bishop of Salamis, Cyprus, in about A.D. 367, and was an intimate friend of Jerome. He is noted for his unique witness to the banishment of John: He states twice that it was during the emperorship of Claudius.[26] He writes that John "prophesied in the time of Claudius . . . the prophetic word according to the Apocalypse being disclosed."

A number of scholars see Epiphanius's statement not so much as an extravagant tradition, as a rare designation of Nero. Some have suggested that Epiphanius may have used another of Nero's names, rather than his more common one. Nero is often called by his adoptive name "Claudius" on inscriptions. For instance, he is called "Nero Claudius" and "Nero Claudius Caesar" in certain places. Even late-date advocates Donald Guthrie, Robert Mounce, and James Moffatt recognize that this was probably what Epiphanius intended.[27]

Clearly Epiphanius stands solidly in the early date tradition—whether we interpret his statement as referring to the emperor Claudius (doubtful[28]) or to Nero Claudius (probable). Furthermore, it is extremely unlikely that he simply created his "evidence" out of the blue.

The Syriac Tradition

A strong Syriac tradition for the early date exists. The *History of John, the Son of Zebedee* refers to John's banishment under Nero: "After these things, when the Gospel was increasing by the hands of the Apostles, Nero, the unclean and impure and wicked king, heard all that had happened at Ephesus. And he sent [and] took all that the procurator had, and imprisoned him; and laid hold of S. John and drove him into exile; and passed sentence on the city that it should be laid waste."[29]

In addition, late-date scholar David E. Aune notes: "John's exile to Patmos is set during the reign of Nero in the title of two Syriac versions of Revelation."[30] Their titles read: "written in Patmos, whither John was sent by Nero Caesar."[31]

Arethas

According to A. R. Fausset, Arethas, who wrote a commentary on Revelation in the sixth century, "applies the sixth seal to the destruction of Jerusalem (70 A.D.), adding that the Apocalypse was written before that event."[32] On Revelation 6:12 Arethas writes: "Some refer this to the siege of Jerusalem by Vespasian." On Revelation 7:1 he notes: "Here, then, were manifestly shown to the Evangelist what things were to befall the Jews in their war against the Romans, in the way of avenging the sufferings inflicted upon Christ." Of Revelation 7:4 we read: "When the Evangelist received these oracles, the destruction in which the Jews were involved was not yet inflicted by the Romans."[33]

In his comments on Revelation 1:9, Arethas says: "John was banished to the isle of Patmos under Domitian, Eusebius alleges in his Chronicon."[34] Clearly Arethas is not satisfied with what Eusebius "alleges." This is all the more evident in his comments on various passages in Revelation.

Theophylact

A much later witness is Theophylact of Bulgaria, a noted Byzantine exegete (d. 1107). He also gives evidence of a dual tradition on John's banishment. Aune observes: "Theophylact, the bishop of Achrida during the eleventh century A.D., also places John's exile during the reign of Nero in the preface to his commentary on the Gospel of John."[35] In his *Preface to Commentary on the Gospel of John,* Theophylact puts the banishment of John under Nero when he says John was banished thirty-two years after the ascension of Christ.

Conclusion

The above survey shows that early church tradition is not uniformly set against the early date of Revelation, as some imply. Indeed, when carefully scrutinized, the evidence even tilts in the opposite direction. Thus, Guthrie's statement does not appear to be well founded: "It would be strange, if the book really was produced at the end of Nero's reign, that so strong a tradition arose associating it with Domitian's."[36] In a review of my larger work, *Before Jerusalem Fell,* Oxford Revelation scholar J. P. M. Sweet commented: "a thorough study of the primary sources and secondary literature (of all complexions), and demolition of some bad but often repeated arguments for a Domitian date. He makes a strong case for the early external evidence, including that of Irenaeus." Professor J. Christian Wilson commented on my study of the external evidence: "Gentry's work on the external evidence is particularly valuable. . . . I think that Gentry's book has the most thorough treatment of the external evidence available. . . . I have been very grateful for his work."

Some early witnesses strongly hint at a pre-A.D. 70 dating for Revelation, such as *The Shepherd of Hermas* and Papias. Other sources are even more indicative of a Neronic banishment: the Muratorian Canon and Tertullian. These at least suggest either an early competition between theories, or a double banishment of John, once under Nero and later under Domitian. Undeniably supporting a Neronic date are Epiphanius, Arethas, the Syriac *History of John,* Clement of Alexandria, and the Syriac versions of Revelation.

Notes

1. J. P. M. Sweet, *Revelation* (Philadelphia: Westminster, 1979) 27.G. K. Beale, *The Book of Revelation* (NIGTC) (Grand Rapids: Eerdmans, 1999), 27.

2. Andre Feuillet, *The Apocalypse* (Staten Island: Alba, 1965), 92.

3. Henry B. Swete, *Commentary on Revelation* (Grand Rapids: Kregel, [1911] 1977), xcix ff.

4. R. H. Charles, *A Critical and Exegetical Commentary on the Revelation of St. John*, 2 vols. (Edinburgh: T. & T. Clark, 1920), 1:xci.

5. Michael W. Holmes, ed., *The Apostolic Fathers: Greek Texts and English Translations* (Grand Rapids: Baker, 1999), 328.

6. J. R. Michaels, "Apostolic Fathers," in Geoffrey W. Bromiley, ed., *The International Standard Bible Encyclopedia*, 2nd ed. (Grand Rapids: Eerdmans, 1982), 1:213.

7. A. Cleveland Coxe, in Alexander Roberts and James Donaldson, eds., *The Ante-Nicene Fathers*, 10 vols. (Grand Rapids: Eerdmans, n.d. [rep. 1975]), 5:600.

8. Edgar J. Goodspeed, *The Apostolic Fathers* (New York: Harper, 1950), 97.

9. John Lawson, *A Theological and Historical Introduction to the Apostolic Fathers* (New York: Macmillan, 1961), 220. M. H. Shepherd, Jr., "Hermas, Shepherd of," in George Arthur Buttrick, ed., *The Interpreter's Dictionary of the Bible* (Nashville: Abingdon, 1990), 584.

10. Donald B. Guthrie, *New Testament Introduction*, 4th ed. (Downers Grove, Ill.: Inter-Varsity, 1990), 931–932. Compare Robert Mounce, *The Book of Revelation* (Grand Rapids: Eerdmans, 1977), 36–37.

11. J. B. Lightfoot and J. R. Harmer, *The Apostolic Fathers* (Grand Rapids: Baker, [1891] 1984), 293–294.

12. Lightfoot and Harmer, *Apostolic Fathers.*, 294.

13. Philip Schaff, *History of the Christian Church*, 3rd ed. (Grand Rapids: Eerdmans, 1910), 1:687ff.

14. Tertullian, *Orations* 16.

15. Arthur S. Barnes, *Christianity at Rome in the Apostolic Age* (Westport, Conn.: Greenwood, [1938] 1971), 212ff.; and John A. T. Robinson, *Redating the New Testament* (Philadelphia: Westminster, 1976), 319-320.

16. Michael W. Holmes, ed., *The Apostolic Fathers: Greek Texts and English Translations* (Grand Rapids: Baker, 1999), 1:331. J. R. Michaels, "Apostolic Fathers," in Geoffrey W. Bromiley, ed., *The International Standard Bible Encyclopedia*, 2nd ed. (Grand Rapids: Eerdmans, 1982), 1:213.

17. Swete, *Revelation*, clxxix–clxxx.

18. Schaff, *History*, 1:776.

19. The seven churches addressed by Paul would be Rome, Corinth, Galatia, Ephesus, Philippi, Colossae, and Thessalonica.

20. E. Earle Ellis, *The Making of the New Testament Documents* (Boston: Brill, 1999), 143. Richard Longenecker, "Paul, the Apostle," in Merrill C. Tenney and Steven Barabas eds., *The Zondervan Pictorial Encyclopedia of the Bible* (Grand Rapids: Zondervan, 1976), 5:654. Walter A. Elwell and Robert W. Yarbrough, *Encountering the New Testament: A Historical and Theological Survey* (Grand Rapids: Baker, 1998), 255.

21. Jerome, *Lives of Illustrious Men*, 5.

22. Tertullian, *Exclusion of Heretics*, 36.

23. Jerome, *Against Jovinianum* 1:26.

24. Tacitus, *Annals* 15:44.

25. Schaff, *History* 1:428.

26. *Heresies* 51:12, 33.

27. Among these we may list late date advocates Guthrie, *Introduction*, 957; Mounce, *Revelation*, 31; and James Moffatt, *The Revelation of St. John the Divine*, in W. Robertson Nicoll, ed., *The Expositor's Greek Testament*, vol. 5 (Grand Rapids: Eerdmans, rep. 1980), 505; as well as early date advocates F. J. A. Hort, *The Apocalypse of St. John, I–III* (London: Macmillan, 1908), xviii, and Robinson, *Redating*, 224.

28. Though Aune notes that Stolt and Karrer hold this view. Aune, *Revelation*, 1:lix. See: J. Stolt, "Om dateringen af Apokalypsen, *Dansk teologisk tidsskrift* 40 (1977); and M. Karrer *Die Johannesoffenbarung als Brief: Studien zu ihrem literarischen, historische und theolgischen Ort*. (Göttingen: Vandenhoeck & Ruprecht, 1986), 18n. 6

29. William Wright, *Apocryphal Acts of the Apostles* (Amsterdam: Philo, [1871] 1968) 2:55–57.

30. Aune, *Rvvelation*, 1:lx. See also: Arthur S. Peake, *The Revelation of St. John* (London: Joseph Johnson, 1919), 76–77.

31. Moses Stuart, *Commentary on the Apocalypse*, 2 vols. (Andover: Allen, Monrill, and Wardwell, 1845), 1:267.

32. A. R. Fausset, in Robert Jamieson, A. R. Fausset, and David Brown, *A Commentary Critical an Explanatory on the Old and New Testaments*, 2 vols. (Hartford: Scranton, n.d.), 2:548.

33. Cited in P. S. Desprez, *The Apocalypse Fulfilled*, 2nd ed. (London: Longman, Brown, Green, Longmans, 1855), 7.

34. Stuart, *Apocalypse* 1 :268.

35. Aune, *Revelation*, lxi. See also: Peake, *Revelation*, 77.

36. Guthrie, *Introduction*, 957.

The Patristic Objection

And I, John, am the one who heard and saw these things
Rev. 22:8a

I have shown that, contrary to sweeping assertions made by late-date advocates, a variety of external evidences support an early date for Revelation. I will now analyze the purported late-date witnesses from church history.

The statements confidently cited by late-date scholars almost invariably include the following church fathers: Irenaeus of Lyons (A.D. 130–202), Clement of Alexandria (A.D. 150–215), Origen (A.D. 185–254), Victorinus of Pettau (*ca.* A.D. 304), Eusebius of Caesarea (A.D. 260–340), and Jerome (A.D. 340–420). Without a doubt these names represent the mainstays of the late-date position. For example, the following biblical scholars list all or most of these church fathers as the leading witnesses from church tradition. Among conservatives we find: Henry B. Swete, Robert H. Mounce, Albert Barnes, B. B. Warfield, Henry C. Thiessen, Donald B. Guthrie, John F. Walvoord, and G. K. Beale, to name but a few.[1] From among liberal commentators we note

R. H. Charles, James Moffatt, J. W. Bowman, and David E. Aune.[2] Let us survey the evidence.

Irenaeus

As we begin analyzing the historical evidence for the date of Revelation, the obvious starting point is with the Bishop of Lyon, Irenaeus, the famed heresiologist. Beyond any shadow of doubt, Irenaeus is the key witness for the late date of Revelation. The strong reliance on Irenaeus is clearly indicated by Thompson ("the most compelling evidence for dating the book"), Guthrie ("earliest and weightiest"), and Beale ("the most decisive and earliest").[3] Most recent scholarship tends to rely heavily upon Irenaeus,[4] with some citing *only* Irenaeus.[5] Irenaeus's famous statement is found in Book 5 of his work entitled *Against Heresies*.

Irenaeus is an important witness and deserves initial consideration for several reasons: (1) He seems to speak directly to the issue at hand. (2) He wrote the very work in question at a rather early date, between A.D. 180 and 190.[6] (3) He claims to have known Polycarp, who in turn may have known the Apostle John.[7] Thus, the long-standing heavy reliance on Irenaeus is not unreasonable.

Irenaeus's Statement

The evidence from Irenaeus is found in Book 5, Chapter 30, Paragraph 3 of his *Against Heresies*. Although originally composed in Greek, today this work exists in its entirety only in Latin translation. Thankfully, however, the particular statement in question is preserved for us in the original Greek twice in Eusebius's *Ecclesiastical History*, at 3:18:3 and 5:8:6.

Irenaeus's crucial statement occurs at the end of a section dealing with the identification of "666" in Revelation 13, which he applies to the Antichrist. That statement is generally translated into

English as follows:

> We will not, however, incur the risk of pronouncing posi-
> tively as to the name of Antichrist; for if it were necessary that
> his name should be distinctly revealed in this present time, it
> would have been announced by him who beheld the apocalyp-
> tic vision. For that was seen no very long time since, but almost
> in our day, towards the end of Domitian's reign.

The late-date advocate argues that this serves as compelling evidence
that John "saw" the Revelation "at the end of the reign of Domitian."

How shall early date advocacy deal with such strong and forthright
testimony by this noteworthy early church father—especially since he
is "by far the most important theologian of the second century"?[8] As a
matter of fact, several problems arise which tend to reduce the usefulness of Irenaeus for late-date advocacy. Late-date proponent Sweet admits that "Irenaeus's date is open to question."[9] I will summarize just a
few of these problems here.[10]

First, the translational problem. The most important matter facing
us is the proper translation of Irenaeus's statement. The phrase "that
was seen" or "it was seen" (as it is often translated) is our crucial concern. This statement is commonly considered to refer back to the immediately preceding noun from the preceding sentence. That noun
means either: "apocalyptic vision" or "Revelation." But as John A. T.
Robinson has observed regarding the commonly accepted translation:
"This translation has been disputed by a number of scholars."[11] Compounding this problem are several contextual matters and a certain internal confusion in Irenaeus regarding the incompatibility of his statements on Revelation.

Second, the grammatical problem. Indisputably, the most serious
potential objection to the common translation is the proper understanding of the Greek verb *heorathe,* "was seen." What is the subject of this

verb? Is it "he who saw the Revelation" (*i.e.,* John) or "Revelation" it self? Either one will work grammatically because Greek is an inflected language that has no need of separate pronouns (although it does have them). The verb endings often serve in lieu of a pronoun and with an implied subject. The verb before us is found in the third person singular form. Considered alone and divorced from its context, it may be translated either "it was seen" or "he was seen." Hence the reason for our inquiry. Which of the two antecedents—"he who saw" (*i.e.,* John) or "Revelation"—"was seen" almost in Irenaeus's time and near the end of the reign of Domitian?

Let us paraphrase the possible translations of this statement in order to clarify our question. Did Irenaeus mean: "the *Revelation* was seen in a vision by John almost in our own generation"? This is the commonly accepted view. Or was he saying "*John,* who saw the Revelation, was seen alive almost in our own generation"? This is a grammatically possible view—one which I hold to be preferable.

Such questions are all the more significant when we consider the observations of the editor of the first English translation of Irenaeus. A. Cleveland Coxe has noted that "Irenaeus, even in the original Greek, is often a very obscure writer. At times he expresses himself with remarkable clearness and terseness; but, upon the whole, his style is very involved and prolix."[12] In an obscure writer such as Irenaeus, questions of translation of unclear grammatical usage become quite important.

Third, the syntactical problem. Moving beyond the grammatical ambiguity of the verb, we must consider the structural flow of the passage cited. We have to explain properly the conjunction "for" (Greek: *gar*) in Irenaeus's statement.[13] This conjunction is grammatically difficult to account for if we accept the common translation. If, however, it introduces a statement which refers back to the *main* idea of the preceding statement, then all becomes simple.

But what is the main idea? Irenaeus's main idea may be illustrated in a paraphrase of his point: "It is not important for us to know the name of the Beast (or Antichrist), which was hidden in the number 666. Were it important, why did John not tell us? After all, he lived almost to our own era, and spoke with some men that I have known." The main idea involves John himself. *Irenaeus is speaking of John and his knowledge of the name of the Beast.* It seems quite clear that he is exhorting the reader not to worry about the name of the Beast. We should not trouble ourselves with the matter because even John, who lived a long time after writing Revelation, did not tell anyone the identity.

Fourth, the contextual problem. In his *Ecclesiastical History* (5:8:5, 6) Eusebius again cites Irenaeus's statement, this time with more of the context:

> These things were said by the writer [*i.e.,* Irenaeus] referred to in the third book of his treatise which has been quoted before, and in the fifth book he discourses thus about the Apocalypse of John and the number of the name of the Antichrist. "Now since this is so, and since this number is found in all the good and ancient copies, and since those who have seen John face to face testify, and reason teaches us that the number of the name of the beast appears according to the numeration of the Greeks by the letters in it. . ." [*Heresies* 5:30:1].

And going on later [*Heresies* 5:30:3] he says concerning the same point: "We therefore will not take the risk of making any positive statement concerning the name of the Antichrist. For if it had been necessary for his name to have been announced clearly at the present time, it would have been spoken by him who also saw the Revelation; for it was not even seen a long time ago, but almost in our own generation towards the end of the reign of Domitian."[14]

We must note the *personal* knowledge emphasized by Irenaeus. It seems clear that the verb "was seen" is but the dim reflection of his preceding statement's more expansive and precise statement: "those who have seen John face to face testify." In fact, the very same Greek verb (*heorathe*, "seen") is used in both statements! Surely it speaks of John in both instances.

Fifth, the argumentative problem. What was the intent of Irenaeus? The proposed reinterpretation of Irenaeus is characteristic of Irenaeus's thought. By this I mean that *Irenaeus constantly emphasizes the organic and living unity of the Church's life*. According to church historian Philip Schaff, Irenaeus's work sought to demonstrate that "the same gospel which was first orally preached and transmitted was subsequently committed to writing and faithfully preserved in all the apostolic churches through the regular succession of the bishops and elders."[15] Thus, the most natural interpretation of Irenaeus's statement would be that he was referring to John's being alive to communicate the number of Beast-Antichrist to his hearers.

Sixth, the contradiction problem. At *Against Heresies* 5:30:1 Irenaeus writes: "Such, then, being the state of the case, and this number [666] being found in all the most approved and ancient copies [of the apocalypse], and those men who saw John face to face bearing their testimony [to it]." As Guthrie notes: "Since he [Irenaeus] also mentioned ancient copies of the book, it is clear that he knew of its circulation at a much earlier time."[16]

Irenaeus's mention of "ancient copies" of Revelation may suggest the date. This reference to "ancient copies" definitely indicates that the original manuscript of Revelation is ancient. Surely "ancient *copies*" demand a *more ancient* original. It would seem that the "ancient" character of the "copies" would imply something more ancient than the "end of Domitian's reign" which Irenaeus speaks of as "almost in our own generation"—does he consider himself "ancient"? If Revelation was written pre-A.D. 68, then its date would be about three decades older still.

Seventh, the eyewitness problem. In *Against Heresies* we read a very unusual historical statement:

[Christ] came to Baptism as one Who had not yet fulfilled thirty years, but was beginning to be about thirty years old. ... But the age of 30 years is the first of a young man's mind, and that it reaches even to the fortieth year, everyone will allow: but after the fortieth and fiftieth year, it begins to verge towards elder age: which our Lord was of when He taught, as the Gospel and all the Elders witness, who in Asia conferred with John the Lord's disciple, to the effect that John had delivered these things unto them: for he abode with them until the times of Trajan. And some of them saw not only John, but others also of the Apostles, and had this same account from them, and witness to the aforesaid relation.[17]

The careful detail he meticulously recounts in his argument, and the reference to the eyewitness accounts, should be noted. Yet, no respected New Testament scholar asserts that the biblical record allows for a fifteen year or more ministry for Christ, or his having attained the age of fifty. With Schaff we must heartily agree that Irenaeus was "strangely mistaken about the age of Jesus."[18] If this "eyewitness" account of Christ's age and length of ministry could be so woefully in error, why not his "eyewitness" sources for John's banishment?

Conclusion

A careful scrutiny of the Irenaean evidence for a late date for Revelation tends to render any confident employment of him suspect. The proper translation of Irenaeus's statement is the leading obstacle to confident use of him in the debate. He may not have meant that Revelation was seen by John during Domitian's reign. He may have meant to press the point that *John* was seen alive in Domitian's reign.

Origen

Origen of Alexandria lived from A.D. 185–254. He was a disciple of Clement of Alexandria and wrote a great number of works, many of which we still have. As noted earlier, Origen is usually cited as among the leading external witnesses to a late date for Revelation. The "evidence" from Origen's *Commentary on Matthew* (at Matthew 16:6ff.) reads as follows:

> The King of the Romans, as tradition teaches, condemned John, who bore testimony, on account of the word of truth, to the isle of Patmos. John, moreover, teaches us things respecting his testimony [*i.e.*, martyrdom], without saying who condemned him when he utters these things in the Apocalypse. He seems also to have seen the Apocalypse . . . in the island.

Needless to say, early-date advocates find the use of Origen questionable, in that it is not at all clear that he had in mind Domitian as "the King of the Romans." Indeed, many late-date advocates even admit that this "leading evidence" is based on *presumption*. R. H. Charles, for instance, writes: "Neither in Clement nor Origen is Domitian's name given, but it may be *presumed* that it was in the mind of these writers."[19] H. B. Swete and Mounce agree.[20]

Thus we come again upon a widely acclaimed late-date witness which is wholly unconvincing. Additional arguments against the reading of Origen as a late-date witness may be garnered from the following material on Clement of Alexandria, in that Clement was not only the precursor and teacher of Origen, but is equally nondescript.

Clement of Alexandria

Clement of Alexandria (A.D. 150–215) was a prominent and learned scholar in early Christianity. The evidence from Clement almost universally is cited by late-date advocates as supporting their view. Clement's statement is found in his *Who is the Rich Man that shall be Saved?*, Section 42:

Hear a story that is no mere story, but a true account of John the apostle that has been handed down and preserved in memory. When after the death of the tyrant he removed from the island of Patmos to Ephesus, he used to journey by request to the neighboring districts of the Gentiles, in some places to appoint bishops, in others to regulate whole churches, in others to set among the clergy some one man, it may be, of those indicated by the Spirit.

The critical phrase here is "after the death of the tyrant he [John] removed from the island of Patmos to Ephesus."

Despite widespread employment of Clement's statement, a close scrutiny destroys its usefulness in the debate. Furthermore, some quite logical considerations actually tilt Clement's evidence in an early date direction.

Read the text for yourself. John is said to return from Patmos after the death of "*the tyrant.*" It is painfully obvious that the required name "Domitian" is absent, just as in the case with his disciple, Origen. Yet H. B. Swete calls Clement one of "the chief authorities" from tradition for the late date![21] But who was this "tyrant"? Late-date advocate Aune confesses that "Clement neglects to specify which tyrant he has in mind."[22] Can we confidently cite Clement's nebulous statement about a "tyrant" as evidence for a Domitianic date for John's banishment? These questions are all the more relevant when we realize that *Nero* above all other emperors best meets up to the billing of a notorious tyrant. Let us see why.

The Universal Fear of Nero

First, even outside Christian circles Nero's infamous evil was greatly feared. As I noted in Chapter 4, Roman writers such as the historian Tacitus,[23] biographer Suetonius,[24] naturalist Pliny the Elder,[25] satirist Juvenal,[26] and philosopher Philostratus wrote of Nero's tyranny.

Philostratus (*fl.* 210–220) wrote that in his day Nero was "commonly called a Tyrant."[27] This is a most fascinating observation, in that Philostratus wrote during the time of Clement of Alexandria—he died just two years after Clement.

Nero scholar Miriam T. Griffin analyzes the presentation of Nero in the ancient at tragedy *The Octavia* (second century), noting: "Nero is, in fact, the proverbial tyrant, robbed of any personal characteristics, a mere incarnation of the will to evil, unaffected by advice or influence."[28] Nero's emperorship long stained the memory of the empire. Perhaps this is why Clement could write merely "the tyrant" when he made reference to the emperor of the banishment. This is at least as reasonable as assuming he meant Domitian.

The Feared Return of Nero

Second, Nero was so dreaded by many that soon after his death haunting rumors began circulating regarding his destructive return, either from the grave or from his place of hiding. This *Nero-redivivus* myth can be found in the writings of Tacitus, Suetonius, Dio Cassius, Zonaras, Dion Chrysostom, Augustine, and other ancient writers.[29] In the *Sibylline Oracles* (Second to Seventh Centuries A.D.) Nero appears as a constant threat to the world. Sibylline scholar J. J. Collins has noted in this regard that "there is the prominence of Nero as an eschatological adversary throughout the Sibylline corpus."[30]

The Christian Hatred of Nero

Third, as noted earlier, Christians particularly detested Nero as the Arch Tyrant and enemy of God. Many of the early church fathers remembered Nero with loathing. I will cite just a few:

• Eusebius speaks of Nero's "depravity," "the perversity of his degenerate madness, which made him compass the unreasonable destruction of so many thousands," and his being "the first of the emperors to be pointed at as a foe of divine religion."[31]

• Lactantius (A.D. 240–320) observes that Nero was a tyrant: "He it was who first persecuted the servants of God . . . and therefore this tyrant, bereaved of authority, and precipitated from the height of empire, suddenly disappeared."[32]

• Sulpicius Severus (A.D. 360–420) writes that Nero was "the basest of all men, and even of wild beasts," that "he showed himself in every way most abominable and cruel," and that "he first attempted to abolish the name of Christian."[33]

The Evil Paradigm of Nero

Fourth, the traditions about Domitian's alleged persecution warranted his being called a "Nero" by many, Christian and non-Christian alike. That Domitian was known as a "Nero," indicates Nero's name was paradigmatic of anti-Christian tyranny, not Domitian's. Tertullian (a contemporary with Clement of Alexandria and early Christendom's greatest apologist) spoke of Domitian as not only "somewhat of a Nero in cruelty,"[34] but a "*sub-Nero*."[35] He speaks of Domitian much more favorably than of Nero: "Domitian too, who was somewhat of a Nero in cruelty, had tried it [*i.e.*, persecution], but forasmuch as he was also a human being, he speedily stopped the undertaking, even restoring those whom he had banished."[36]

In his *Sacred History* Sulpicius Severus reserves two chapters for considering Nero's reign, and only three sentences to Domitian's. Severus extols the sainted life of Martin of Tours by noting that he would have gladly suffered for the Faith, even under the two worst persecutors of the Church: "But if he had been permitted, in the times of Nero and of Decius [A.D. 249–251], to take part in the struggle which then went on, I take to witness the God of heaven and earth that he would freely have submitted."[37]

Is Nero not a prime candidate for Clement's designation "the tyrant"? Where is Domitian as scathingly treated as Nero? Ask anyone on the street who Nero and Domitian were. You will discover Nero's name is known even today, whereas Domitian's is largely forgotten. Go to your local library and try to check out some books on Domitian. You will find very few. But you very likely will find several on Nero. Nero gained himself great notoriety as a tyrant burned into the memory of history. But there is more.

The Contextual Difficulty Supporting Nero

To further compound the problem for late-date employment of Clement, another difficulty surfaces in the context of his famous statement. The context following the critical statement is more easily believable if John were about thirty years younger, as he would have been in A.D. 65–66 as opposed to A.D. 95–96.

In connection with John's returning from banishment under the "tyrant," Clement informs us of John's activities. These activities are wholly incredible if performed by a man in his nineties (which John must have been, if Revelation was written in A.D. 95–96). I will cite the passage again:

> When after the death of the tyrant he removed from the island of Patmos to Ephesus, he used to journey by request to the neighboring districts of the Gentiles, in some places to appoint bishops, in others to regulate whole churches, in others to set among the clergy some one man.[38]

In further illustration of his activities, Clement immediately added to the account a story in which John, disturbed by a young church leader's forsaking of the faith, chased him on horseback: "But when he recognised John as he advanced, he turned, ashamed, to flight. The other followed with all his might, forgetting his age, crying, 'Why, my son, dost thou flee from me, thy father, unarmed, old? Son, pity me.'"[39]

This is quite strenuous missionary activity for a man who by that time had to be in his 90s! And that he had forgotten his "age" does not indicate he may have been ninety. Paul calls himself "the aged" while nowhere near that old (Philem. 9). The whole episode is much more believable if speaking of a man much younger than in his nineties, perhaps in his sixties.

The Cessation of Revelation Under Nero

The evidence thus far should give us pause when we hear that Clement supports a Domitianic date for John's banishment. But if not, then the following should totally reverse his usefulness in the debate.

In *Miscellanies,* Book 7, Clement deals with the perversion of truth by heretics. Their error is that "they do not make a right but a perverse use of the divine words." In his debate with them, he states that *apostolic revelation has ceased:* "For the teaching of our Lord at His advent, beginning with Augustus and Tiberius, was completed in the middle of the times of Tiberius. And that of the apostles, embracing the ministry of Paul, *ends with Nero.*"[40]

Beyond all doubt, Clement considers the Apostle John as Revelation's author. This may be seen in two of his writings: *Who is the Rich Man?* (Sec. 42) and *Miscellanies* (6:13). Yet here at *Miscellanies* 7:17 it is equally plain that he also holds that revelation through the apostles ceased *under Nero.* How could he have made this statement if John's Revelation had been written about thirty years *after* Nero?

Conclusion

When all the Clementine evidence is considered together, it is obvious that Clement should be removed as a late-date witness: The crucial statement by Clement lacks (1) specificity (it does not mention

Domitian) and (2) credibility (if, in fact, it does refer to a Domitianic banishment we would be left with a record of incredible feats by a ninety-year-old John).

Not only so, but Clement even serves as a positive external witness to the early-date composition of Revelation, for the following reasons: (1) The non-specific statement is more easily applied to Nero than Domitian (Nero is the classic and paradigmatic tyrant in ecclesiastical history) and (2) Clement teaches that divine revelation ceased with Paul under Nero (yet Clement accepts Revelation as having been written by John).

This evidence is from a church father not far removed in time from Irenaeus—and one much closer to the region where John labored.

Victorinus

Victorinus (d. A.D. 304), bishop of Pettau, is another of the mainstays of the late-date argument from tradition. Victorinus's relevant statement is found in his *Commentary on the Apocalypse* at Revelation 10:11:

> When John said these things he was in the island of Patmos, condemned to the labour of the mines by Caesar Domitian. Therefore, he saw the Apocalypse; and when grown old, he thought he should at length receive his quittance by suffering, Domitian being killed, all his judgments were discharged. And John being dismissed from the mines, thus subsequently delivered the same Apocalypse which he had received from God.[41]

It is abundantly clear that Victorinus taught that John was banished by Domitian.

What is striking about this traditional evidence, however, is that John, who was doubtless well into his nineties, could be *condemned to the mines and live*. This difficulty is similar to that regarding Clement of Alexandria. Such difficulties tax to the very limit the credibility of the reference.

Eusebius Pamphili

Eusebius (A.D. 260–340), Bishop of Caesarea in Palestine, is known as "the Father of Church History." In his *Ecclesiastical History* he writes:

> Domitian ... finally showed himself the successor of Nero's campaign of hostility to God. He was the second to promote persecution against us, though his father, Vespasian, had planned no evil against us.
>
> At this time, the story goes, the Apostle and Evangelist John was still alive, and was condemned to live in the island of Patmos for his witness to the divine word. At any rate Irenaeus, writing about the number of the name ascribed to the anti-Christ in the so-called Apocalypse of John, states this about John in so many words in the fifth book *Against Heresies*.[42]

As we analyze the weight of this evidence, we must bear in mind that *Eusebius clearly declares his dependence upon Irenaeus* in this matter. Whatever difficulties there may be with Irenaeus (see previous discussion), such must necessarily apply to Eusebius. Furthermore, we may discern some additional perplexities in Eusebius's writings, even apart from his founding his view on Irenaeus.

Inconsistent Usage of Irenaeus

In the first place, despite Eusebius's express dependence upon Irenaeus, he disagrees with Irenaeus on an extremely important and intimately related question. Eusebius denies what Irenaeus clearly affirms: that John the Apostle wrote Revelation.[43] This poses a problem. In another place in his book, Eusebius establishes the Apostle John's longevity based on Irenaeus's confident statement that John lived through Domitian's persecution.[44] But he disagrees with Irenaeus's teaching that John wrote Revelation, even though both ideas are found in the same place in Irenaeus. If Eusebius believed the one report, why not the other? The two issues—(1) that the Apostle John wrote Revelation (2) during Domitian's reign—are bound up together in Irenaeus. To doubt one would seem necessarily to entail the doubting of the other.

Contradictory Assertions in Eusebius

In the second place, Eusebius contradicts himself in his writings on John's banishment. It is clear in his *Ecclesiastical History* that Eusebius believes John was banished under Domitian. But in *Evangelical Demonstrations* 3:5, he speaks of the execution of Peter and Paul in the same sentence with the banishment of John. This clearly implies the events happened together. Thus, it indicates that when he wrote *Evangelical Demonstrations,* he was convinced of a Neronic banishment of John.

Thus, again we discover that one of the leading witnesses from tradition for the late date of Revelation is not all that solid a piece of evidence.

Jerome

As a number of late-date proponents argue, Jerome seems to regard John as having been banished by Domitian.[45] Due to its context, however, this evidence may not be as strong as many think. The context tends to confuse the matter by giving evidence of Jerome's confounding of two traditions. In his *Against Jovinianum* we read that John was

> a prophet, for he saw in the island of Patmos, to which he had been banished by the Emperor Domitian as a martyr of the Lord, an Apocalypse containing boundless mysteries with the future. Tertullian, moreover, relates that he was sent to Rome, and that having been plunged into a jar of boiling oil he came out fresher and more active than when he went in.[46]

As shown above, the reference from Tertullian strongly suggests a Neronic date. Thus, Jerome's evidence seems confused, indicating two competing traditions regarding the date of John's banishment, and, hence, the date of Revelation.

Conclusion

I cannot see how the external evidence can be used with much credence by late-date advocates. Irenaeus's statement is grammatically ambiguous and easily susceptible to a most reasonable re-interpretation, which would eliminate him as a late-date witness. Origen and Clement of Alexandria's evidence are more in the mind of the modern reader than in the script of the ancient text. The important references from both of these two fathers wholly lack the name "Domitian." Victorinus is a sure witness for the late date, but requires incredible implications. Eusebius and Jerome provide us with conflicting testimony.

We have weighed the evidence in the balance and found it wanting.

Notes

1. Henry B. Swete, *Commentary on Revelation* (Grand Rapids: Kregel, [1911] 1977), c. Robert Mounce, *The Book of Revelation*, 2nd ed. (Grand Rapids: Eerdmans, 1998), 17. Albert Barnes, *Barnes' Notes on the New Testament*, 1 vol. ed. (Grand Rapids: Kregel, rep. 1962), 1531ff.. B. B. Warfield, "Revelation, Book of", in Philip Schaff, ed., *A Religious Encyclopedia: Or Dictionary of Biblical, Historical, Doctrinal, and Practical Theology* (New York: Funk and Wagnalls, 1883), 3:2035. Henry C. Thiessen, *Introduction to the* New Testament (Grand Rapids: Eerdmans, 1943), 317ff. Donald B. Guthrie, *New Testament Introduction*, 4th ed. (Downers Grove, Ill.: InterVarsity Press, 1990), 956–957. John F. Walvoord, *The Revelation of Jesus Christ* (Chicago: Moody Press, 1966), 13ff. Merrill C. Tenney, "Revelation, Book of," in Merrill C. Tenney, ed., *The Zondervan Pictorial Bible Dictionary* (Grand Rapids: Zondervan, 1967), 721. A. T. Robertson, *Word Pictures in the New Testament*, (Nashville: Broadman, 1933), 6:275. G. K. Beale, *The Book of Revelation* (NIGTC) (Grand Rapids: Eerdmans, 1999), 19.

2. R. H. Charles, *A Critical and Exegetical Commentary on the Revelation of St. John* (Edinburgh: T. & T. Clark, 1920) 1:xciii. James Moffatt, *The Revelation of St. John the Divine*, vol. 5 in W. Robertson Nicoll, ed., *The Expositor's Greek Testament* (Grand Rapids: Eerdmans, rep. 1980), 320. David E. Aune, *Revelation 1-5* (Dallas: Word, 1997), lviii–lix. J. W. Bowman, "Revelation, Book of," in George Arthur Buttrick, *The Interpreter's Dictionary of the Bible* (Nashville: Abingdon, 1990), 60.

3. Leonard L. Thompson, *The Book of Revelation: Apocalypse and Empire* (New York: Oxford, 1990), 15. Guthrie, *New Testament Introduction*, 956. Beale, *The Book of Revelation*, 19.

4. Mounce, *Revelation*, 32; Sweet, *Revelation*, 21; Guthrie, *New Testament Introduction*, 956–957; Kümmel, *Introduction to the New Testament*, 466–467; William Hendriksen, *More Than Conquerors* (Grand Rapids: Baker, 1967), 19–20.

5. Leon Morris, *The Revelation of St. John*, rev. ed (Grand Rapids: Eerdmans, 1987), 35. J. P. M. Sweet, *Revelation* (Philadelphia: Westminster, 1979), 21. Charles Caldwell Ryrie, *Revelation* (Chicago: Moody, 1968), 8. Alan F. Johnson, *Revelation* (Grand Rapids: Zondervan, 1983), 12. Werner Georg Kümmel, *Introduction to the New Testament*, trans by. Howard Clark Kee (17th ed.: Nashville: Abingdon, 1973), 446. Hendriksen, *More Than Conquerors*, 20. George Eldon Ladd, A Commentary on the Revelation of John (Grand Rapids: Eerdmans, 1972), 8. G. R. Beasley-Murray, *The Book of Revelation* (Grand Rapids: Eerdmans, 1974), 37. Marvin R. Vincent, *Word Studies in the New Testament* (Grand Rapids: Eerdmans, [1887] 1985), 2:3.

6. Donald K. McKim, ed., *Historical Handbook of Major Biblical Interpreters* (Downers Grove, Ill: InterVarsity, 1998), 39. W. H. C. Frend, *The Rise of Christianity* (Philadelphia: Fortress, 1984), 921.

7. Irenaeus, *Against Heresies* 3:3:4. See: Johannes Quasten, *The Beginnings of Patristic Literature from the Apostles Creed to Irenaeus* (Allen, Tex.: Christian Classics, n.d.), 1:287–88.

8. Quasten, *The Beginnings of Patristic Literature from the Apostles Creed to Irenaeus*, 1:287. Seventeen full two-column pages are given over to "Irenaeus" in Henry A. Wace and William C. Piercy, *A Dictionary of Christian Biography* (Peabody, Mass.: Hendrikson, [1911] 1994), 520–536.

9. J. P. M. Sweet, "Revelation, Book of," in Bruce M. Metzger and Michael D. Coogan, eds., *The Oxford Companion to the Bible* (New York: Oxford University Press, 1993), 653.

10. Other problems are discussed in my *Before Jerusalem Fell: Dating the Book of Revelation*, 3rd ed. (Atlanta: American Vision, 1998), 47–66.

11. John A. T. Robinson, *Redating the New Testament* (Philadelphia: Westminster, 1976), 221.

12. Coxe, in *Ante-Nicene Fathers*, 1:312, 313.

13. Aune, *Revelation 1–5*, lix.

14. Translation by Lake.

15. Philip Schaff, *History of the Christian Church*, 3rd ed. (Grand Rapids: Eerdmans, [1910] rep. 1950) 2:753. See also: E. Ferguson, "Irenaeus," in Sinclair B. Ferguson, David F. Wright, and J. I. Packer, eds., *New Dictionary of Theology* (Downers Grove, Ill: InterVarsity, 1988), 340. Mary Ann Donovan, "Irenaeus," David Noel Freedman, *The Anchor Bible Dictionary*, 6 vols. (New York: Doubleday, 1992), 3:460. E. Venables, "Irenaeus," in Wace and Piercy, *A Dictionary of Christian Biography*, 522.

16. Guthrie, *Introduction*, 931.

17. Irenaeus, *Against Heresies* 2:22:5.

18. Schaff, *History* 2:751.

19. Charles, *Revelation*, xciii. Emphasis added.

20. Swete, *Revelation*, xcix, n. 2; Mounce, *Revelation*, 16.

21. Swete, *Revelation*, xcix.

22. Aune, *Revelation 1–5*, lix. Oddly though, Aune mentions Origin as late-date evidence— though without any such qualifying statement.

23. *Histories* 4:7;4:8.

24. Suetonius, *Nero* 7:1; 27:1.

25. Pliny, *Natural History*, 7:45; 22:92.

26. *Satire* 7:225; 10:3 36ff.

27. Philostratus, *Life of Apollonius* 4:38.

28. Miriam T. Griffin, *Nero: The End of a Dynasty* (New Haven: Yale University Press, 1984), 100.

29. Tacitus, *Histories* 1:78; 2:8; Suetonius, *Nero* 57; Dio Cassius, *Xiphilinus* 65:9; Zonaras, *Annals* 11:15-18; Dion Chrysostom, *Orations* 21; Augustine, *The City of God* 20:19:3.

30. J. J. Collins, "Sibylline Oracles," in *Apocalyptic Literature and Testaments*, vol. 1 of James H. Charlesworth, ed., *Old Testament Pseudepigrapha* (Garden City, N.Y.: Doubleday, 1983), 360.

31. Eusebius, *Ecclesiastical History* 2:25:2, 3.

32. *On the Death of the Persecutors* 2.

33. Sulpicius Seven is, *Sacred History* 2:28.

34. *Apology* 5.

35. *On Size Mantle* 4.

36. Tertullian, *Apology* 5.

37. Sulpicius Severus, *Letters* 3 (To Deacon Aurelius).

38. Clement of Alexandria, *Who Is the Rich Man that Shall be Saved?*, 42.

39. Clement, *Who Is the Rich Man?*, 42

40. Clement of Alexandria, *Miscellanies* 7:17.

41. Victorinus, *Revelation* 10:1.

42. Eusebius, *Ecclesiastical History* 3:17–18.

43. Eusebius, *Eccl. Hist.* 3:29:1, 2, 5, 6.

44. Eusebius, *Eccl. Hist.*, 3:18:1–3; 5:8:5.

45. See Swete, Charles, Mounce, Moffatt, Warfield, and Tenney.

46. Jerome, *Against Jovinianum* 1:26.

15

The Theoretical Problems

He who has an ear, let him hear what the Spirit says to the churches
Rev. 2:16

Despite the wealth of evidence from within Revelation supporting its early date, since the beginning of the twentieth-century late-date advocacy has persisted among the majority of both liberal and conservative scholars. "During much of the nineteenth century, however, the prevailing view held that Revelation was written between A.D. 64 (in response to the Neronian persecution) and A.D. 70, i.e., the destruction of Jerusalem. . . . The critical tide turned toward the beginning of the twentieth century, when major commentators again began to date Revelation toward the end of the reign of Domitian."[1] In the nineteenth century the evidence cited in defense of a late date for Revelation was derived almost exclusively from church tradition. Milton S. Terry, author of a much used text on the principles of biblical interpretation, wrote in 1898: "No critic of any note has ever claimed that the later date is required by any internal evidence."[2] This is no longer true today.

Though depending mostly on evidence from tradition, current late-date literature does attempt to build a case from Revelation's self-witness. In order to better secure the early date argument in terms of the self-witness evidence, I will address the major contrary arguments put forward by late-date advocates.

The modern case for the late date of Revelation concentrates upon four basic arguments. These have been ably summarized by noted evangelical scholar and late-date advocate Leon Morris. I choose to investigate Morris's approach for two basic reasons. He has rightfully earned an international reputation among both evangelical and liberal scholars; and he has a demonstrated competence in the field of New Testament studies, having even produced an excellent commentary on Revelation itself. The order of my listing of these evidences will follow Morris's, which is based on his scholarly estimation of their priority.

Emperor Worship

First, Morris begins with what he calls "the principal reason for dating the book during" Domitian's reign: Revelation "contains a number of indications that emperor-worship was practised, and this is thought to have become widespread in Domitian's day."[3] James Moffatt insisted that the role of emperor worship in Revelation was virtually conclusive: "When the motive of the Apocalypse is thus found in the pressure upon the Christian conscience exerted by Domitian's emphasis on the imperial cultus, especially as that was felt in Asia Minor, any earlier date for the book becomes almost impossible."[4] This argument is also held by Robert H. Mounce, R. H. Charles, H. B. Swete, Donald B. Guthrie, W. G. Kümmel, M. Eugene Boring, and William Barclay. References in Revelation which seem to reflect emperor worship are found in scattered places: Revelation 13:4, 8, 12, 15; 14:9, 11; 16:2; 19:20; 20:4. The most noteworthy passage is found in Revelation 13, where worship of the "beast" is compelled.

In effect, this objection has already been met in Chapter 6 above. There I showed that the worship of the emperor dates back to Julius Caesar and that Nero endorsed it. The emperor cult had a prominent role in the political and social life of the Roman empire well before Domitian, and even before Nero. Although it is true that historical development continued to introduce new features and requirements into the practice, after 30/29 B.C. "we can observe a swift spread of the emperor cult throughout the Roman Near East."[5] As even late-date advocate James Moffatt wrote: "The blasphemous title of *divus*, assumed by the emperors since Octavian (Augustus = *sebastos*) as a semi-sacred title, implied superhuman claims which shocked the pious feelings of Jews and Christians alike. So did *theos* [god] and *theou huios* [son of god] which, as the inscriptions prove, were freely applied to the emperors, from Augustus onwards."[6]

The appearance of emperor worship in Revelation is held by many late-date theorists as the strongest evidence for a date during the last year of the reign of Domitian (A.D. 81–96). It is true that Domitian required people to address him as "Lord and God." Certainly the emperor cult was prominent in his reign. Yet when we scrutinize the historical evidence we discover abundant testimony to emperor worship at various stages of development well before both Domitian and Nero. Indeed, such clear statements exist of so many aspects of the emperor cult, it is surprising this argument is used against the early date. That it is deemed "the principal reason" (Morris) that makes it "almost impossible" (Moffatt) for the early date view to stand is wholly incredible.

Persecution in Revelation

Second, Morris discovers "indications that Revelation was written in a time of persecution." This evidence is felt to accord "much better with Domitian."[7] W. G. Kümmel is quite confident that "the picture of the time which the Apocalypse sketches coincides with no epoch of the primitive history so well as with the period of Domitian's persecution."[8] Morris, Kümmel, and a number of other scholars list this as among their leading arguments for the A.D. 95–96 date.

Again, in effect, I have already spoken to this matter in Chapter 5. I agree that it seems clear enough that in Revelation imperial persecution against the faith has begun. But the evidence heavily favors a Neronic (A.D. 64–68) persecution rather than a Domitianic (A.D. 95–96) one.

As noted in Chapter 5 it is extremely difficult to even prove a Domitianic persecution—secular history is totally silent on the matter. Surprisingly, when we turn to Morris's own presentation, we are frustrated as we seek sure conviction: "While later Christians sometimes speak of a persecution under Domitian the evidence is not easy to find."[9] Many scholars understand Domitian's violent conduct in A.D. 95 as a paranoid outburst.[10] It seemed to concentrate on "selected individuals whom he suspected of undermining his authority."[11] The problem with the evidence for this "persecution" is that it proceeds solely from Christian sources—sources somewhat later than the events. A Domitianic persecution is not mentioned by any secular historian of the era.

Though the historicity of a Domitianic persecution of Christianity is questioned, such cannot be the case with the persecution under Nero. Although many scholars argue that the Neronic persecution was confined to Rome and its environs, the indisputable fact remains: Nero cruelly persecuted Christianity, taking even the lives of its foremost leaders, Peter and Paul. The evidence for the Neronic persecution is overwhelming and is documentable from heathen, as well as Christian, sources.

In Chapter 5 I showed clear evidence of a Neronic persecution from the writings of several pagan and Christian writers of the era. To that list let me now add Tertullian (A.D. 150–220), who was a lawyer who wrote in Latin, the legal language of the Roman Empire. In defending Christianity, he challenged men to search the archives of Rome for the proof that Nero persecuted the Church: "And if a heretic wishes his confidence to rest upon a public record, the archives of the empire will speak, as would the stones of Jerusalem. We read the lives of the Caesars: At Rome Nero was the first who stained with blood the rising faith."[12] Surely he would not issue a challenge to search the archives of Rome, which could easily be taken and just as easily refuted, were his statement untrue.

Indisputably, the sheer magnitude, extreme cruelty, and paradigmatic role of Nero's persecution of Christianity fit well the role required in Revelation. Thus, we are led again to repeat: The Domitianic evidence is doubtful and, if accepted at all, pales in comparison to Nero's. Interestingly, late-date advocate Robert Mounce, like so many others, admits that "the evidence for widespread persecution under Domitian is not especially strong." Yet, he goes on rather boldly to add that "there is no other period in the first century in which it would be more likely"![13] No other period?

The late-date use of the persecution theme in Revelation can neither establish the late date for Revelation, nor compete with the early date evidences.

The Nero Redivivus Myth

Third, a most unusual phenomenon seems to appear in Revelation, according to Morris. His third argument is very popular among late-date theorists. This evidence regards the remarkable and ancient legend known as the *Nero Redivivus* myth. Morris briefly explains the myth and confidently employs it: "Again, it is urged that the book shows evidence of knowledge of the Nero *redivivus* myth (e.g. xvii. 8, 11). After Nero's death it was thought in some circles that he would return. At first this appears to have been a refusal to believe that he was actually dead. Later it took the form of a belief that he would come to life again. This took time to develop and Domitian's reign is about as early as we can expect it."[14]

In providing the myth as late-date evidence David Aune boldly claims that "it is not likely that the Nero *redivivus* or Nero *redux* myth was widely circulated until the end of the first century A.D."[15] In Moffatt's commentary on Revelation 17 he speaks strongly of the myth's role in interpreting the passage, when he noted that "the latter trait is unmistakably due to the legend of Nero redivivus, apart from which the oracle is unintelligible."[16]

Nero so fearfully impressed the world in his era that pagan, Jewish, and Christian legends quickly sprang up around his death. These legends asserted themselves among the general populace throughout the far-flung reaches of the empire. In the pagan literature references to the expectation of Nero's return after his fall from power may be found in the writings of Tacitus, Suetonius, Dio Cassius, Xiphilinus, Zonaras, and Dion Chrysostom.[17] Among the Jews the myth surfaces in the Talmud. In Christian circles, it is mentioned in books by Lactantius, Sulpicius Severus, Jerome, and Augustine.[18] Several *Sibylline Oracles* of various origins—Christian, Jewish, and pagan—use the myth as well.[19]

Interestingly, the myth was not simply a "wives' tale" of little significance. It had a measurable impact even on political affairs. Pretenders to the imperial throne, claiming to be Nero used the myth in quests for power.[20]

Clearly the existence, spread, and influence of the *Nero Redivivus* myth cannot be disputed. It is one of the most fascinating and best-known legends in all of political history. But the questions with which we must deal are: Does the myth appear in Revelation? And if so, does this necessitate a late date for the composition of Revelation?

Despite the confidence with which some late-date advocates employ the *Nero Redivivus* myth, two intriguing facts arise regarding its use by biblical scholars.

First, not all late-date proponents allow the argument as helpful to the question of the dating of Revelation. Donald B. Guthrie, a most able late-date adherent, carefully considers the merits of the *Nero Redivivus* argument, but discourages its endorsement in the debate: "If then an allusion to the Nero myth is still maintained as underlying the language of Revelation xiii and xvii, it must be regarded as extremely inconclusive for a Domitianic date. The most that can be said is that it may possibly point to this."[21] In fact, some admit it could arise soon after Nero's death: "Given the presence of this legend, the Book of Revelation cold not have been written in its present form before 68 CE when Nero died, but the legend could have spread quickly after Nero's death."[22]

Second, a number of *early-date* advocates believe the myth appears in Revelation, but still maintain the Neronic dating position. John A. T. Robinson is a case in point: "As virtually all agree, there must be a reference to Nero *redivivus* in the beast that 'once was alive and is alive no longer but has yet to ascend out of the abyss before going to perdition.'"[23]

It is most interesting to find proponents of *both* dating positions able to admit the presence of an element which the late-date school proffers as a leading proof for its position! Beyond these two initial problems, however, significant and reasonable possibilities available to hand wholly undermine the *Nero Redivivus* argument for a late date.

Despite the intriguing correspondences between the *Nero Redivivus* myth and some of Revelation prophecies, the two are not related. We may easily interpret the relevant passages in a way that has nothing whatsoever to do with the *Nero Redivivus* myth. In addition, this interpretation is more appropriate, not only in regard to one of the major events of the first century, but also to the theme of Revelation. The interpretation of which I speak is given in Chapter 7 above, on the revival of the Beast. What John is speaking about is not a myth, but the historical phenomena associated with the death of Nero, the near demise of Rome, and its reestablishment under Vespasian.

Late-date proponent James Moffatt is particularly interesting at this point. He attempts to hold to the best of both worlds: (1) He vigorously attests that the *Nero Redivivus* myth appears in Revelation 13 and 17. He urges that its appearance helps establish the late date for Revelation, in that its highly developed form is not possible until Domitian's reign (A.D. 81–96).[24] (2) But then he also adopts the interpretation of Revelation 13 and 17 like I suggest: That the death wound and revival of the beast refer to the Roman Civil Wars of A.D. 68–69. Notice his comments on Revelation 13:3:

> The allusion is . . . to the terrible convulsions which in 69 A.D. shook the empire to its foundations (Tac *Hist.* i. 11). Nero's death with the bloody interregnum after it, was a wound to the State, from which it only recovered under Vespasian. It fulfilled the tradition of the wounded head.... The vitality of the pagan empire, shown in this power of righting itself after the revolution, only added to its prestige.[25]

Thus, a vigorous late-date advocate and *Nero Redivivus* enthusiast admits that the references allude to the Roman Civil Wars and Rome's revival under Vespasian. This is a telling admission.[26] If the references in question can be applied to the Roman Civil Wars of A.D. 68–69, how can these same references point to *Nero Redivivus* and demand an A.D. 96 date for the book?

If the verses in Revelation can properly be understood as referring to the earth-shaking historical events of the era, why would any commentator employ a myth to make sense of the passages? And this being the case, how can the myth be used as a major chronology datum from the internal evidence?

From our observations, it is obvious that the *Nero Redivivus* myth cannot be used with any degree of success to establish a late date for Revelation. There is good reason to doubt that it even appears in

Revelation. The presumed evidence based on this myth cannot undermine the facts derived from the documented historical matters by which we may establish its early date.

The Condition of the Seven Churches

Fourth, the historical situations of the seven churches (Rev. 1:4; 2; 3), suggest a late date. Since these are historical churches to which John wrote, the letters may contain historical allusions helpful in dating Revelation. As Morris states it, the "indication is that the churches of Asia Minor seem to have a period of development behind them. This would scarcely have been possible at the time of the Neronic persecution, the only serious competitor in date to the Domitianic period."[27] Mounce, Swete, Kümmel, Guthrie, and Beale employ the same argument.

Since I have not previously touched upon this evidence it deserves a little lengthier treatment. I will consider the four strongest arguments from this perspective, once again following the order found in Morris's work on Revelation.

The Wealth of Laodicea (Rev. 3:17)

The first evidence Morris offers in this regard is drawn from Revelation 3:17: "Because you say, 'I am rich, and have become wealthy, and have need of nothing,' and you do not know that you are wretched and miserable and poor and blind and naked." Morris notes that in this letter the Laodicean church is spoken of as "rich," but "as the city was destroyed by an earthquake in AD 60/61 this must have been considerably later."[28] All late-date advocates follow Morris's approach.

According to Tacitus, Laodicea was destroyed by an earthquake about this time.[29] The idea behind the argument is that such a devastating event as an earthquake necessarily must have severe and long-term economic repercussions on the community. And in such a community, the minority Christians could be expected to have suffered, perhaps even disproportionately. If Revelation were written prior to A.D. 70, it is argued, the time frame would be insufficient to allow for the enrichment of the church at Laodicea. But by the time of Domitian a few decades later, such would not be difficult to imagine.

Despite the initial plausibility of this argument it is not as strong as it appears. In the first place, who is to say that the reference to "riches" mentioned by John is not a reference to *spiritual* riches? After all, such language is used in Scripture of those who glory in their presumed spiritual riches: Luke 12:21; 16:15; 18:11, 12; 1 Corinthians 1:5; 13:12; 2 Corinthians 8:9. In fact, this language is used in a way very similar to Revelation in 1 Corinthians 4:8 and Hosea 12:8. If the spiritual riches view is valid, then the entire force of the late-date argument would be dispelled. Surprisingly, this is even the view of late-date advocate Robert Mounce: "The 'wealth' claimed by the Laodicean church, however, was not material but spiritual." And this despite the fact he uses the wealth of Laodicea as a late-date evidence.[30]

Second, fascinating historical evidence undermines the whole foundation of the late-date point, even if material riches are in view: Laodicea had a relatively effortless, unaided, and rapid recovery from the earthquake. Tacitus reports that the city did not even find it necessary to apply for an imperial subsidy to help them rebuild, even though such was customary for cities in Asia Minor.[31] Thus, despite the earthquake, economic resources were so readily available within Laodicea that the city easily recovered itself from the damage.

Third, who can say that the *Christian community* was necessarily overwhelmed by the quake in that city? In Revelation 3:17 the *church* is in view, not the city. Even the horribly destructive earthquakes in Mexico City on September 19 and 20 of 1985 did not destroy *every* sector of the city. Perhaps, by the grace of God, the Christians were in areas less affected by the quake, as Israel was in an area of Egypt unaffected by the plagues (Ex. 8:22; 9:4, 6, 24; 10:23; 11:27). If the Laodicean church had been spared the effects of the quake, would this token of God's providence lead the Laodiceans to a too proud confidence in their standing, as in Revelation 3:17? Perhaps a roughly analogous situation is found with the situation at Corinth, which Paul set about to correct (1 Cor. 4:6–8). Such boastful pride is ever a danger to those blessed of God (Deut. 8:18, cp. vv. 11–17).

The Existence of the Church in Smyrna

Morris's second argument is that "the church at Smyrna seems not to have been in existence in the days of Paul."[32] Obviously, if the church mentioned in Revelation 2:8–11 did not exist until after Paul's death it could not have been founded before Paul's martyrdom, which occurred in A.D. 67 or 68. Thus Revelation's date could not precede A.D. 67/68. (It would not necessarily affect, however, a date after A.D. 68 and before A.D. 70.)

This late-date objection is based on a statement by Polycarp in a letter written to the church at Philippi:

> But I have neither perceived nor heard any such thing among you [*i.e.,* the church at Philippi], among whom the blessed Paul laboured, who are praised in the beginning of his Epistle. For concerning you he boasts in all the churches who then alone had known the Lord, for we had not yet known him.[33]

Polycarp (*ca.* A.D. 69–155) was the bishop of the church at Smyrna and is thought to have been the disciple of John. He seems to refer here to the Smyrna church when he writes "*we* had not yet known him." By this statement he may mean the church at Smyrna was not yet founded while Paul was alive. Several late-date advocates consider this among their strongest arguments. Nevertheless, serious objections undermine its usefulness.

First, it is not at all necessary that Polycarp's statement be interpreted in the manner demanded by Morris and others, *i.e.,* as indicating that the church was founded after Paul died. Re-read the statement for yourself. Does it demand that Paul was dead before the church at Smyrna was founded? Or could it easily be interpreted to mean that Paul *praised* the church at Philippi in his letter before the church at Smyrna was founded? It is much easier to understand Polycarp to be merely stating that Paul praised the Philippians for their conversion, which praise occurred before the Smyrnaeans were even converted. Polycarp would not then be saying that the Smyrnaeans church was founded after Paul died.

In the second place, most probably Smyrna was evangelized soon after Ephesus. We say this in light of the statements in Acts 19:10, 26. The Acts account emphasizes in conjunction with Paul's labors in Ephesus, that "all who lived in Asia heard the word of the Lord Jesus" and that "in almost all of Asia" Paul was making progress in the promotion of the Gospel. Smyrna is one of the cities of Asia (Rev. 1:4, 11). If Smyrna was evangelized soon after Ephesus, then this would put Smyrna's founding *before* the year 60. No necessity exists for assuming a late date for Revelation based on John's letter to Smyrna and Polycarp's letter to the Philippians.

The Spiritual Decline in Ephesus, Sardis, and Laodicea

The most familiar of the evidences from the Seven Letters is derived from warnings of spiritual decline at Ephesus, Sardis, and Laodicea. Obvious spiritual decline is noted in Revelation 2:4, 5; 3:1-2, 15-18. Morris states the late-date position thus: "All the churches in chapters ii and iii appear to have had a period of history. Especially is this the case with those of whom things could be said like 'thou hast left thy first love' (ii. 4)."[34]

Late-date theorists insist that the spiritual decline manifested in the churches demands a period of time more readily available if John wrote during Domitian's reign. It seems reasonable that the early fervency of a newfound faith would wane only after the passing of various perils encountered over an extended period of time.

Despite all the vigorous assertions, however, a major objection destroys this argument: Granting a marked deterioration in the churches, the whole question of the length of time necessary for such lies at the heart of the situation. How long does it take for faith to wane? Was not Paul surprised at the rapid decline among the Galatians when he wrote: "I am amazed that you are so quickly deserting Him who called you by the grace of Christ, for a different gospel"?

Consider also Paul's concern over the multitude of troubles within the church of Corinth. This church was founded in A.D. 49 and Paul wrote to it with heavy heart in A.D. 57. Apparently, Paul anticipated such problems among churches virtually as soon as he left the scene, as he noted to the elders of the church at Ephesus (Acts 20:29ff). Was not Timothy urged to remain at Ephesus because of the entry of false doctrine within Paul's lifetime (1 Tim. 1:6)?

Paul also experienced distressing defections from fidelity to him as a servant of Christ within his ministry (2 Tim. 4:10). Paul expresses concern over the labors of Archippus at Laodicea (one of the churches in question) when he warns him to "take heed to the ministry which you have received in the Lord, that you may fulfill it" (Col. 4:13-17).

How much more would such a problem of slackened zeal be aggravated by the political circumstances generated from the initiation of the Neronic persecution in A.D. 64? Did not Jesus' teaching anticipate such (Matt. 13:20, 21; 24:9, 10)? No compelling reason whatsoever requires rejecting the early date of Revelation on the basis of the spiritual decline in certain of the Seven Churches. After considering this line of argument, late-date advocate Aune confesses: "Both lines of argument are capable of a variety of interpretations, so that a firm date late in the first century A.D. cannot be based on these arguments."[35]

Conclusion

A careful consideration of the merits of the major arguments from the Seven Letters demonstrates their inconclusive nature. Neither the arguments individually, nor all of them collectively compels acceptance of the Domitianic date of Revelation. This is all the more obvious when their inconclusive nature is contrasted with the wealth of other internal considerations for an early date, as rehearsed heretofore in the present work.

In fact, the Seven Letters even have elements suggesting a period prior to the destruction of the temple: (1) The presence of strong Judaistic elements in the churches (Rev. 2:9; 3:9). This bespeaks an early period of Christian development prior to the cleavage between Jew and Christian in the A.D. 60s.[36] (2) John's exhortation to the churches anticipates the "judgment coming" of Christ (Rev. 2:5, 16; 3:3, 10). No events expected in Domitian's day approached the magnitude and significance—either culturally or theologically—of the Neronic persecution, the death of Nero and the extinction of the Julio-Claudian imperial line, the destruction of Judaism's temple, and the near demise of Rome in the Civil Wars of A.D. 68–69.[37]

The early date stands, despite the attempted objections on the foregoing bases.

Notes

1. David E. Aune, *Revelation 1–5* (Dallas: Word, 1997), lvii.

2. Milton Terry, *Biblical Hermeneutics* (Grand Rapids: Zondervan, undated reprint), 240.

3. Leon Morris, *The Revelation of St. John*, 2nd ed. (Grand Rapids: Eerdmans, 1987), 35.

4. James Moffatt, *The Revelation of St. John the Divine*, vol. 5 in W. Robertson Nicoll, ed., *The Expositor's Greek Testament* (Grand Rapids: Eerdmans, rep. 1980), 317.

5. Doron Mendels, *The Rise and Fall of Jewish Nationalism: Jewish and Christian Ethnicity in Ancient Palestine* (Grand Rapids: Eerdmans, 1992), 278

6. Moffatt, *Revelation*, 429. See also: Aune, *Revelation 1–5*, lxviii; Leonard L. Thompson, *The Book of Revelation: Apocalypse and Empire* (New York: Oxford, 1990), 104–190.

7. Morris, *Revelation*, 37.

8. W. G. Kümmel, *Introduction to the New Testament*, trans. Howard Clark Kee, 17th ed. (Nashville: Abingdon, 1973), 328.

9. Morris, *Revelation*, 36. Other similar references can be found in Chapter 5.

10. For example, J. Ramsey Michaels, *Revelation* (Downers Grove, Ill.: InterVarsity Press, 1997), 19. M. Eugene Boring, *Revelation: Interpretation: A Bible Commentary for Teaching and Preaching* (Louisville: John Knox, 1989), 17.

11. Glenn W. Barker, William L. Lane, and J. Ramsey Michaels, *The New Testament Speaks* (New York: Harper and Row, 1969), 368.

12. Tertullian, *Scorpion's Sting* 15.

13. Robert Mounce, *The Book of Revelation*, 2nd ed. (Grand Rapids: Eerdmans, 1998), 34.

14. Morris, *Revelation*, 37.

15. Aune, *Revelation 1–5*, lxi. See also: Moffatt, *Revelation*, 317.

16. Moffatt, *Revelation*, 450.

17. Tacitus, *Historic* 1:2; 2:8, 9; Suetonius, *Nero* 40, 57, *Domitian* 6; Dio Cassius, *Roman History* 63:9:3; 66:19:3; Xiphilinus 64:9; Zonaras, *Annals* 11:151–58; and Dion Chrysostom, *Orations* 1.

18. Lactantius, *On the Death of the Persecutors* 2; Sulpicius Severus, *Sacred History* 2:28; Jerome, *Daniel* 11:28; and Augustine, *The City of God* 20:19:3.

19. Sibylline Oracles 3:63ff; 4:115ff; 5:33ff; 8:68ff; 12:78; 13:89ff.

20. Tacitus, *Histories* 1:78; 2:8; Suetonius, *Nero* 57.

21. Donald B. Guthrie, *New Testament Introduction*, 4th ed. (Downers Grove, Ill.: Inter-Varsity, 1990), 953.

22. Leonard L. Thompson, *The Book of Revelation: Apocalypse and Empire* (New York: Oxford, 1990), 14.

23. John A. T. Robinson, *Redating the New Testament* (Philadelphia: Westminster, 1976), 245. Moses Stuart and E. Earle Ellis are orthodox early-date scholars who allow that the myth appears in Revelation. Moses Stuart, *Commentary on the Apocalypse* (Andover: Allen, Morrill, Wardwell, 1845). E. Earle Ellis, *The Making of the New Testament Documents* (Boston: Brill, 1999), 212.

24 Moffatt, *Revelation*, 317.

25. Moffatt, *Revelation*, 430.

26. Interestingly, Mounce does the same thing: On page 19 of his work, he employs the myth to demonstrate a late date for Revelation, but in his commentary at Revelation 13 and 17 he opts for the revival-of-the-Empire interpretation (*Revelation*, 248, 318).

27. Morris, *Revelation*, 38.

28. Morris, *Revelation*, 38.

29. Tacitus, *Annals*, 14:27.

30. Mounce, *Revelation*, 19, 110.

31. Tacitus, *Annals*, 14:27.

32. Morris, *Revelation*, 37.

33. Polycarp, *Letter a the Philippians*, 11:3.

34. Morris, *Revelation*, 38.

35. Aune, *Revelation*, *1–5*, lxiii.

36. See Chapter 12.

37. See Chapter 9

Conclusion

And he said to me, "Do not seal up the words of the
prophecy of this book, for the time is near"
Rev. 22:10

I have been considering two of the most interesting and debated questions regarding Revelation: Who is the Beast haunting its pages? And when did John write this terrifying work? Our journey has been a long and arduous one. We have dug deeply into Revelation and have traveled far and wide in ancient Church and Roman history. I now come to the end of the investigation, hoping that this inquiry was both profitable and convincing. If so, perhaps it will help to unseal the meaning of Revelation for you.

The Importance of the Questions

The proper identity of the Beast and the appropriate date of composition are not simply trivia questions. Large issues hang in the balance. If the views I have presented in this book are correct, then Revelation was written about a terrible Beast that would afflict the people of God *before* and *in anticipation* of the fall of Jerusalem and the destruction of the temple in A.D. 70.

That being the case, then, we do not have the Beast and a "Great Tribulation" to look forward to in our future. The Beast—ancient Rome (generically) and Nero Caesar (specifically)—has already lived and the Tribulation has already occurred, as Scripture said it would, in the first century "birth pangs" of Christianity (Matt. 24:8, 21; cp. v. 34[1]). Revelation, then, does not leave us with biblical warrant to view earth's future as a "blocked future" of despair. The woes of Revelation have already occurred!

If these views are correct—and I am convinced beyond any doubt that they are—then Revelation was given as God's divinely inspired and inerrant pre-interpretive word on the destruction of the temple order and the divorce of Israel as God's covenant wife.[2] We have God's word that this was brought about in the first century by the decree of the Lord Jesus Christ.

In Revelation we have a biblical explanation of the catastrophic events of the A.D. 60s. The watershed events of that era included: the outbreak of the first, precedent-setting imperial persecution of Christianity; the death of Christianity's first and most heinous Roman persecutor, Nero Caesar; the subsequent near collapse of Rome, followed by its revival under the non-persecuting emperors (Vespasian and Titus); the destruction of Jerusalem and the temple; and the hope for the increase throughout the earth of God's New Creational salvation.[3]

The Evidence for Our Answers

Our convictions regarding the identity of the Beast and the date of Revelation's composition have not been demanded merely by our theological perspective or sociological outlook. The relief we may experience regarding the vanished prospect of sending our children into such a dismal future is a happy *side-effect* of our inquiry. Now that we have looked rather carefully at the arguments for the date of Revelation, I believe we are compelled by historical and exegetical evidence to assert that Revelation was written in the A.D. 60s—not in the A.D. 90s.

It is my deep conviction that much of the decline of the influence of orthodox Christianity on our culture today is due to a pervasive, pessimistic eschatology. As dispensationalist R. A. Torrey loved to say at the turn of the century: "The darker the night gets, the lighter my heart gets."[4] If Christians refuse to be the light of the world, no wonder the nights get so dark! And what is the point of attempting to scatter the darkness if the darkness is a sign of the Lord's soon return? As Hal Lindsey has told tens of millions of Christians in our era: "We should be living like persons who don't expect to be around much longer" because Jesus is coming soon to snatch us "out of the world as it plunges toward judgment."[5] Why should Christians engage themselves in slow, long-term cultural reconstruction if we are soon to vanish from the earth? The success of the *Left Behind* series of novels is not happy evidence of evangelical Christendom's interest in Revelation. Rather it serves as a sad illustration of her hopelessly naive confusion.

Too often pessimistic eschatology is demanded by a wrong approach to Revelation, which sees the Beast as looming in our future. And a wrong approach to Revelation is often encouraged by a misconception of Revelation's date. But Revelation is clear: Its prophecies were to occur soon after John wrote, not millennia later (Rev. 1:1, 3; 3:10; 22:6–11). The events symbolized in Revelation were earth shaking, but they are now past events.

Summary of Evidence for the Beast

Perhaps the most important initial evidence pointing to the Roman Empire (generically) and Nero Caesar (specifically) is the matter of the *relevance* of the Beast. John clearly and emphatically expected the events of Revelation—a number of which were associated with the Beast—to begin transpiring "soon" (Rev. 1:1, 3; 22:6ff).[6] This evidence clears away 99.9% of the modern suggestions regarding the identity of the Beast, suggestions demanding hundreds and thousands of years for accomplishment.

But this evidence alone does not demand Nero Caesar as the specific reference—although it does strongly indicate the Roman Empire is the generic referent. When we calculate the *number 666* and discover that it adds up to the first century Jewish spelling of Nero's name, however, we are getting somewhere.[7] And when the *character* of the Beast is matched to Nero's infamous conduct, we become more confident still.[8] Nero was clearly a beastly character possessed with a horrendously sinful will to evil and holding great power to unleash his base desires.

In addition I noted the remarkable correspondence between the *war* of the Beast with the persecution of Christians by Nero.[9] This correspondence may easily be adapted to the forty-two month time frame in Revelation (Rev. 13:5): November, A.D. 64, to June, A.D. 68. Filling out the evil character of the Nero-Beast was the Roman practice of *emperor worship*, which alluded to in Revelation 13.[10] And then to top it all off, one of the most unusual features of the Beast—his death and "resurrection"—finds remarkable fulfillment in the events of the A.D. 60s after the death of Nero. Rome was buckling to her knees, fainting to her death with the demise of her sixth head, Nero, during the Civil Wars of A.D. 68–69. But the empire—the Beast generically considered —was revived under Vespasian, to the "wonder" of the world.[11]

The Beast is clearly the Roman Empire, particularly expressed in its most evil head, Nero Caesar. This Beast has lived and died, according to the infallible prophecy of Scripture. But, of course, all of this evidence for the identity of the Beast depends on the date of Revelation's composition. For if it were written almost thirty years after his death, the whole structure holding Nero before us would collapse. So, I presented the case for the early date of Revelation in the pre-A.D. 70 era.

Summary of Evidence for Revelation's Date

The evidences for Revelation's early-dating during the reign of Nero Caesar are numerous, varied, clear, and compelling. In addition to all the positive evidence for Nero Caesar as the Beast (which itself indicates a pre-A.D. 70 composition), additional compelling evidences appear to the alert interpreter.

The Evidence from Within Revelation

The thematic evidence:[12] Revelation insists upon the soon coming of certain events resulting in the judgment-coming of Christ. That judgment-coming necessarily involved the destruction of the temple and the punishment of the first-century Jews, the crucifiers of Christ. This had to be the final destruction of the temple in Jerusalem and the devastation that accompanied it in A.D. 67–70. Jesus clearly prophesied it (Matt. 24; Mark 13; Luke 21), and so did John (Revelation).

The political evidence:[13] Revelation clearly asserts that the sixth emperor of Rome was living at the very time John wrote (Rev. 17:9–10). Historically, Nero was the sixth emperor of Rome, which corresponds perfectly with the early-date, preterist interpretation of the Beast. In addition, he was followed by a seventh ruler who reigned but a short while: Galba (17:11). These political statements regarding imperial Rome's rule are objectively datable.

The architectural evidence:[14] One of the great examples of architecture of the ancient world was still standing as John wrote—the temple in Jerusalem (Rev. 11:1, 2). The destruction of this structure is datable from both documentary and archaeological evidence. It was destroyed, never to be to built again, in August, A.D. 70, by General Titus of the Roman Empire.

The ecclesiastical evidence:[15] The Christianity in John's day was at an early stage of development. Christians were obviously still intermingling with the Jews and presenting themselves as "true Jews" (Rev. 2:9; 3:9). Christian Jews are portrayed as the fullness of the Twelve Tribes of Israel (7:4). The language of Revelation has a strongly Hebraic cast.

The Evidence from Church History

Despite much of current opinion, neither is the evidence from church tradition capable of overthrowing the self-witness evidence. The strongest witnesses for Revelation's late-dating are fraught with interpretive difficulties (Irenaeus) or are ambiguous (Clement of Alexandria and Origen). Or they are internally contradictory (Eusebius). Another involves improbable actions (Victorinus). Still another seems to confuse both traditions into one (Jerome).[16]

Although the early date view prefers Revelation's own self-witness, it easily discovers evidence from tradition, as well. One late-date witness even has an observation that demands all revelation ceased under Nero (Clement of Alexandria). The contradiction in one witness provides a statement supportive of the early date (Eusebius).

But beyond these we find clear statements demanding a pre-A.D. 70 date for Revelation in a number of early witnesses (*Muratorian Canon*, Epiphanius, Syriac writers, Arethas). In addition there are strong implications of an early date in still others (Papias, *Shepherd of Hermas*, Tertullian).[17]

A Plea for a Hearing of the Evidence

I do hope from this inquiry that thinking Christians will reconsider the issues. At the very least I trust that any hasty dismissal of the identity of the Beast and the early date for Revelation will be pre-empted. Discussion of the matter of Revelation's date should not be closed with a "thus saith current opinion."

Not all scholars hold to the futuristic identity of the Beast or the Domitianic date of Revelation. Nor is there anything approaching a unanimity of opinion in ancient church history in either direction. Nor may we dismiss the self-witness of Revelation as obscure or inconsequential.

Regarding the date of Revelation, when even liberals are considering the fallacy of the late date (e.g., C. C. Torrey, John A. T. Robinson, Rudolf Bultmann) and opting for the early date, orthodox Christians should take notice. Revelation was written just prior to the initial outbreak of the Tribulation-wrath of God against the Jews, for John was already enmeshed in its harbingers as he wrote (Rev. 1:9). The Tribulation was immediately preceded by the Beast's "war against the saints" (ch. 13), which started with the Neronic persecution in November, A.D. 64. Revelation *anticipates* the destruction of the Temple (August, A.D. 70) in Chapter 11, the death of Nero (June, A.D. 68) in Chapter 13, *and* the formal imperial engagement of the Jewish War (Spring, A.D. 67) in Chapters 6-7. Hence, Revelation was written sometime between November, A.D. 64 and Spring, A.D. 67— probably in A.D. 65.

The evidence permeates Revelation. We have simply been letting the blind lead the blind, causing both to fall into the ditch. Or should we say they both fall into the same old rut? For much of late-date advocacy is simply a rehearsing of time-worn but unconvincing arguments.

Notes

1. For more information see: Kenneth L. Gentry, Jr., *Perilous Times: A Study in Eschatological Evil* (Texarkana, Ark.: Covenant Media Press, 1999), chs. 2 and 3. Gary DeMar, *Last Days Madness: Obsession of the Modern Church*, 4th ed. (Powder Springs, Ga.: American Vision, 1999). For a debate on the subject see: Thomas Ice and Kenneth L. Gentry, Jr., *The Great Tribulation: Past or Future?* (Grand Rapids: Kregel, 1999).

2. See my forthcoming commentary: *The Tale of Two Cities: A Commentary on Revelation* (Powder Springs, Ga.: American Vision, 2002).

3. Cp. Revelation 21–22 with 2 Corinthians 5:17; Galatians 6:15; Matthew 13:31ff.; 2 Corinthians 5:21ff. See: Kenneth L. Gentry, Jr. in C. Marvin Pate, ed., *Four Views on the Book of Revelation* (Grand Rapids: Zondervan, 1998), 86–90.

4. Cited in Dwight Wilson, *Armageddon Now!* (Grand Rapids: Baker, 1977), 37.

5. Hal Lindsey, *The Late Great Planet Earth* (Grand Rapids: Zondervan, 1970), 145, 186.

6. See Chapter 2.

7. See Chapter 3.

8. See Chapter 4.

9. See Chapter 5.

10. See Chapter 6.

11. See Chapter 7.

12. See Chapter 9.

13. See Chapter 10.

14. See Chapter 11.

15. See Chapter 12.

16. See Chapter 14.

17. See Chapter 13